T0306150

BEYOND E-BUSINESS

In *Beyond E-Business: Towards Networked Structures* Paul Grefen returns with his tried and tested BOAT framework for e-business, now fully expanded and updated with the very latest overview of digitally connected business; from business models, organization structures and architecture to information technology.

What used to be termed 'e-business' is now simply business as usual. Today's successful organizations are complex; they are part of dynamic business networks built on digital channels, going far beyond traditional e-business. This text provides invaluable insights of modern e-business integrated with networked business, going much further than the usual analysis of traditional e-business texts. Included is coverage of the Big Five – social media, mobile computing, big data, cloud computing and the internet of things – as well as service-oriented business and technology.

This essential text provides a compact roadmap to networked e-business for engineering, information systems or business students as well as professionals in the field.

Paul Grefen is Professor at the School of Industrial Engineering of Eindhoven University of Technology, the Netherlands. He has extensive teaching and research experience in electronic business, networked business processes and information systems, through which he has collaborated with many international business and research organizations.

BEYOND E-BUSINESS

Towards networked structures

Paul Grefen

Routledge
Taylor & Francis Group

LONDON AND NEW YORK

First published 2016
by Routledge
2 Park Square, Milton Park, Abingdon, Oxon OX14 4RN

And by Routledge
711 Third Avenue, New York, NY 10017

Routledge is an imprint of the Taylor & Francis Group, an informa business

British Library Cataloguing in Publication Data
A catalogue record for this book is available from the British Library

Library of Congress Cataloging-in-Publication Data
Grefen, Paul.
    Beyond e-business : towards networked structures / Paul Grefen.
        pages cm
    Includes bibliographical references and index.
    1. Electronic commerce—Management.   2. Computer
networks.   3. Information technology—Management.   I. Title.
    HF5548.32.G7447 2015
    658.8'72—dc23
    2015002449

ISBN: 978-1-138-80176-9 (hbk)
ISBN: 978-1-138-80177-6 (pbk)
ISBN: 978-1-315-75469-7 (ebk)

Typeset in Bembo
by Apex CoVantage, LLC

CONTENTS

FIGURES AND TABLES

Figures

Tables

PREFACE

In modern-day business we can observe two major developments that have taken place simultaneously in the past two decades and are still taking place with an ever increasing speed. First, electronic business (e-business) has pervaded society, moving many aspects of business into the digital domain from the perspective of channels for business communication and collaboration. The internet has become the backbone for many kinds of business, both in business-to-business and business-to-consumer settings. Second, business has become highly networked from the perspective of topologies in business communication and collaboration. Successful business organizations nowadays typically do not operate in stand-alone mode or in simple supply chains. They are organized in business networks that often have a dynamic character and can reach a high level of complexity. This book is about the kind of business that is rooted in both these developments: *networked e-business*. The book combines insights in e-business and highly networked business in an integrated way, thereby going beyond treatments of traditional e-business. Using this combination of insights is the only way to truly understand and design modern business.

This book provides a view on networked e-business that is different from views found in other textbooks on electronic business. The core of this view consists of two observations. The first is the observation that modern networked e-business is a complex, multi-faceted field that goes beyond 'standard' e-business as we have known it for about two decades now. In this field, it is most important to understand high-level, conceptual structures in terms of essential elements and relationships between these elements. By understanding the overall structure, it is easy to understand further details of the field, as well as cases and developments in the field. The second observation is that networked e-business can only be completely understood by having a well-balanced, integrated treatment of the entire spectrum from business elements via organization and architecture elements to information technology elements. Concentrating on business aspects only with some illustration of operational and technical aspects will not do the job – and neither will the reverse.

This preface explains the background and intended audience of this book – thereby also further explaining its view and its aim. After that, a short reading guide is presented.

About the background of this book

The early roots of this book can be found in a framework reader for the *Electronic Business Architectures and Systems* (EBAS) course taught at the School of Industrial Engineering at Eindhoven University of Technology (TU/e, Netherlands). The EBAS reader has also been used at the Department of Supply Chain & Information Systems of Pennsylvania State University (PSU, USA), at the Economics and Management School of Beijing University of Technology (BJUT, China) and in collaboration with industry. The EBAS course at TU/e is the successor of the *e-Commerce* course previously taught at the University of Twente (UT, Netherlands). The author of this book was responsible for the design of both courses. As such, there are almost two decades of teaching experience behind this book. Although the material was developed in the Netherlands, it has been given an explicit international orientation from the very beginning: networked e-business is a very international affair.

About this book

The book you are currently holding is a follow-up of the book *Mastering e-Business*, which was published in 2010 by Routledge Publishers – and as the title suggests, it goes substantially beyond this predecessor [Gref10]. On the one hand, *Beyond e-Business* adds the aspect of networked business much more explicitly. On the other hand, *Beyond e-Business* is a major rework and extension of the topics covered by its predecessor. Like its predecessor, *Beyond e-Business* keeps the approach to explain its domain without touching too many volatile details – hence, it is less susceptible to the erosion of time than a book based on many time-dependent details of specific business cases or technology developments.

Beyond e-Business builds on the same proven overall structure of *Mastering e-Business*, but contains a major overhaul and extension of that structure. This makes *Beyond e-Business* more complete and gives it full alignment with the latest developments in its field. The main improvements and extensions are briefly explained here.

First, the book has been completely updated to be current and state-of-the-art. This is reflected in its new title and subtitle, stressing that the 'networking' aspect is far more important nowadays than the 'electronic' aspect that is becoming increasingly the default. But more importantly, the updates are reflected in the entire body of the book.

The book has been extended with an extensive coverage of the major IT-related developments that influence the organization of networked e-business (which we call the *Big Five*): social media, mobile computing, cloud computing, big data and the internet of things. The Big Five are introduced in chapter 2, referenced and used in the other chapters and discussed in detail from the technology point of view in chapter 8.

The discussion on the business aspect of the BOAT framework is fully updated, more complete and much better structured in chapter 5. Most importantly, the material on business models has been completely rewritten and is now based on a proper taxonomy of business models. A new chapter 10 has been added, discussing the role of business strategy as an 'umbrella' for the development and management of new business models in a business organization.

The book has further been extended with an elaborate discussion of the service-oriented view in the organization (O) aspect and the architecture (A) aspect of the BOAT framework. For this purpose, new sections have been added to chapters 6 and 7. To complement this extension in the technology (T) aspect, a discussion of service-oriented technology has been added to chapter 8, focusing on topics such as *managed service platforms* and *enterprise service busses*.

Finally, a third running case study has been added to the book, discussing a highly networked e-business scenario in the travel services industry. The two existing case studies have been updated to reflect new developments.

Intended audience and setting

This book has been developed primarily to be used in M.Sc. courses (or advanced B.Sc. courses) in programs such as industrial engineering, (business) information systems, management science, and computer science. The book is, however, also well suited for professionals in the field of networked business and electronic business, and managers of organizations engaging in networked e-business. For these readers, it provides a structured treatment of the field that is a strong basis for developing networked business models and their supporting infrastructure.

To understand the book, only a basic level of prior knowledge of business structures and information technology is required. This makes the book equally suitable for readers with a technical background who want to broaden their view on business aspects and for readers with a business background who want to further dive into the technical aspects of networked e-business.

As explained before, this book provides a general framework on the topic of networked e-business in which a complete spectrum of topics is discussed with explicit attention to their interrelationships – ranging from business to information technology aspects. As such, the individual topics are not treated at the highest possible level of detail – the aim is to provide a complete and cohesive overview of the domain. The reader is expected to find more detailed material himself or herself based on the framework offered – the reference list at the end of this book provides an elaborate point of entry into the literature about networked e-business and related fields.

Reading guide

The first four chapters of this book lay the conceptual basis for the rest of the book (the 'head' of the book). In the first three chapters, we introduce networked e-business, discuss its practical context and explain how to classify networked e-business scenarios. The cornerstone of the book is the BOAT framework, which is introduced in chapter 4. The BOAT framework distinguishes four aspects of networked e-business (which explain the acronym): business, organization, architecture and technology.

After the conceptual basis has been treated, the structure of the 'body' of the book follows the structure of the BOAT framework. Each of the four BOAT aspects is treated in a separate chapter: chapter 5 discusses the business aspect, chapter 6 discusses the organization aspect, chapter 7 deals with the architecture aspect and chapter 8 is devoted to the technology aspect.

After the body of the book, we discuss two additional topics that are of high relevance for the use of the BOAT framework in practice (the 'tail' of the book). Chapter 9 discusses approaches for the analysis and design of networked e-business scenarios. Chapter 10 pays attention to the role of business strategy in the context of networked e-business. Finally, chapter 11 ends the book with concluding remarks. An overview of the structure of the book is shown in the following figure.

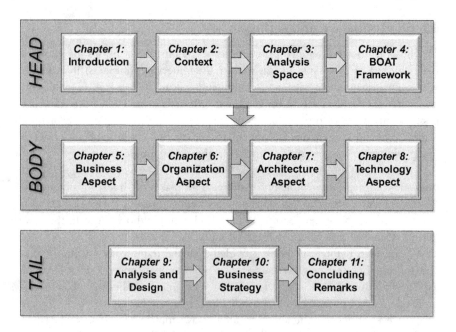

To get the most benefit from the approach of this book, the reader can best read the chapters in the sequence in which they are organized. The chapters discussing the four BOAT aspects contain sections that summarize the relationships between these aspects, as such paying explicit attention to dependencies among aspects. Also, references between elements in the chapters are explicitly included in the text. It is possible, however, to focus on one or more individual aspects of the BOAT framework when reading this book. In this case, the reader is advised to start with the first four chapters and then continue with the chapter(s) of interest. To best appreciate the last two chapters, it is advised to read all other chapters first.

Each chapter starts with a set of learning goals that serves as an advanced organizer for the reader. Each chapter (apart from the concluding one) is ended with a summary of the chapter and a set of questions and exercises to apply the knowledge from the chapter. To enable the use of this book as a reference guide as well, an extensive index and a list of figures and tables are included in the book, providing easy access to the discussion and illustration of major concepts. The field of networked e-business is riddled with acronyms – so many of these are found in this book. For easy reference, the expansion of most acronyms is included in the index of this book (and from the expanded version, references to the book text are provided).

The reader is wished a good deal of reading pleasure into the dynamic world of networked e-business.

Paul Grefen
Eindhoven, 2015

ACKNOWLEDGMENTS

A number of people have contributed in an important way to making the book into what is in front of you now.

Colleagues who have provided input and feedback to the predecessor of this book and thereby indirectly to this book are Samuil Angelov, Rob Kusters, Ricardo Seguel and Egon Lüftenegger of Eindhoven University of Technology (by the time that book was written); Akhil Kumar of Penn State Smeal College of Business and Ria Marinussen of the University of Twente.

Akhil Kumar of Penn State Smeal College of Business and Claudia Chituc of Eindhoven University of Technology are thanked for their helpful feedback on the manuscript of this book. The many people in industry and academia with whom I have collaborated in national and international research projects in the past years are thanked for their contribution to ideas portrayed in this book.

The (anonymous) reviewers of the proposals for this book are thanked for their feedback and suggestions. The publishing team at Routledge is thanked for the pleasant cooperation in realizing this book. Last, but certainly not least, Ilonka is thanked for being such a positive influence on my mood (again) during the writing period of this book.

1

SETTING THE SCENE

Learning goals

- *Be able to precisely define and explain what basic e-business and networked e-business is.*
- *Know the essentials of the history of e-business and networked e-business.*
- *Be able to explain the relation of the concept of networked e-business to other concepts in the field.*
- *Understand the role of business and technology in networked e-business.*

1.1 Introduction

This book is on networked e-business – doing business in business networks using digital means for communication, collaboration and the execution of business transactions. Networked e-business is all around us – both in private and business settings. As consumers, we buy all kinds of things through electronic channels: books, music, electronics, airplane tickets, complete holidays and so on. We receive more and more information from a broad spectrum of organizations in 'the digital way'. Companies collaborate more and more using automated systems that exchange information digitally to support effective and efficient business operation. They also engage in business networks that become increasingly dynamic and complex to enable the production of highly integrated products and services. Government organizations are moving to digital business processes, creating *e-government* initiatives. The internet and the web are the default means of communication for many – be it for professional or private goals. We all live and work in the so-called *global village*, which has been enabled by the advance of information technology (IT) and is characterized by previously unseen levels of interconnectedness (typically with the internet at its foundation).

Although the extreme electronic business hype (also referred to as the *internet bubble* [Perk99]) of the turn of the century has passed, it is clear that the combination of computers, networks and business has a high impact on how the modern economy (and the entire society, for that matter) operates [Piep01]. Some argue that electronic business and networked business actually constitute *the* most important business developments of the past decades. But when one takes a more thorough look around, the question "what exactly is networked e-business?" quickly comes to mind. Clearly, not any combination of computers and business constitutes networked e-business – if this were the case, we would have had networked e-business back in the 1950s and 1960s, when computers started to be used to support basic administrative tasks.[1]

In the following section we deal with the question of what networked e-business is and try to provide some clarity. In section 1.3 we briefly discuss the history of networked e-business. In section 1.4 we compare the term *networked e-business* to a number of related terms. Then, in section 1.5 we take a closer look at the relationship between business and technology in the context of networked e-business. In section 1.6 we explain the purpose and structure of our exploration of networked e-business and hence the structure of this book. Section 1.7 ends the chapter with a summary and a set of questions and exercises related to the contents of this chapter.

1.2 What exactly is networked e-business?

As we have stated earlier, networked e-business is not just any combination of computers and business. A company that only uses a computer to perform its salary administration clearly does not constitute networked e-business. In this section we first work towards a basic definition that distinguishes e-business from non-e-business. Next, we extend this definition to identify networked e-business, the topic that we address throughout this book.

1.2.1 Towards a basic definition

In this section we develop a basic definition of e-business. To start, we must observe that we don't use the term *e-business* to denote an organization form or a class of information technology. The term *e-business* denotes a specific kind of business activity performed by one or more organizations with the use of information technology. To call a combination of business activities and information technology *e-business*, a number of criteria have to be met to make sure that we deal with a truly important combination of business and information technologies.

1. The activities must be *core activities* (also called *primary activities*) for the business; that is, they must be directly related to the reason for the existence of the

involved organization(s). For example, for an airline company selling tickets and transporting people are core activities, but bookkeeping and cleaning their offices are not.

2. The use of information technology must be essential for the way the activities are performed; that is, the activities must be *IT-enabled*. Activities for which efficiency or effectiveness are only improved by the use of IT are called *IT-supported* activities – hence, they do not qualify as e-business.[2]

3. The information technology must be used in an *integrated fashion* for both the processing and communication of information. In other words: information must be both transformed and transported digitally. If only one of these two aspects is enabled by IT, we do not call it e-business.

These criteria lead to the following basic definition of e-business that we use in this book (we extend it in the following section):

Electronic business is conducting core business activities in a way that is enabled by the integrated use of information technology for processing and communication of information.

If you prefer ultra-short definitions, the following abbreviation may be used:

E-business is IT-enabled business.

Given this definition, the use of IT is the discriminating factor that distinguishes e-business from 'traditional' business. As we see in the remainder of this book, this discriminating use of IT can either be realized by using 'general' IT in a way that is specific for e-business or by using new types of IT in a *technology push mode* – we revisit this issue in section 1.5.

1.2.2 Towards an extended definition

The previous definition separates e-business from non-e-business by listing the minimum requirements that have to be met. Using minimum requirements in the definition, including the not-so-interesting cases. To distinguish the not-so-interesting cases from the really interesting ones we have to discuss two aspects: *scope of activities* and *dynamism of relations*.

The *scope of activities* determines whether e-business activities are executed entirely within the boundaries of a single organization (*intra-organizational*) or are executed across the boundaries of several organizations (*inter-* or *cross-organizational*). If activities are inter-organizational, they are part of a collaboration between organizations. Collaboration between organizations is of increasing importance for the delivery of complex products and services. In traditional e-business a customer buys a stand-alone product (or service), whereas in contemporary e-business a consumer buys a product (or service) that is integrated in a 'web' of related services (and products).

For example, a consumer buys an e-reader (a product) that is connected to an online content delivery service, to an online software update service, and to a social network for discussing the use of the device. As such, a business network is required in which the device-provider organization, the content and software providers and the social network operator collaborate. In business-oriented markets we see similar developments. An example is the mobility market, in which simple car-leasing services (providing a product: the lease car) are replaced by integrated mobility solutions that include services such as shared cars, public transportation, flexible meeting-rooms support, teleconferencing and travel planning [Lüft14].

Inter-organizational e-business helps in transforming the nature of collaboration in business markets. Inter-organizational e-business has much greater consequences for these markets than intra-organizational e-business, making things more complex but also more interesting.

The *dynamism of relations* determines how dynamic the relations are between organizations that together engage in e-business activities. E-business facilitates the dissolution of long-term, static dependencies between organizations because it enables organizations to easily find new partners to work and connect with. This allows for new temporary forms of collaborations, which can lead to highly dynamic partnerships. In the mobility market example mentioned earlier, we see that collaboration networks change as customer requirements to mobility change: new service providers are added to a collaboration (e.g., a rental bike provider); other service providers are discarded from a business network. Dynamism of relations is obviously only of interest to inter-organizational e-business.

Highly dynamic partnerships are more interesting than static partnerships from an e-business perspective because they have to rely to a larger extent on specific characteristics of e-business (such as easily finding new partners to collaborate and connect with). But more importantly, from a business perspective highly dynamic partnerships are becoming increasingly important to deal with the dynamism of contemporary markets – think for example of the rapid developments in the telecommunication and entertainment markets.

Given the previous discussion of *scope* and *dynamism*, we provide an extended version of the basic definition of e-business given earlier, which delineates the *interesting* field of networked e-business for this book.[3]

Networked electronic business (e-business) is conducting inter-organizational core business activities in dynamic business collaborations, such that these activities are enabled by the integrated use of information technology for both communication and processing of information.

Note that we assume dynamic collaborations implicitly in the term *networked e-business*: to keep terminology short, we don't use the term *dynamic networked e-business*.

1.2.3 E-business scenarios

To actually conduct networked e-business, two or more parties engage in a concrete collaboration with a specific goal, specific characteristics and a specific context.

In our terminology, networked e-business is conducted in *e-business scenarios*, which we define as follows:

An e-business scenario is a setting in which two or more parties engage in networked e-business to achieve a specific business goal.

We use the term *party* in this definition to include both business organizations, non-business organizations (such as government organizations) and individuals (e.g., consumers). For reasons of brevity, we don't prefix the term *e-business scenario* with *networked* (we consider this implicitly understood). Examples of simple e-business scenarios include a web shop that collaborates with a logistics company to sell and deliver products to consumers (a three-party scenario) and an organization that offers financial services through the internet to other organizations (a two-party scenario). We will see more elaborate examples throughout this book.

The definition of e-business scenario implies that one organization (or individual) can be involved in more than one e-business scenario at the same time (to achieve more than one business goal). This is illustrated in Figure 1.1. Here, we see five parties *A*, *B*, *C*, *D* and *E*, and three e-business scenarios *1*, *2* and *3*. Parties *B* and *E* are each involved in two e-business scenarios. As an example, party *B* may be a logistics service provider that provides different logistics solutions in different scenarios. Note that scenarios *1* and *3* are two-party scenarios, and scenario *2* is a three-party scenario (a scenario can have any number of parties greater than two). Given the dynamic nature of networked e-business, parties engage in e-business scenarios and leave e-business scenarios as new business goals dictate.

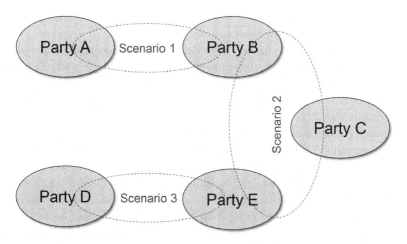

FIGURE 1.1 Parties in networked e-business scenarios.

In this book we concentrate on networked e-business conforming to the definitions outlined in this section. We start the discussion of the networked e-business domain in the next section with a brief outline of its history.

1.3 A brief history of networked e-business

Although e-business in general is not per se coupled to the use of the internet (as we have seen in the definitions of the previous section), its development is closely related to the development of the internet. Therefore, the development of the internet plays an important role in the history of networked e-business. In this section we first briefly look at e-business before the internet era. Then we discuss how the internet became the communication platform of choice for e-business. After that, we pay attention to two important periods after these initial developments: the e-business hype around the turn of the century and the 'steady times' that have been witnessed after the hype. In these steady times the networked character of e-business becomes evident.

1.3.1 Before the internet

The use of information technology to allow companies to collaborate in business can be traced back to the previous century. In the early days of this development, we find dedicated systems for very specific business activities. An example is the SABRE airline booking system, which was used starting in the early 1960s to connect airline ticketing offices to a central data center [Wik14f].[4] Another example is electronic business between banks, which since the 1970s has been supported by the network of the Society for Worldwide Interbank Financial Telecommunication (SWIFT) [Wik14g].

Before the rise of the internet, high-volume e-business scenarios typically relied on dedicated digital communication channels; that is, communication channels that were created for specific business activities between specific pairs of business partners. Low-volume e-business typically relied on using existing phone lines and modems to connect computers to each other.

Often, communication channels were dedicated both conceptually and physically; that is, both in their logical design and in their realization in hardware (physical wires). With these channels, standards such as *electronic data interchange* (EDI) [Soko95] and *electronic funds transfer* (EFT) [Kirk87] were supported to allow business organizations to perform business transactions in an electronic fashion.

The dedicated channels were usually very expensive and time-consuming to set up (and maintain). Therefore, they typically only supported long-term, stable business collaborations between pairs of large organizations. Because of this, e-business was only available to a small set of business organizations. Also, this form of e-business only conforms to our basic definition of e-business, as discussed earlier in this chapter, as e-business relations were far from dynamic. The rise of the internet in the final two decades of the twentieth century changed the e-business landscape dramatically.

1.3.2 The rise of the internet

The history of the internet starts in the 1960s [Wik14c], long before the days of modern e-business. The predecessor of the internet, ARPANET, was established as a research network at the end of the 1960s, linking only a few research institutions in the Untied States. ARPANET grew both in size and in technology and was linked to NSFNet (the network of the American National Science Foundation) in the late 1980s. At about that time the name *internet* started to be used for a global network based on standardized TCP/IP technology (we discuss this technology in section 8.2.1). At the same time, this global network started to rapidly grow in size.

The growth in the size of the internet is shown in Figure 1.2.[5] In this figure the vertical axis shows the number of internet hosts; that is, the number of computers connected to the internet. The curved line gives a rough indication of the number of hosts through the years. Note that the vertical axis has a logarithmic scale: the figure shows that the internet has undergone an exponential growth since the early 1980s. Somewhere around 2013 the internet reached one billion hosts [ISC14].

The growth of the internet has enabled the pervasiveness of internet computing. Currently, the internet is 'always everywhere' – making the word 'ubiquitous' literally true.[6] It is hard to find places in the so-called civilized world that do not have internet access. The CIA World Factbook gives a list of internet connectivity (measured in number of internet hosts) per country. The list is topped in 2014 by

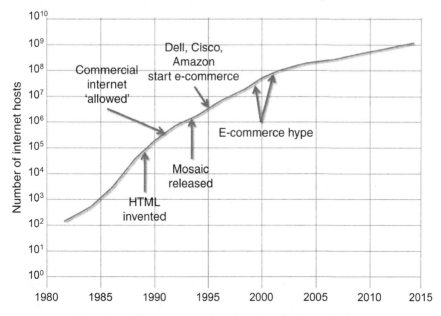

FIGURE 1.2   Overview of internet growth and major e-business developments.

the United States, with about half a billion hosts (at the bottom of the list is the Marshall Islands, with three hosts in 2012) [CIA14]. The growth of the internet continues – it is not even constrained by the number of people on the planet, as more and more devices and machines become connected to the internet – both of the human-operated kind and of the fully automated kind.

With the advent of the internet, a ubiquitous and inexpensive infrastructure became available for business transactions. Figure 1.2 shows two important technology milestones: the definition of HTML as a standard web markup language in 1989 and the release of Mosaic [Rauc95] as the first web browser in 1993. Together, these two milestones enabled the development of the *world wide web* (WWW), one of the technology cornerstones of modern e-business (we revisit the technology of the WWW in detail in section 8.2.2). Its presence has become so generally accepted that it is commonly referred to as simply 'the web' – without anybody asking 'which web?' (the odd arachnologist excluded, of course).

Figure 1.2 also shows that commercial use of the internet only has been allowed from the early 1990s. Among the first large commercial parties taking advantage of the possibilities of the internet were Dell [Dell06], Cisco [Paul01] and Amazon [Marc05]. The fact that two of these three are IT companies is not a coincidence, as using e-business was still highly technology-dominated in those days. A few years later, however, many business organizations were venturing commercially into the internet, leading to the *internet hype* or *e-commerce hype*.

1.3.3 The e-commerce hype

Towards the turn of the century, the development of e-business (then often labeled 'e-commerce') resulted in a hype of tremendous (if not ridiculous) proportions. Many were convinced that prefixing any business idea with an *e-* would lead to immediate success and, of course, great wealth for the inventor. As prefixing a business idea with *e-* usually led to setting up a website with an address ending in *.com*, the e-commerce hype is also known as the *dot-com hype*. During the hype period, the number of e-business companies grew at an exponential rate, not unlike the rise of the internet that provided the technical infrastructure for them.

The hype period, however, lasted only a few years until people realized that not all that shines (or appears to shine) is gold. Many internet startups went bankrupt after very short operating periods. Or, as a coined phrase states, the internet bubble burst. A typical and well-known example is Pets.com, an online retail store for pet supplies that went online in 1998 and was liquidated in 2000 after having 'burned' substantial capital [Wik14j].

After the bubble burst, many were disillusioned, thinking that the days of e-business were over. But this wasn't the case at all: digital castles in the air were simply separated from realistic e-business developments – and these realistic developments were actually doing well, moving into steady times for networked e-business. One may note that the three pioneering companies mentioned earlier are all still in healthy existence at the time of this book's publication.

1.3.4 Into steady times

After the burst of the internet bubble, e-business has been growing steadily and has taken a solid position in the global economy. In many domains, e-business has become the primary way of doing business; for example, in the banking, insurance and travel industries. Other domains are currently in a transition phase; for example, the music, television and publishing industries – here we observe a growing use of digital communication media, more interactivity and more *on-demand* services. Today, anything can be traded using e-business, from simple pencils to complete islands (see Figure 1.3). Providing complex, solution-oriented services is becoming a major part of networked e-business. It is this mature, integrated version of e-business that we deal with in this book.

In these steady times, however, e-business still is a constantly and swiftly changing domain. From the business perspective, the role of dynamic business networking is growing to create business collaborations that can deal with fluid market conditions and quickly changing customer requirements: networked e-business is moving beyond 'traditional' e-business. From the technology perspective, changes are highly influenced by a set of major IT-driven developments: mobile computing, social media, cloud computing, big data and the internet of things. We call these developments the *Big Five* and we discuss them in detail in section 2.2.

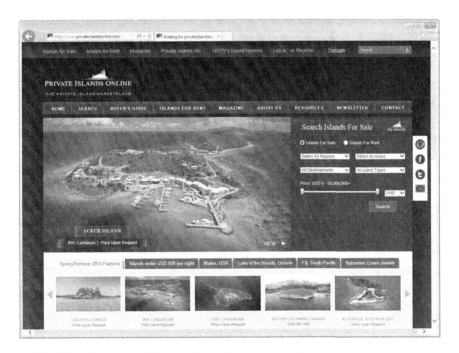

FIGURE 1.3 (Almost) anything can be traded using e-business.

1.4 Networked business, e-business, e-commerce and other terms

The term e-business is used (and misused) in many different ways. The same goes for quite a few related terms. We have defined our use of the terms *e-business* and *networked e-business* in section 1.2. In the current section we place our interpretation of the term e-business in the context of a number of related terms to obtain clarity in terminology.

A term that is often used as a synonym of e-business is *electronic commerce* or *e-commerce*. We, however, see e-commerce as a subset of e-business; that is, all e-commerce is e-business but not the other way around. In our use the term e-commerce implies explicit trading of objects (which can be physical or non-physical objects, see section 3.5 for a further discussion). So, we have the following definition of e-commerce:

Electronic commerce is e-business in which objects are explicitly traded between participating parties.

E-business may include trading, but it doesn't have to. Collaborative product design through electronic channels is an example of e-business in which there is no explicit trading. One may argue, however, that there is implicit trading in collaborative design as parts of designs are exchanged between organizations. Note that other visions on the relationship between the terms e-business and e-commerce exist in literature. According to one view, e-business refers to intra-organizational activities and e-commerce to inter-organizational activities [VanH03]. Obviously, this latter view conflicts with the one of this book.

The term e-business does not imply anything about the nature of the digital communication channel used to communicate between involved organizations. If we restrict the channels to wireless channels, we restrict electronic business to *mobile business* or *m-business*. As such, m-business is a subset of e-business. So, we have the following definition of m-business:

Mobile business is e-business in which a substantial part of collaboration between participating parties is realized through wireless channels.

If m-business is about explicit trading of objects, we speak of *mobile commerce* or *m-commerce*. As such, m-commerce is a subset of both m-business and e-commerce. Worded more precisely, m-commerce is the intersection of m-business and e-commerce.

The subset relations between e-business, m-business, e-commerce and m-commerce are shown in Figure 1.4 (as a Venn diagram [Wik14l]).

Apart from the terms introduced here, many other related terms have been invented, such as *internet commerce* (or *i-commerce*), *digital commerce*, *cyber commerce*, *cyber business*, *virtual commerce*, *online commerce*, *online business* and so on. To make matters

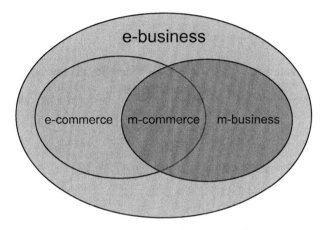

FIGURE 1.4   Subset relationships between some terms.

worse, these terms are used differently in different places. Hence, we don't try to discuss and define them all.

In this book we stay with the basic terms and relationships shown in Figure 1.4, adding the *networked business* aspect to arrive at *networked e-business.* The network aspect can be added to the other three terms as well to explicitly indicate the collaborative character, thus arriving at *networked e-commerce, networked m-business* and *networked m-commerce.*

1.5 Business versus technology

In the developments in the field of networked e-business, business and technology aspects are strongly interwoven. In many other fields business developments create new requirements to technology. In other words: technology follows business. In the field of e-business, however, many business developments have taken place because the enabling technology created the opportunity. A well-known and very clear example is the development of the use of the web for retailing applications: the web was not developed because business demanded it; rather, the mere existence of the web pushed business into new directions.

Consequently, developments in networked e-business are driven by two concurrently operating forces that reinforce each other: a market pull (also called requirements pull) force and a technology push force (see Figure 1.5). Both forces are strong in the sense that they are driven by rapid developments. Developments are easily observable not only on the technology side[7] but also on the market (business) side. These developments cause e-business to change at a pace that is sometimes hard to keep up with.

In trying to understand the fast developments in networked e-business, we must always be aware of the dual force field shown in Figure 1.5. Focusing on

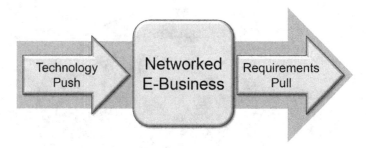

FIGURE 1.5 Technology push and requirements pull.

technology only may mean that one forgets to understand what the market wants. Many e-business initiatives have died this way. Focusing on the market side only may mean that one forgets to adequately use new technological possibilities. Many traditional business organizations have lost large market shares by disregarding technological developments. In chapter 2 we discuss five major technology-inspired developments in networked e-business that shape part of its development.

1.6 Goal and structure of this book

Now that we have a first impression of the domain of networked e-business, it is time to see what and how this book contributes to our further understanding of this domain. To do so, we discuss in this section the goal and the structure of this book.

1.6.1 Goal of this book

The goal of this book is to explain the domain of networked e-business in a well-structured way, covering the complete spectrum from business to technology aspects. Note that many explorations of the domain do already exist, but in isolation most are not fit for our purposes. Often, they have a more narrow main focus; for example, mainly on business aspects [Phil03, McKa04], sometimes explicitly with a case-based orientation [Elli02, Jela08], or mainly on technology aspects [VanS03]. Often, they do not follow a well-defined structure that indeed helps in clearly and unambiguously charting the territory of networked e-business. To achieve a clear structure, in chapters 3 and 4 of this book introduces a three-dimensional analysis space and a four-aspect framework.

Note that the purpose of this book is to also provide a time-independent framework for the networked e-business domain. This implies that the focus is not so much on the many volatile technical details or business case studies that exist – for this, the reader is referred to the heaps of related material (the rest of the book provides many references for this goal). The focus of this book is on concepts and relations between concepts that withstand the erosion of time.

The book is aimed at both students at the senior undergraduate or graduate level and professionals operating in the e-business field. Understanding this book requires only basic prior knowledge of business structures and information technology, such that it is useful for both readers with a technology-oriented background and readers with a business-oriented background.

1.6.2 Structure of this book

In this chapter we have provided an introduction to the field of networked e-business. In the rest of this book, we explore this field in a systematic way.

We start in chapter 3 by identifying a space for three description dimensions for classifying scenarios in networked e-business. In chapter 4 we extend these three dimensions by adding a fourth for the structured analysis or design of e-business scenarios. This dimension uses the *BOAT framework* to distinguish aspects of e-business scenarios. This fourth dimension is chosen as the leading dimension for the structure of the remainder of this book (as the text in a book is in principle one-dimensional, one leading dimension is clearest).

The BOAT framework distinguishes between four aspects of e-business: *business*, *organization*, *architecture* and *technology*. These aspects are each discussed in more detail in chapters 5 to 8. Because the BOAT framework is also explicitly concerned with relating aspects, we pay explicit attention to mapping each discussed aspect to the other aspects in chapters 6 to 8.

In chapter 9 we provide an approach to use the classification space and the BOAT framework as an analysis instrument for the assessment of existing e-business scenarios and a design instrument for the design of new e-business scenarios. Chapter 10 is devoted to business strategy. In it we show how business strategy is a context in which business models for networked e-business are developed. Chapter 11 concludes this book by presenting some final observations.

Throughout the book we use three running example cases to illustrate the introduced concepts and models. These cases are introduced in the next chapter and are further elaborated on at the end of each chapter.

Each chapter of this book is concluded with a chapter end section, which includes a short chapter summary and a set of questions and exercises to actively apply the knowledge of that chapter.

1.7 Chapter end

Here we present a brief chapter summary containing the main messages of this chapter. We then provide a set of questions and exercises to apply the concepts from this chapter.

1.7.1 Chapter summary

E-business is the type of business that is enabled by the use of information technology. In e-business information technology is used both for processing and for communication of information. This book focuses on dynamic, inter-organizational scenarios for e-business, which we label as *networked e-business*. E-business (following this focus) is a relatively young domain, which started around 1995. After a hype period around the turn of the century, we have arrived at a productive field of networked e-business.

E-commerce is the subdomain of e-business that explicitly aims at trading objects. *M-business* is the subdomain of e-business that relies on mobile devices for communication between business parties. *M-commerce* is the intersection of e-commerce and m-business.

Networked e-business develops quickly as a consequence of the sum of technology push and requirements pull forces, which reinforce each other.

1.7.2 Questions and exercises

1. Find four organizations in practice that are involved in three different e-business scenarios (in the manner shown in Figure 1.1).
2. Select a well-known networked e-business organization and reconstruct its development. Establish whether it is a new organization (a so-called *greenfield operation*) or a pre-existing organization that (partly) has converted to networked e-business.
3. In section 1.3 we have sketched the history of networked e-business and pointed out that this is still a short history that is quickly developing (given the ubiquitous nature of e-business nowadays). Compare the history and development of networked e-business with those of other areas that have had a development with technology push elements, such as railroad transport or telecommunication.
4. Try and make an 'educated prediction' of the further growth of the size of the internet (in terms of number of internet hosts) beyond the graph shown in Figure 1.2. Are there parameters or factors constraining the future size of the internet? Note that there are not only 'traditional computers' connected to the internet but also other devices (both in the business world and in the personal world). Try and use sources of information (e.g., [daCo13]).
5. Try to get numbers on the 'size' of (networked) e-business in terms of the total turnover of e-business transactions per year (for a large e-business organization or for a country). Note that the numbers obviously heavily depend on the exact definition of the term (networked) e-business.

Notes

1 One of the milestones in this development were UNIVAC computers [Wein52], the first line of general-purpose computers for commercial use [Wik14o].
2 In the sequel to this book we make an exception to this rule for activities for which efficiency is *dramatically* improved, as this enables truly new forms of business – we address this point in chapter 5.

3 Note that this definition of e-business is not shared by all. Many others use a much broader definition, sometimes as broad as 'e-business is doing business with computers'. Obviously, almost all business is covered by such a broad definition, as there is hardly any contemporary business in which computers do not play a role.
4 The SABRE system (obviously in a much more modern version) is still in use. It now supports many more travel-related business activities than airline booking [Wik14f].
5 This figure was constructed from several sources.
6 Ideas exist to even extend the internet beyond planet Earth [Wik14k], although the use of that extension for e-business purposes can be questioned, obviously.
7 Information and communication technologies come and sometimes go at rapid rates. Development and acceptance of new technologies are very nicely illustrated by the *hype cycle* model developed by Gartner [Fenn05].

2

THE PRACTICAL CONTEXT

Learning goals

- Know the most important IT-related developments (the Big Five) that influence the current state and future of networked e-business: social media, mobile computing, cloud computing, big data and the internet of things.
- Know the relation of the Big Five developments to networked e-business and to each other.
- Understand the basics of a number of e-business scenarios that cover the spectrum from 'traditional' e-business (taking place between two or three parties) to highly networked e-business (taking place in a network of many parties).

2.1 Introduction

In this chapter we discuss the practical context of networked e-business. We do this from two perspectives: technology and business. The technology perspective is covered in section 2.2. Here, we introduce the five main IT-related developments that influence the current state and future of networked e-business (which we call the Big Five). Section 2.3 is devoted to the business perspective of the practical context. In this section we introduce the three running case studies that we use throughout this book to illustrate the practical side of networked e-business: POSH, TTU and TraXP. We present the main characteristics of each individual case study and discuss the main differences among them. As in the previous chapter we end this chapter with a summary and a set of questions and exercises related to the contents of the chapter, which are provided in section 2.4.

2.2 Main IT-related developments: the Big Five

Currently, many changes in networked e-business are strongly influenced by a set of main IT-related developments that we call the *Big Five*[1]: social media, mobile computing, cloud computing, big data and the internet of things (see Figure 2.1). All of these developments have a technology aspect and a business aspect (as discussed in the previous chapter), although they were initially mainly developed from the technology perspective. We discuss each of the Big Five developments in more detail in the following sections.

2.2.1 Social media

Perhaps the most visible and most discussed IT-driven development is the rise of social media. This rise has been enabled by the fact that individuals have obtained direct access to easy-to-use computing devices connected to the internet on a very large scale and at relatively low costs. The visibility of the rise of social media is – quite obviously – caused by the fact that social media are directly used by individuals in all kinds of facets of daily life.

We can distinguish between several classes of social media: *community-oriented*, *messaging-oriented* and *media-oriented*. Boundaries among the classes are blurring, however, as applications in these three classes are almost constantly expanding their functionality, incorporating elements from other classes. This is illustrated in Figure 2.2.

The *community-oriented* class of social media primarily targets the support of communities or networks of humans beings. This class of social media allows users to create groups of individuals (or organizations) around specific individuals, organizations or themes. Within a group, status updates of various kinds can be shared and augmented with messages and media. Well-known examples are Facebook (www.facebook.com), which typically targets private communities and networks,

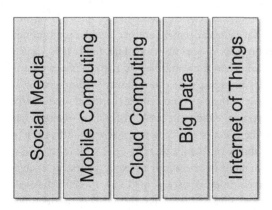

FIGURE 2.1   The Big Five.

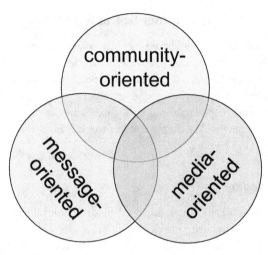

FIGURE 2.2 Classes of social media.

and LinkedIn (www.linkedin.com), which typically targets professional communities and networks.

The *message-oriented* class of social media primarily aims at the support of message-based communication between individuals or groups of individuals. Messaging is typically asynchronous (transmission of a message without required receipt confirmation), but can be used as a basis for interactive conversations. Well-known examples are Twitter (www.twitter.com; mostly for one-to-many communication on a subscription basis) and WhatsApp (www.whatsapp.com; mostly for one-to-one communication on a direct addressing basis).

The *media-oriented* class of social media primarily aims at facilitating the sharing of multimedia files, such as photographs and videos. Sharing is supported by offering large repositories for media that have a centralized appearance to users. Media repositories offer facilities to store (upload), search and retrieve (download) media. In this class, YouTube (www.youtube.com) is a well-known example of video sharing and Flickr (www.flickr.com) is a well-known example of photo sharing.

Social media have created large internet-based communities that are related to networked e-business in various ways. This holds for e-business activities targeted *towards* a community, for e-business activities *within* a community or external e-business activities emerging *from* a community. With respect to activities towards a community, the size of the user communities of social media makes them attractive for marketing purposes of different kinds by business organizations. As an example, Facebook has on the order of one billion active users at the time of this book's publication. The availability of data on users in a network (either provided by the users themselves or generated by the social network operator) enables highly directed marketing. Within communities, social media are used for the evaluation, discussion and promotion of all kinds of products and services, thereby providing (implicit) e-business services. With respect to e-business activities from a community, users of social media can organize themselves to engage group-wise into e-business with third parties.

2.2.2 Mobile computing

In the previous section we have mentioned that the rise of social media is perhaps the most visible and most discussed of the Big Five. However, the development of mobile computing may be a big contender too. By *mobile computing* we refer to the availability and use of computing facilities that are not bound to a static location. And as this book is about networked e-business, we mainly focus on mobile computing facilities that are connected to the internet in some way (either on a continuous basis or on an intermittent basis).

Mobile computing has mainly been enabled by two distinct technology developments: the development of mobile computing devices and the development of wireless networks that can be used by these devices. We can roughly say that the early days of mobile computing correspond to the final decades of the twentieth century. In these days, mobile computing devices were mainly based on portable computers (e.g., laptops) and *personal digital assistants* (PDAs), and networking often had to rely either on wired connections or on modems and phone networks. In the beginning of the twenty-first century we have seen a confluence of computing devices and communication devices – resulting in the well-known and extremely popular smartphone [Ahma11]. We have also seen the developments of light-weight mobile devices such as tablets with built-in communication capabilities. For networking, these devices typically rely both on Wi-Fi connections (when in the vicinity of Wi-Fi internet access points) and on cellular data connections (using 3G or 4G cellular data networks). One of the major enabling sub-technologies for mobile computing that may be less visible is power management and battery technology.

The advent of mobile computing has caused a disconnection of computing and internet access from fixed work places, giving way to the always-and-everywhere-connected paradigm. This has changed (and will further change) the nature of e-business, since it enables conducting e-business transactions at the time and spot that is most convenient for a customer – or the most profitable for a provider.

2.2.3 Cloud computing

Based on the definition by the US National Institute of Standards and Technology (NIST), *cloud computing* is a computing paradigm for enabling ubiquitous, convenient on-demand network access to a shared pool of configurable computing resources and services [Mell11]. Or, in simpler terms, we can say that cloud computing makes shared, remote computing facilities easily accessible. Cloud computing aims to achieve a number of advantages for users with computing requirements: lowering technology entry thresholds, lowering costs through large-scale sharing and adapting available computing performance to dynamically changing usage requirements (referred to as *elasticity*).

Cloud computing is enabled by the combination of two main elements:

- the use of flexible, remote computing infrastructures (platform virtualization); and
- the use of remote application functionality (application virtualization).

Here we discuss both elements in a nutshell. For more details, see [Armb09, Armb10].

Platform virtualization is the use of remote computing platforms instead of local computing platforms. These remote platforms are typically operated by platform service providers that are external to the user organization. The user organization can run its software on these platforms as if it has these platforms installed locally: the platforms are virtual. The 'amount' and 'quality' of platform available to a user is specified in a service-level agreement (SLA). A computing platform refers to the technical infrastructure required to run application programs. In a narrow sense, it consists of computing hardware, data storage and computer networks. In a broader sense, it also includes security facilities, back-up facilities, power and cooling facilities and personnel to maintain all these facilities. A platform service provider typically offers its services to a number of user organizations. This is in a sense comparable to a power company offering power (such as electricity) to a number of users. Therefore, platform virtualization is also referred to as *utility computing*. In platform virtualization, a distinction is often made between *infrastructure as a service* (IaaS) and *platform as a service* (PaaS). IaaS is the most basic model, based on providing computers (and other resources). Provided computers can be physical, but more often they are virtual machines. PaaS is a more advanced model in which cloud providers deliver a complete computing platform. This platform typically includes an operating system, a programming language execution environment, a database server and a web server.

Application virtualization is the use of (business) application software that is installed remotely – in the context of cloud computing on a virtualized platform run by a provider. For personal computing, application virtualization is currently very popular. Well-known examples can be found in personal communication applications such as Outlook (www.outlook.com) or Gmail (www.gmail.com), where the application software runs remotely and is accessed by a web browser. Application virtualization can in principle be used in two basic forms: using partly virtualized applications and using completely virtualized applications. With partially virtualized applications part of the business functionality is run on local platforms. This local functionality makes use of other functionality that is offered remotely. This form can be realized using service-oriented computing and can hence be seen as service outsourcing. With completely virtualized applications, the entire business functionality is run on remote platforms – locally, only the user interface is supported. This form is typically referred to as application hosting or, more popularly, as *software as a service* (SaaS). To make SaaS as effective as possible, the user interface layer should be as 'thin' as possible; that is, require as little as possible specific functionality. In the ultimate case, the user interface is completely realized using web technology, such that a standard web browser suffices for application use.

Cloud computing empowers ubiquitous end-user computing for consumers, such as the email services we have mentioned earlier. It also powers social media platforms as discussed in section 2.2.1. Cloud computing is very relevant for enterprise computing, however, and hence for networked e-business applications. Platform virtualization allows for quick setup of computing facilities without large upfront investments, thereby facilitating the quick launch of new e-business initiatives. Usage elasticity allows an e-business organization to have the 'size' of its computing facilities follow the 'size' of its business in fluid markets. Software as a service allows an e-business company to use virtualized standard software without installation or maintenance effort – and hence concentrate on those software assets that set it apart in a market.

2.2.4 Big data

The term *big data* refers to the acquisition, processing and use of (very) large amounts of data. These large amounts of data may originate from a single source, but they may also be produced by multiple sources. The term is used both for scientific domains (such as astronomy, where automated digital telescopes produce huge amounts of data) and for business domains (such as telecommunication and retail, where large business organizations produce huge amounts of data). It is – obviously – the latter domain that is interesting in the context of this book. The advent of big data is powered by the automated recording of data, as the involved amounts of data cannot be entered manually. Note that either data from automated sources (such as the previously mentioned digital telescopes) can be recorded automatically, or data from activities of large groups of human beings (such as their telecommunication behavior).

The size of databases in business is quickly increasing. As an example, *The Economist* reported in 2010 that Wal-Mart, a very large retail organization, handles more than one million customer transactions every hour, feeding databases estimated at more than 2.5 petabytes[2] [Econ10]. Social media (as discussed earlier in this section) generate huge amounts of data that can be of business interest. This holds for data that are explicitly uploaded by users, but certainly also for data that are logged as a result of activities of users (the trail of clicks of internet users is sometimes referred to as *data exhaust* [Econ10]).

Big data can be used in networked e-business for various purposes. It can be used in marketing as input for advertising campaigns. It can be used in new business developments for spotting emerging business or consumer trends. It can be an important input in customer relationship management (CRM) for detecting and analyzing customer group behavior.

The advent of big data brings all kinds new possibilities, such as the ones mentioned earlier. It also, however, brings new problems. An obvious problem is storing and processing enormous amounts of information – both from a technical and a financial point of view. Another problem is in selecting the interesting data and the interesting information distilled from it – the availability of data becomes a problem in itself (this is referred to as the *information overload* problem). A third (and often difficult) problem lies in dealing with ownership, confidentiality and security of data.

2.2.5 Internet of things

In the development of *internet of things* (IoT), an integration is created of the digital and the physical world [Kell13]. This can in principle be accomplished in two ways. The first way is to make physical objects 'intelligent' by embedding computing and communication facilities into them and connecting these to the internet. The second way is to attach tags to physical objects, such that sensors that are connected to the internet can read these tags and generate information about the objects. Likewise, actuators internal or external to physical objects can change their physical state.

A well-known and relatively simple class of tags and sensors is found in *radio-frequency identification* (RFID) technology. By equipping physical objects with RFID tags, their movements can be automatically fed to the internet when they pass by RFID readers. RFID is, for instance, applied in logistics scenarios [Jone07].

The use of networked, location-aware devices can also be seen as part of the internet of things when it applies to physically tracking these devices. This use applies to persons with networked, global positioning system (GPS)-enabled smartphones (thus creating an 'internet of persons') and to vehicles with networked, GPS-enabled devices such as digital driving assistants (thus creating an 'internet of vehicles').

The internet of things is applied in domains such as transport, logistics and manufacturing. In these domains, the development enables automatic registration of the transport of products from their source to their destination, allowing providers, transporters and consumers to track transport in a real-time fashion without human intervention.

Applications in the internet of things can serve as sources of big data (as discussed earlier in this section). For example, the automatic tracking of products (and vehicles) in large logistics companies can generate huge amounts of logistics data. Cloud computing can be used as an enabler of the internet of things by making data-processing capabilities available in a ubiquitous fashion.

2.2.6 Relating the Big Five

In this section we have discussed the Big Five technology-inspired (but business-related) developments that influence the development of networked e-business. In the discussion we also have indicated a few relationships among developments in the Big Five. In Figure 2.3 we show a complete overview of the relationships in the context of networked e-business. We have classified the relationships into two categories: 'enables' and 'feeds data'. In the first category one development technically enables the other. In the second category applications in one development generate data that can be used by applications in the second development.

Cloud computing is a basic technology class in this context: it does not rely on any of the other four classes. Both mobile computing and social media rely heavily on cloud computing: both classes make use of platforms and functionalities that are offered 'in the cloud'. This is caused by the fact that they typically use *thin clients*; that is, relatively simple software that provides user interface functionality and relies on remote software for the support of the actual core application functionality. Applications in the big data class often rely on cloud computing to have distributed means for data capture and flexible means for high-volume data processing. Applications in the internet of things class rely on mobile computing for interaction with mobile objects. They also rely on cloud computing to enable the distributed data processing that is typical for this class.

Depending on the business domain, applications in the big data class can be fed with data that are generated by applications in the mobile computing, social media or internet of things classes (or combinations of these). For example, in the e-business marketing business domain, big data applications for analysis of customer behavior can be fed by data generated by social media applications.

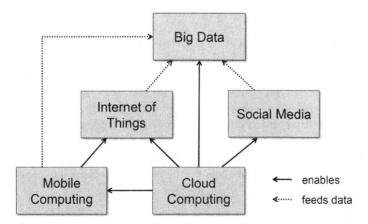

FIGURE 2.3 Relationships among the Big Five.

2.3 The running cases of this book

In this book we use three example cases to illustrate most of what we introduce in the various chapters. We use multiple case studies to show how networked e-business can be different depending on the business domain and the business goals of an organization. The case studies are based on fictive companies to allow for full freedom of discussion. The companies are described such, however, that they conform to real-world, networked e-business as much as possible.

The first case study is the Perfect Office Solution House (POSH), a company specializing in office solutions. POSH is making the move from the 'old economy' to the 'new economy' by introducing e-business concepts. The second case study is TalkThroughUs (TTU), a newly established company specializing in business services for interpretation and translation between various languages via the internet. The third case study is TraXP, a new spin-off in the travel industry that offers highly integrated travel solutions for various customer segments.

For reasons of clarity and brevity, the discussion of the cases throughout the book is simplified with respect to real-world scenarios – the complete and detailed description of one e-business scenario elaboration easily fills a book by itself. In the following sections we introduce each of the three cases. After this, we briefly compare them. They are individually elaborated further in the rest of the book.

2.3.1 POSH

The Perfect Office Solutions House (POSH) is a chain of stores that supplies complete office solutions, consisting of supplies from simple pens and notepads to complete sets of office equipment and office furniture, complemented with professional service and advice. POSH supplies to both consumers and companies, focusing on the high-end market (that is why they are happy with the abbreviation of their name) – they do not compete on price, but on quality. POSH has been in the market for several decades now.

POSH has five large stores and three smaller branch offices around the country. The large stores have most of their products physically on display. The smaller branch offices mostly work with catalogs. POSH's head office and central warehouse are co-located with one of the large stores. POSH has a turnover of about $850 million per year and employs about 750 staff. Currently, POSH sells both out of its own stores and branch offices and through selected retailers (third parties to whom it acts as a wholesaler).

Seeing that e-business can bring new business opportunities, POSH has decided to launch a new business master plan for the company to open new opportunities. It has two major directions in which it wants to go:

1. Directly sell to all customers nationwide without the intervention of the third-party retailers so as to increase its profit margin or be able to make more compelling offers to large companies by lowering its prices.

2. Offer a more complete spectrum of services to its customers, such as office design advice and inventory management (such that their customers can look up what they have exactly bought at POSH and easily adapt new purchases to this).

We analyze these new business goals in chapter 5 after we have discussed the theory of the business aspect in networked e-business.

2.3.2 TTU

TalkThroughUs (TTU) is a recently established company that aims at offering language services in the context of a global economy. With companies doing more and more business across country borders, language boundaries become more of a problem in the global economy. Although many around the globe speak English, the language is not yet common in many countries, and where it is common, the mastery of the English language is often too poor to be a basis for conducting business. This holds both for written and spoken communication. Therefore, TTU wants to provide translation and interpretation services through the internet. They call this the IT^2 *concept*: interpretation and translation through information technology. TTU tries to offer language services between any pair of major languages around the globe.

A relatively new company, TTU is still in an expanding phase. They have one central head office combined with their research and development (R&D) division. The R&D division is responsible for both the development of new business models and for the introduction of new information technology into TTU's operation. Apart from the head office, TTU currently has five international offices around the world (they have plans to expand this number). Currently, they employ about 150 staff, of which almost two-thirds are working at the central location. Apart from their staff, they have an extensive network of more than 1,000 freelance interpreters and translators all over the world. The turnover of TTU has grown quickly since the company started and currently is about $72 million per year.

TTU interpretation services allow customers to have TTU interpreters support electronic business meetings between parties that don't share a common language in an adequate way. Interpretation services are based on interpreters engaging live in electronic meetings using digital conference systems – both telephone-based conferences and videoconferences. For supporting videoconferences, TTU relies on cloud computing–based platforms (as discussed in section 2.2.3). As TTU aims at the business market where confidential matters may be discussed in meetings, explicit confidentiality of their services is of utmost importance.

TTU translation services allow customers to send documents in one language to TTU to be translated into another language. Translation services are preferably based on electronic exchange of documents: customers send input in digital format and TTU returns the output in digital format as well. For electronic documents, TTU strives for very short translation turnaround times: short documents can typically be translated within one hour. To comply with more traditional markets and historic documents, TTU also offers translation of physical documents. These translation services can be ordered through the internet. Obviously, transport of physical documents (typically by post) implies that turnaround times are much longer than for electronic documents. Nonetheless, TTU guarantees quick responses. For urgent, high-priority orders pertaining to physical documents, TTU employs a high-quality, third-party courier service for document transport.

We further discuss and analyze the business goals of TTU in chapter 5.

2.3.3 TraXP

TraXP is a new spin-off of a major player in the international travel market. In this market, a number of service providers operate that offer more or less integrated travel booking functionality (e.g., to book combinations of air travel and hotel stays). But according to TraXP, there is demand for travel services that offer a truly seamless travel experience. The seamless travel experience consists of a complete spectrum of highly integrated travel services, support for both travel booking and travel execution plus a high level of customer intimacy. For TraXP, *customer intimacy* means that they know their customer's travel preferences such that they only have to state the *essence* of their travel wishes at travel booking time. TraXP aims at offering this complete seamless Travel eXPerience (hence their name) in both the business-to-consumer (B2C) and business-to-business (B2B) travel markets. As TraXP is in the starting phase, they don't yet have a stable revenue stream.

TraXP's working slogan is: 'TraXP does not support a trip but a traveler'. Like Spotify (www.spotify.com), which offers a seamless music-listening experience, TraXP offers a seamless travel experience that integrates a broad spectrum of services in a tightly integrated way. The high-level business vision of TraXP is shown in Figure 2.4.

TraXP realizes that the travel market is a very dynamic market in which offerings change fast. Therefore, the mission of TraXP is to realize their vision in a highly agile way based on the use of highly networked e-business. As illustrated by Figure 2.5, TraXP has the ambition to be the central party (orchestrator) of complex travel services for a customer, where a network of partners provide component services that are integrated by TraXP. Note that the figure only shows a subset of partners of TraXP – there are more, such as taxi service providers, boat charter services and holiday home brokers. Note also that the partners shown in the figure are actually *partner classes*, and each can contain multiple concrete partners. For example, TraXP works with several rental car providers, depending on the geographic location of a travel destination. Altogether, TraXP has an extensive partner network.

The technological basis of TraXP is strongly related to the development of the Big Five, as we have discussed earlier in this chapter. One of the basic starting

- Offer a seamless, complete travel experience to various customer groups
- Base that on advanced customer profiles that record preferences
- Use a broad spectrum of travel services that can be flexibly combined
- Execute the combinations in a highly networked, real-time fashion
- Be the central orchestrator in these networks

FIGURE 2.4   TraXP business vision.

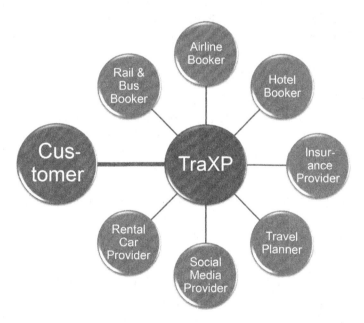

FIGURE 2.5   Part of the TraXP e–business network.

points of TraXP is that travel must be integrated in a traveler's life. This is demonstrated by the fact that TraXP considers social media providers as important business partners (as illustrated in Figure 2.5). Mobile computing is important to

TraXP to stay in touch with its customers during the execution of a trip. TraXP uses developments in the big data field as a basis for its business intelligence – for example, in the context of the construction of customer profiles. Finally, cloud computing is important to TraXP to achieve flexibility (elasticity) in its computing resources.

2.3.4 Comparing the three cases

In this section we have seen three cases of e-business. Of the three, POSH represents the most traditional e-business case. In this case we see a limited amount of networking, as POSH does collaborate with manufacturing partners and transport providers in an e-business fashion. The set of partners is limited, though, and the collaborations are not very dynamic. One might say that POSH represents a hybrid case of traditional, non-e-business thinking and modern e-business thinking – something that is typical in business domains that are based strongly on trading physical objects.

TTU represents a more networked case, because they rely on a network of autonomous service providers (the individual translation and interpretation professionals). This network is large and very dynamic at the level of collaboration with individuals in the class of translaters and interpreters (as these professionals join and leave TTU's network with a high frequency). In terms of classes of partners with which TTU collaborates, the network is relatively simple.

Of the three cases, TraXP is clearly the most networked. TraXP relies on an elaborate, dynamic business network with many different types of partners to provide their e-business services. The nature of the network depends on the exact market offerings that TraXP develops: when traveler needs change, new component services can be added to composed services (and hence partners to the network) to offer the seamless travel experience, whereas other component services may be dropped (and hence partners deleted from the TraXP network).

Figure 2.6 shows the comparison of the three case studies with respect to their level of networking and their level of dynamism. The bottom-left area of the figure below the dotted line represents traditional e-business, whereas the area above the dotted line represents networked e-business as we have defined it in chapter 1. The arrows with the three cases indicate developments for each case. POSH is still in the area of traditional e-business, but is slowly increasing its levels of dynamism and networking. TTU and TraXP are both well in the domain of networked e-business, where TTU concentrates on increasing its level of dynamism (to be able to adapt to business requests with dynamic non-functional characteristics, such as time and location) and TraXP concentrates on increasing its level of networking (to be able to adapt to business requests with dynamic functional characteristics, such as spectrum of services delivered).

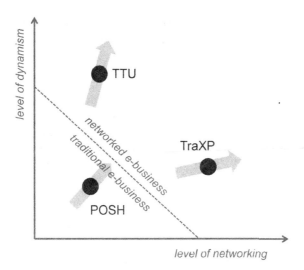

FIGURE 2.6   Three case studies compared.

2.4 Questions and exercises

1 A distinction that is often made in cloud computing is between *public clouds* and *private clouds* (and *hybrid clouds* as a form in between). Find out what these terms mean and how this distinction is related to networked e-business.

2 In the discussion of the internet of things we have mentioned RFID as a technology to automatically track the movement of physical products. Find another technology for the same purpose and discuss its advantages and disadvantages with respect to RFID, both from the technical and the economical perspectives.

3 In Figure 2.3 we see eight relationships between developments in the Big Five. Provide a practical example for each relationship in the context of electronic retailing (i.e., the use of web shops).

4 What are the major differences between POSH, TTU and TraXP (as described in the previous section) from an e-business point of view? Formulate your answer both in terms of their current business operations and their business innovation characteristics. Take both the individual companies and the markets in which they operate into account. Make assumptions where necessary.

5 The only development of the Big Five that is not mentioned in TraXP's brief profile (see section 2.3.3) is the internet of things. Describe a context in which the internet of things can indeed become important for TraXP as well.

6 In Figure 2.6 the three running cases of this book are plotted with respect to their levels of networking and dynamism in collaboration. Find three other

real–life e-business cases and plot them in the figure too. In doing so, try and compare their levels of networking and dynamism to those of POSH, TTU and TraXP.

Notes

1 Note that this name has been adopted for this book. Other names or acronyms exist; for example, the acronym SMAC, which stands for *social, mobile, analytics* and *cloud* (where *analytics* is related to our class of *big data* and the class of the internet of things is omitted).
2 A petabyte (PB) contains 1,000 terabytes (TB) or 1,000,000 gigabytes (GB).

3

CLASSIFYING NETWORKED E-BUSINESS

Learning goals

- *Understand the goal of classifying networked e-business scenarios.*
- *Know the main dimensions for classification of networked e-business scenarios.*
- *Be able to classify a networked e-business scenario in terms of participating parties.*
- *Be able to classify a networked e-business scenario in terms of traded objects.*
- *Be able to classify a networked e-business scenario in terms of time scopes.*

3.1 Introduction

The networked e-business domain is a complex field in which many elements and aspects play a role and in which many interrelationships among these exist. To explore e-business scenarios in this domain in a well-structured, systematic way we need an instrument to clearly organize the relevant characteristics of these scenarios. In other words, we need a tool enabling us to clearly classify specific e-business scenarios. In this chapter we introduce such a tool – a three-dimensional classification space of e-business characteristics. In section 3.2 we first have a close look at what exactly we are classifying – and why. In section 3.3 we describe the nature and structure of this three-dimensional space. In the next three sections we go into the details of each of the three classification dimensions identified in the space: parties, objects and time scopes.

In chapter 4 we will see how the three classification dimensions are complemented by a fourth dimension, which is the analysis dimension that we use as the basis for the structure of the remainder of this book. Further, the classification space of this chapter is an ingredient for the analysis and design approach that we discuss in chapter 9.

3.2 What exactly are we classifying?

Before we start the discussion of the classification space for e-business scenarios, it is good to know what exactly in an e-business scenario we are classifying. As we have discussed before, networked e-business entails dynamic business networks of organizations and/or individuals that collaborate via electronic means. These networks may be simple and consist of a provider and a customer only. But often in modern e-business these networks consist of more organizations. A provider may use the capabilities of other providers (which we call *auxiliary providers*) to construct its offering towards the client. One or more organizations may be used as *intermediaries* between provider and customer to accommodate the collaboration. This is illustrated in Figure 3.1.

Even though all parties in the network of an e-business scenario are important, we classify the scenario only on the basis of the collaboration between main provider and customer – shown as the dotted classification scope in Figure 3.1.

The main reason for this limited scope is the fact that the nature of relationship between provider and customer determines the nature of the rest of the business network to a high degree. It is in the relationship between provider and customer where the actual value of networked e-business is created.

Note that the classification of an e-business scenario therefore can significantly differ from the characteristics of the collaboration between a provider and its auxiliary providers.

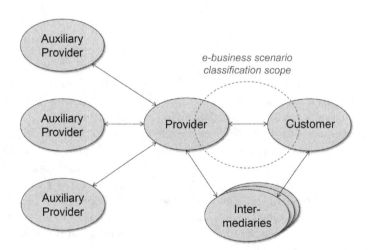

FIGURE 3.1 Scope of e-business scenario classification.

3.3 Structure of the classification space

When exploring the complex field of networked e-business, it is important to distinguish the various dimensions in which an e-business scenario can be described. Having multiple dimensions allows us to use a clear separation of concerns in classifying an e-business scenario. Each dimension describes specific characteristics of a scenario. A proper classification of a scenario is the basis for the subsequent analysis or design of a scenario.

When thinking about the characteristics of e-business scenarios, the questions *who?*, *what?* and *how?* are obvious.[1] These questions pertain to the performers (also called *actors*) of a scenario, the objects that are handled by them and the way they perform the scenario. There are many aspects to the *how*, not all of which can be easily classified. One thing that e-business scenarios have in common, however, is that the *time aspect* is very important in the *how*, as e-business changes the relative importance of time.[2]

Based on the previous observations, we use a networked e-business classification space consisting of three dimensions that describe the basic characteristics of e-business scenarios:

Parties in networked e-business: this dimension contains the options (values) for the combinations of parties that perform the e-business activities; that is, engage together in an e-business scenario. This dimension is elaborated further in section 3.4

Objects of networked e-business: this dimension contains the options (values) for the type of object that is primarily manipulated (traded, for instance) by e-business activities in a scenario. We further discuss this dimension in section 3.5.

Time scopes of networked e-business: this dimension contains the options (values) to classify an e-business scenario with respect to the time scope of e-business activities; that is, the duration of the relationship between the involved e-business parties. The time scopes dimension is discussed in section 3.6.

The three dimensions describe characteristics of e-business scenarios that are in principle mutually independent. In other words, the three dimensions are orthogonal.[3] Consequently, we can depict the e-business classification space that they create as a three-dimensional space, as illustrated in Figure 3.2. Each e-business scenario can be positioned (given a value) along each of the three dimensions (axes), giving it a position in the three-dimensional space. In the figure, this is shown, for example, for an abstract e-business scenario labeled scenario A. This scenario has value *p1* in the *parties* dimension, value *o1* in the *objects* dimension and value *t1* in the *time scopes* dimension – hence position *[p1,o1,t1]* in the classification space. These dimension values are abstract here – in the rest of this chapter we discuss the real values.

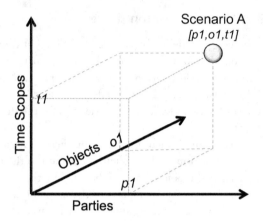

FIGURE 3.2   E-business scenario classification dimensions.

As we will see in the remainder of this book, many developments in networked e-business are related to shifts of e-business scenarios in the classification space of Figure 3.2. For example, market conditions in a business domain may become more volatile, making business relations more dynamic. This means that e-business scenarios in this business domain are shifted 'up' along the *time scopes* axis of Figure 3.2. In the case that a business domain is being 'virtualized', we see that the nature of objects can change from physical to digital objects, such as digital media objects. This means that e-business scenarios in this domain are shifted along the *objects* axis of Figure 3.2.

The *parties*, *objects* and *time scopes* classification dimensions of networked e-business are discussed in detail in the following three sections. At the end of this chapter we apply the classification to our three running cases – POSH, TTU and TraXP – to have concrete examples of the introduced concepts.

3.4 Parties in networked e-business

In the previous section we have seen the three dimensions that are the basis for the networked e-business analysis space. In this section we elaborate the *parties* dimension by analyzing which combinations of parties can engage in e-business relationships. We perform a general analysis of the dimension first and then discuss the most important values in the dimension.

3.4.1 Values in the parties dimension

In general, the following three types of main parties (within a classification scope, as shown in Figure 3.1) can be involved in a networked e-business collaboration:

Business (B) party: a commercial organization of any size and any type, ranging from a multi-national to a one-person company.

Consumer (C) party: an individual acting as a private person (note that this is different from an individual acting on behalf of a business organization).

Government (G) party: (a part of) a government organization (such as a tax office or a municipality office) or a related non-profit organization (such as a public educational organization).

By combining the three types of parties in all possible ways, we get the combinations shown in Table 3.1. In this table the vertical dimension indicates the *initiator* of an e-business activity; that is, the party that starts the activity. The horizontal dimension indicates the *responder*; that is, the party that responds to the initiative by participating in the activity. By having three values along each axis, we find nine pairs of interacting party types that form the values along the *parties* dimension of the networked e-business analysis space.

The most common combinations in the table are shown in bold. Certainly the combinations *business-to-business* (B2B) and *business-to-consumer* (B2C) are coined terms in the e-business world – they form the main classes of networked e-business. Although B2C may be more familiar to many, B2B is by far the most important class when it comes to 'turnover'. *Consumer-to-consumer* (C2C) is the class where consumers perform transactions among one another (we discuss examples further on). Although this class is less important from a large-scale economic perspective (i.e., in financial volumes), it is interesting from an e-business point of view. *Government-to-consumer* (G2C) and *government-to-business* (G2B) are the classes in which government bodies are the main players. These classes get quite a bit of attention in specific circles (often termed *e-government*). We discuss these five important classes in more detail further on. The four less common combinations are printed in italic in Table 3.1. But also of these, examples can be found – we leave this as an exercise for the reader.

Note that for the classification in the parties dimension we focus here on the main parties in a networked e-business scenario; that is, on the main providers and main consumers in a scenario (remember our discussion of the classification scope). We do not include intermediaries or auxiliary providers as parties in the classification, although they can be very important for the implementation of

TABLE 3.1 Overview of e-business types in the *parties* dimension

↓ Initiator	*Responder* → *Business*	*Consumer*	*Government*
Business	**B2B**	**B2C**	*B2G*
Consumer	*C2B*	**C2C**	*C2G*
Government	**G2B**	**G2C**	*G2G*

e-business scenarios. Typical intermediaries are search engine and catalog providers, payment service providers and transport service providers. Auxiliary providers assist the main provider in supplying its offering; for example, by providing a subservice in a complex service offering. In principle, intermediaries and auxiliary providers can also be of business, consumer or government type. One e-business scenario may include multiple intermediaries for various intermediary roles (payment handler, goods transporter, et cetera). It may also include multiple auxiliary providers. Therefore, including these additional elements in the *parties* dimension would make this dimension overly complex. We address intermediaries and auxiliary providers when we discuss networked e-business organization structures in chapter 6.

3.4.2 B2B networked e-business

Business-to-business networked e-business is from an economic perspective by far the most important form of networked e-business in the parties dimension. On a daily basis, large numbers of transactions worth enormous amounts are conducted between companies through e-business channels in trading all kinds of products and services and in performing all kinds of collaborations.

B2B networked e-business can be found in a wide range of business domains. A few example B2B scenarios are:

- supply chains in industry, where e-business systems are used to orchestrate the operation of the links in the chain;
- complex logistics scenarios, where e-business applications are used to place logistics orders, monitor their progress and synchronize parties involved in transportation – an example B2B logistics application is shown in Figure 3.3;
- industry-level marketplaces through which industrial goods are traded in specific industry domains (such as the electronics industry or the petrochemical industry); and
- inter-bank financial traffic, where e-business is the basis for the execution of business transactions among banks all around the globe.

We discuss more examples in the remainder of this book.

In B2B e-business we often find a certain level of symmetry between participating parties in terms of the complexity of a scenario. This means that the complexity of business processes and supporting automated systems for realizing e-business is divided more or less equally between two business parties. The situation is not necessarily completely symmetric, but it can be so. As we will see further on, this symmetry is not present for all values in the parties dimension.

FIGURE 3.3   Example B2B application in the logistics sector

3.4.3 B2C networked e-business

Business-to-consumer networked e-business is the form of e-business that most of us are familiar with. Many of us use web shops on a regular basis to buy a variety of goods – this is the e-retailing business model (which we discuss in more detail in section 5.6.1). We see an example web shop that grew out of a traditional shop in Figure 3.4.

But networked B2C e-business is more than e-retailing – another B2C application that most of us use on a very regular basis, for example, is e-banking. In personal mobility (public transport, shared cars, trip planning, et cetera) B2C networked e-business is currently emerging fast. B2C networked e-business is actively used in many other domains, such as the travel industry.

Characteristic of the B2C scenario is asymmetry in the realization of the scenario between the B party and the C party. The complexity of the scenario arises within the B party: this is where the main part of the business processes takes place and the complex e-business information systems reside. The C party typically has simple processes and a very limited, general-purpose information system

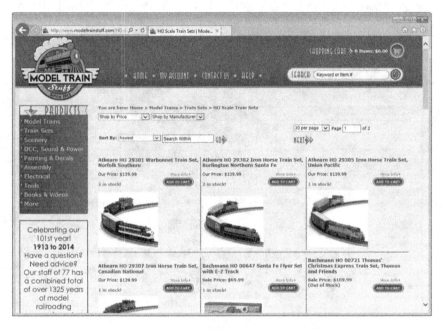

FIGURE 3.4   Example B2C web shop application.

infrastructure (usually, a standard web browser suffices). We revisit this issue when we discuss organization structures for networked e-business in chapter 6.

3.4.4 C2C networked e-business

Consumer-to-consumer networked e-business is the scenario where two customers (individual persons) engage in a business transaction through an electronic channel. Typical examples of the C2C class are electronic marketplaces in which individuals sell or barter[4] (second-hand) goods or offer personal services.

Business networks in C2C scenarios are typically not very complicated, although intermediary parties such as payment and transport providers may be involved. In most C2C scenarios, a third party is involved that facilitates the C2C transactions. This is obvious, as individual consumers do not have the means to realize an e-business information system (and if they do, they typically do not have the volume of business to make this cost effective). The electronic marketplace mentioned earlier is typically set up by such a third party. This third party may have income from advertising or from fees with respect to the transactions conducted through the marketplace. From the third party's point of view, the C2C scenario may also be seen as a B2C scenario – although this also changes the main objects traded (see the next section). A well-known example of a marketplace facilitating both C2C and B2C e-business is eBay (www.ebay.com; see Figure 3.5). Many similar marketplaces exist, often with a regional or national character. Where C2C

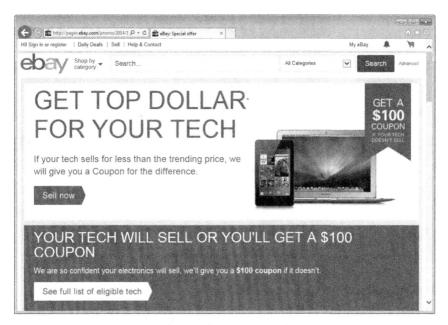

FIGURE 3.5   Example marketplace for C2C and B2C e-business.

marketplaces have frequent interactions between traders in a community, they get some of the characteristics of social media (as discussed in section 2.2.1).

3.4.5 G2C and G2B networked e-business

Government-to-consumer[5] and government-to-business scenarios include a government body as one of the parties. Example government bodies are municipality offices, tax offices and bureaus that give out documents, licenses and permits. Typical G2C examples include electronic tax statement handling and the use of electronic portals through which municipalities serve their citizens in various ways. An example G2C e-government service is shown in Figure 3.6, which is part of an e-government portal of a municipality in the United Kingdom (perhaps not the most appreciated part of their portal, as it handles fines). Comparably, G2B examples include digital handling of business taxes and portals through which business organizations can obtain various kinds of permits.

A special case of e-business scenarios that we can classify as G2C/G2B are the scenarios of charity organizations, which commonly use web-based information systems to inform people, attract members, raise funding and sometimes sell goods. A well-known example is shown in Figure 3.7. Although we classify charity scenarios as either G2C or G2B (depending on their focus), they typically also have characteristics of B2C or B2B scenarios (e.g., they often try to make money, be it for non-profit purposes). The fact that the scenarios are controlled by public organizations and have a non-profit character puts them closer to G2C or G2B, however.

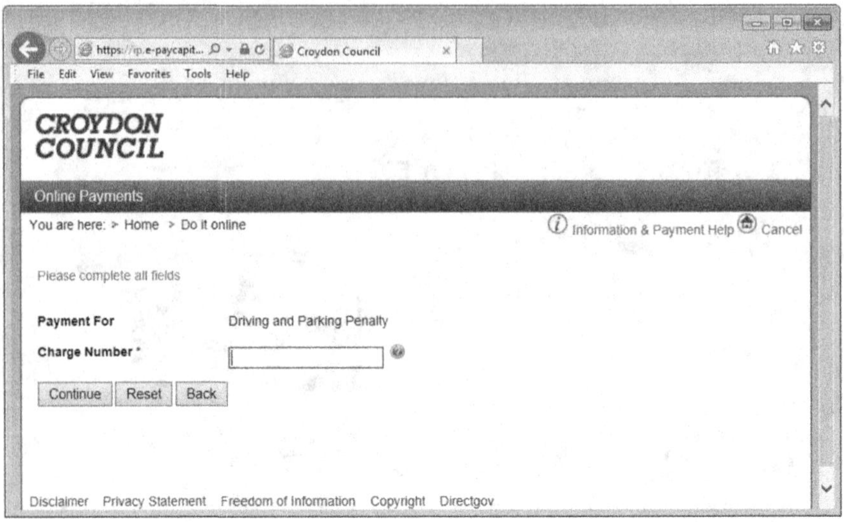

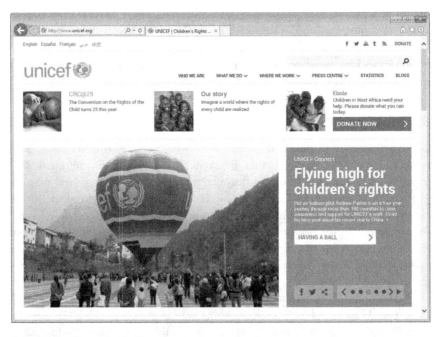

FIGURE 3.6 Example G2C e-government service.

FIGURE 3.7 Example charity organization application.

In many respects, G2C and G2B scenarios are like B2C and B2B scenarios when it comes to operational issues – this is the reason why we do not pay them much dedicated attention throughout the rest of this book. Obviously, the objects traded in G2C and G2B scenarios are typically not of a commercial nature. And also obviously, the G side in these scenarios is often bound to many more regulations than a typical business organization. These characteristics imply that G2C and G2B e-business scenarios are usually not as dynamic as B2B or B2C scenarios.

3.5 Objects of networked e-business

In this section we elaborate the *objects* dimension of the networked e-business analysis space (see Figure 3.2). As with the *parties* dimension in the previous section, we first establish the values in the dimension and then discuss the interesting values in more detail.

3.5.1 Values in the objects dimension

As we have seen, the types of objects that are manipulated (e.g., traded) in e-business are important to characterize an e-business scenario. We distinguish the following basic classes of e-business objects:

- *physical goods* are tangible goods that are physically exchanged between parties in an e-business scenario, such as books, clothing or aircraft engines;
- *digital goods* are intangible goods that are electronically exchanged between parties in an e-business scenario, such as electronic reports or music in MP3 format;
- *services* are activities that one party in an e-business scenario performs for another party, taking relevant characteristics of this other party into account, such as transport or maintenance of physical goods;
- *financial goods* are sums of money or specific forms of guarantees for the later delivery of a sum of money that are transferred between parties in an e-business scenario; and
- *hybrid objects* are combinations of the previous classes; for example, a physical device combined with maintenance services for the device that is exchanged between parties in an e-business scenario.

The boundaries between these classes are not always fully clear. For example, one might argue that a music CD is a hybrid object consisting of a physical information carrier (physical good) and digital content (digital good). The line between digital information and digital services is sometimes hard to establish. An example of an e-business object that fits into these two classes is a personalized holiday weather information service (service) that delivers daily reports (digital goods). These examples are illustrations of the fact that e-business can erase boundaries that used to be clear – proper classification of scenarios thus becomes even more important to keep things as clear as possible.

Note that in e-business scenarios involving trading, typically two kinds of objects are exchanged (each in one direction between the two main parties). Most often, one of the two is a financial good for the payment while the other one is the actual product or service being bought or sold. An exception is when trading has the form of bartering (as mentioned in the previous section), and non-financial goods are exchanged both ways.

We discuss the first three classes of goods in more detail in the following sections to analyze their characteristics in e-business. Financial goods are straightforward and hybrid objects possess the combination of the characteristics of their constituents.

3.5.2 Physical goods

Physical goods are the kinds of goods that have always been traded in 'traditional' business. When trading them in e-business, we usually get a combination of electronic business and 'physical' business. The electronic business part is focused on the actual selling (or buying) of goods; that is, finding a product, finding a business partner, reaching an agreement on a transaction and making a payment. The physical business part is involved because the goods typically need to be transported in some way from seller to buyer. As we will see when discussing business models, these business parts may be allocated to different organizations (goods logistics may be outsourced, for example).

We can distinguish between the following subclasses of physical goods:

* *discrete goods*: goods that are exchanged on a per-piece basis; for example, books, music CD's, office furniture and aircraft.
* *bulk goods*: goods that are exchanged in large quantities on a per-volume or per-weight basis, such as crude oil or bulk food like unprocessed grain.

Discrete goods (or discrete merchandise) are traded both in B2C and B2B scenarios. They are also traded in C2C scenarios; for example, in second-hand goods markets such as e-Bay (see Figure 3.5). Bulk goods are typically relevant in B2B scenarios only. Physical goods hardly play a role in G2B and G2C scenarios. The development of the *internet of things* (as discussed in section 2.2.5) is very relevant when it comes to automatic monitoring of the progress of e-business transactions involving physical goods.

There is a third special class of physical goods with somewhat different properties:

* *immovable goods*: goods that are bound to a specific geographic location, such as land, houses, apartments and industrial estates (also known as *real estate*); we saw an example in Figure 1.3.

Obviously, there is no physical part of the process here to move the immovable goods. Typically, however, there is transport of physical documents that proves transfer and ownership of the immovable good.

3.5.3 Digital goods

Digital goods are a relatively new class of goods that has actually come into existence through the advent of networked e-business. Digital goods have a number of characteristics that distinguish them from physical goods. First, they can be copied in arbitrary numbers (almost) without cost by a producer or a consumer (if not protected by some kind of digital rights management mechanism). Second, they can be transported (almost) instantaneously and (almost) without cost from seller to buyer (using the internet). This enables the creation of business models that are simply impossible for physical goods. We will see this when discussing business aspects of networked e-business in chapter 5.

Although digital goods all consist, in the most basic view, of 'bits and bytes',[6] there are differences to be considered when thinking about e-business. We distinguish among the following subclasses of digital goods:

- *digital content*: copies of published and cataloged (multi-media) content[7]; for example, e-books, digital music (often in the MP3 file format) and on-demand movies – examples of digital content providers are the Apple iTunes store (www.apple.com/itunes) and the Amazon Kindle e-book store (www.amazon.com/Kindle-eBooks).
- *digital information*: on-demand produced informational data; for example, electronic weather forecasts, on-demand stock analyses and personalized travel schemes.
- *software*: copies of software products, such as text-processing programs (e.g., the one this book was written with), multi-media players and financial bookkeeping systems; software is often accompanied by a usage license.

The subclasses of digital goods determine the organization of the business that provides these goods. Digital information is often produced in reply to a specific customer request (in an on-demand fashion), where digital content is often produced for entire markets. Software usually requires a service organization to provide support for software users (such as delivery of updates of the software, a help desk for questions), where this is usually less required for digital content and digital information.

The exact lines between the subclasses of digital goods are not always clear. Software may produce digital information, for example, or digital content may be sold with software to access it. Digital information exists that is actually published without explicit request (e.g., on a periodic basis), making it similar to digital content.

Note that the broad distribution and use of digital goods (certainly in the B2C segment) relies on developments in mobile computing and cloud computing, as discussed in section 2.2. Mobile computing makes digital goods accessible in a ubiquitous way. Cloud computing forms a technical backbone for the processing, storage and communication of digital goods (e.g., in media-oriented social media).

3.5.4 Services

Services are different from goods. When services are traded there is no actual product exchanged between two parties; that is, no object (either physical or digital) is sold by one party to the other. Instead, one party performs a process on behalf of the other (or the two parties do this mutually) such that the other achieves a certain goal.

We distinguish between the following subclasses of services, each having its own types of goals for the service consumer:

- *physical services*: activities that involve manipulation of physical objects that are not exchanged goods; for example, air transportation (where the goal is to move someone or something to a specific destination) or car washing (where the goal is to have a clean car).
- *digital (non-physical) services*: activities that do not involve manipulation of physical objects; for example, financial services, shopping advice (where the goal is to be better informed) and agenda management (where the goal is to be better organized).

As with physical objects, physical services require some physical business activities for their delivery. Digital services can in principle be completely delivered through electronic means. An important example of the digital services class is electronic banking, where services are offered for making electronic payments or electronic money transfers. *Cloud computing* technology (see section 2.2.3) facilitates the development of delivery mechanisms for digital services. Clearly, hybrid forms of physical and digital services exist too.

Financial services are a special kind of digital services because they can be used for reimbursement of other e-business objects. Note that direct payment (by plain

---

Servitization. In the modern economy we see a shift of focus from physical assets to services, a development that is commonly referred to as *servitization*. In the traditional asset-oriented setting, physical assets are acquired (bought) to make use of them. This implies a transfer of ownership of the asset and usually also a change of location. A B2C example is a consumer buying a CD to be able to listen to the music stored on it. A B2B example is a company buying a printer to be able to produce business documents. In the modern service-oriented setting, a service consumer pays a service provider for the delivery of services that involve the use of assets. There is no change of ownership and often no change of location of the assets. A B2C example is a consumer paying a subscription fee for a music-streaming service. The consumer enjoys the music, but does not own it. A B2B example is a company paying for a printing service (e.g., on a per-use basis) to produce its documents. The company will not become the owner of the printer. The location of the printer will depend on the situation: at the premises of the service provider (who transports printed documents to the service consumer) or at the premises of the consumer (but under the control and maintenance of the provider). Servitization typically implies more digital contact between parties; that is, more networked e-business.

money, physical or electronic) is not considered a service but a financial good (as discussed in section 3.5.1). Loan and leasing services can replace direct payments, however. Recent developments (such as digital currency) can blur the difference between financial goods and financial services.

3.6 Time scopes of networked e-business

In this section we elaborate the *time scopes* dimension of networked e-business, as introduced in section 3.3. As with the other two dimensions, we first give an overview of the values we identify in this dimension and then discuss each of these values in more detail.

3.6.1 Values in the time scopes dimension

The time scope of an e-business scenario determines how long a typical e-business collaboration lasts; that is, how long the life cycle of a scenario lasts from first contact between the involved parties until the complete dissolution of the collaboration (note that this can be considerably longer than the execution of the main business transactions in a collaboration).

When analyzing the time scope of an e-business scenario it does not make much sense to use a dimension scaled in absolute time units, such as weeks, days or minutes. Time scales differ immensely depending on the nature of an e-business scenario (and the business domain in which the scenario is positioned). When we are talking about a stock exchange e-business scenario, things have a different scale of time that when we are talking about trading real estate with e-business support (we have seen an example in Figure 1.3). Therefore, we use a relative time scale coupled to the duration of *e-business orders*; that is, the exchange of individual e-business objects as discussed in the previous section. In the stock exchange case, an e-business order is a single transfer of stocks. In the real estate trading case, an e-business order is a single transfer of a unit of real estate (such as a house or an island).

We identify the following values in the time scopes dimension:

- **A static time scope** means that e-business collaboration between the parties in a scenario is of a long-lasting (or even permanent) character, which is not related to individual e-business orders. The selection of parties is performed at a strategic decision level.
- **A semi-dynamic time scope** means that e-business collaborations between business parties are changed periodically, but not on the basis of individual orders. The selection of parties is performed at a tactic decision level.
- **A dynamic time scope** means that e-business collaborations are determined specifically for each individual e-business order. Selection of parties is an operational decision.
- **An ultra-dynamic time scope** means that collaborations are changed even during the execution of an individual e-business order. Selection of parties is a small-scale operational decision.

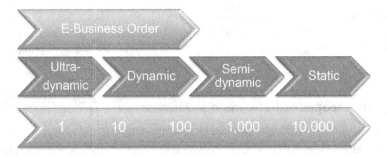

FIGURE 3.8   E-business time scope durations.

The durations of the four time scopes are illustrated in Figure 3.8. The four scopes are shown in the middle row. In the top row we see the duration of an e-business order. In the bottom row we see a very coarse indication of the time periods in abstract time units (as explained, the concrete time unit depends on the application domain). Note that the time scale is logarithmic because the scopes often vary by orders of magnitude.

Given our definition of networked e-business (see section 1.2), it is clear that scenarios with the more dynamic time scopes are the more interesting ones. If a collaboration has a permanent character (the extreme version of a static time scope), it is – strictly speaking – even excluded by our definition of *interesting* e-business.

3.6.2 Static time scope

In the static time scope case, the nature of the collaboration between e-business parties is defined by the long-time relationship between the parties, not by the execution of individual e-business orders. This means that e-business is primarily based on a relational collaboration setting, not on a transactional collaboration set-ting. The static time scope is typically applicable in three kinds of situations

The first situation is that of very stable markets. This means that the players in a market are well known and don't often change the way they do business. This also means that the objects traded in the market (as discussed in section 3.5) have stable characteristics, both in terms of functionality and price. When nothing changes, there is little reason to change collaborations.

The second situation is determined by the fact that specific parties are tied to each other because of an infrastructure they have invested in (a *lock-in* situation). This can be a business infrastructure (such as a long-lasting contractual relation-ship), an organizational infrastructure (such as a business process that was very costly to implement) or a technical infrastructure (such as a shared information system or a shared communication facility). A typical example of a technical infrastructure in 'old-fashioned' e-business is a dedicated *electronic data interchange* (EDI) connection between two organizations.

The third situation is determined by the fact that one or more parties in an e-business collaboration are unique in the market, such that there simply is no alternative to choose from for an e-business scenario. A party is unique because it has unique characteristics, such as unique capabilities (e.g., as a consequence of highly specialized production facilities) or unique branding (it is the owner of a trademark with a highly special position in a market). Note that a party that has a monopoly is by default unique.

3.6.3 Semi-dynamic time scope

In the semi-dynamic time scope the nature of the collaboration is defined both by the relationship between parties and current market circumstances. Characteristics of executed batches of e-business orders or predicted batches of orders to be executed may lead to reselection of partners. For example, when the quality of delivered services is unsatisfactory, a service consumer may select an alternative service provider. Characteristics of individual orders do not lead to a need for partner reselection, however.

The semi-dynamic time scope is typically used in scenarios where parties engage in collaboration for some period of time (where the granularity of the period is determined by the business domain, as discussed before). The length of the period can be fixed at a number of time units (e.g., six months) or a number of e-business orders, such that parties reselect their partners on a regular periodic basis. A period may also end because a specific market characteristic reaches a threshold value (e.g., the price of traded products falls below a threshold value).

As partners are selected more frequently than in the static case, effective means for partner selection are important. Examples of these means are business catalogs (such as electronic yellow pages) and business brokers. Efficiency of these means is not of great importance in semi-dynamic networked e-business because the frequency of partner selection is typically low when compared to the frequency of execution of e-business orders.

3.6.4 Dynamic time scope

In the dynamic time scope case, selection of parties is based on the characteristics of a single e-business order and current market circumstances – therefore, an e-business collaboration is based on a single e-business order. Typically, partner selection has a just-in-time character: a partner is selected only at the moment that its activities are actually needed (such that all up-to-date information can be taken into account). Because partners are selected very frequently and at the last possible moment, partner selection mechanisms must both be effective and efficient. This implies that they typically require adequate automated support.

The well-known web shop scenario is a typical B2C example of e-business with a dynamic time scope (this is the e-retailer business model that we discuss in section 5.5.5). Consumers decide per e-business order (i.e., per object to purchase) and at the latest moment where they will buy this object. Comparison websites enable

---

Dynamic B2B scenarios in the twentieth century. A very explicit example of dynamic networked e-business was already developed in the European CrossFlow research project at the end of the twentieth century [Gref00]. CrossFlow researched the combination of business process management (then called *workflow management*) and networked electronic business (then called *electronic commerce*) [Hof01b]. In this project, two scenarios with dynamic time scopes were constructed and supported by prototype systems for networked e-business. The first scenario concerns logistics for delivery of mobile phones to customers. Here, a telecom operator selling mobile phones can select and contract a logistics provider on a per-order basis (i.e., for each individual mobile phone to be delivered), depending on the characteristics of the delivery and current market circumstances (such as pricing of providers). The second scenario concerns handling damage claim assessment services in car insurances. Here, an insurance company can select and contract a damage assessment expertise provider on a per-claim basis. Both scenarios rely on electronic contracting to enable the required efficiency in collaboration setup [Hof01a]. Even though the technology developed in the CrossFlow project is outdated by now, the networked e-business setting is still state of the art.

---

this dynamic, just-in-time behavior – they are the automated support for partner selection in this case.

Dynamic time scopes are also considered in B2B scenarios; for example, in the real-time outsourcing of services in highly dynamic markets, such as logistics. We present an example in the sidebar: 'Dynamic B2B scenarios in the twentieth century'.

3.6.5 Ultra-dynamic time scope

In the ultra-dynamic time scope case the setup of collaboration parties may change even during the execution of a single e-business order. Reselection of a business party while an e-business order is being executed can happen for two reasons.

First, a party requesting an e-business object may decide to switch the delivery of part of that object to another provider during the execution of the order for that object. In other words, an e-business order may be chopped up into pieces 'on the fly'. An example is a scenario where holiday packages are sold consisting of several elements, such as flight, hotel and rental car. During an e-business order, a customer may decide not to proceed with the purchase of more elements, complete the part of the e-business order so far with the first provider or obtain the other elements through a second provider.

Second, the execution of an e-business order initiated with one partner may be aborted to be restarted with another partner. This is possible with low or zero transaction cost scenarios; for example, in search engine transactions where a customer may switch to another search engine when search results are not satisfactory (or the engine is simply too slow).

Obviously, the ultra-dynamic time scope is used only in extreme e-business scenarios where there are few or no contractual restrictions to 'partner swapping'.

3.7 Running cases

In this section we revisit the three case studies – POSH, TTU and TraXP – that we have introduced in the previous chapter. Using these cases we can apply the concepts of this chapter to the worlds of online furniture retail, online translation and interpretation and online travel services.

3.7.1 POSH

We classify the POSH scenario using the three dimensions that we have introduced in this chapter.

When we look at the *parties* dimension of networked e-business, we classify POSH as both B2B and B2C: they sell both to individual consumers and to business organizations. Note that we do not include B2G in our analysis of the scenario: even if POSH sells furniture to government organizations, the government organization is a 'regular business organization' in such a transaction to POSH.

The *objects* that POSH trades are mainly physical goods; more precisely, discrete goods (office supplies, equipment and furniture). But POSH also provides services supporting these physical goods, so we identify an aspect of hybrid objects as well. Services include, for example, maintenance to equipment and furniture. In the POSH scenario we also see financial goods, as customers have to pay for bought goods – but these are of the trivial kind, so not very interesting to analyze in this scenario.

In the *time scope* dimension, POSH typically works in semi-dynamic and dynamic scenarios. The semi-dynamic time scope is related to project-based collaborations in which a number of individual but related e-business orders are placed by the same business customer – here, a sequence of business transactions is performed in the context of a longer-lasting business relationship. The dynamic time scope is applicable to individual purchases, often by non-business consumers in the B2C segment.

3.7.2 TTU

We also classify the TTU scenario using the three classification dimensions of this chapter.

In the *parties* dimension, TTU is a typical B2B case: they are a business organization that interacts with other business organizations. They might incidentally work for consumers as well (e.g., people who want important private documents translated), but this is not the basis for their business model.

In the *objects* dimension, TTU sells digital services. One might argue that TTU sells digital content (translated documents). Producing new content of documents is not their main activity, however. They primarily transform existing content, which is a clear service functionality. Financial goods play a role for the payment of the services provided by TTU, but in a trivial way.

Time scope wise, TTU works in semi-dynamic and dynamic fashions. As customers have to be registered with TTU to use their services, the e-business relationship has semi-dynamic characteristics. But it is also possible to use TTU for individual activities, creating dynamic characteristics. When TTU delivers interpretation services in a real-time fashion, ultra-dynamic elements may slip in: interpretation sessions may be ended (and diverted to another service provider) before they are completed. TTU does not consider this regular business, however, and hence does not adapt its organization to this aspect.

3.7.3 TraXP

We apply the classification in three dimensions to our third case study, TraXP.

In the *parties* dimension TraXP has explicitly chosen to address both the B2C and the B2B traveler markets; that is, private travelers and business travelers. As we will see in the further discussion of this case (in chapter 5), TraXP does handle different classes of customers in different ways. Similar to the POSH case, government organizations are treated like regular business organizations by TraXP, so B2G business is not an explicit segment for TraXP.

In the *objects* dimension, TraXP provides complex digital services. Part of a complex service is based on TraXP resources, but a large part is based on the resources of third parties with which TraXP collaborates. The nature of the e-business objects dictates a highly networked approach to e-business here.

In the *time scope* dimension, TraXP can be classified as semi-dynamic. TraXP tries to build lasting relationships with its customers (i.e., it tries to move towards a static time scope) but is aware that they operate in a market with fierce competition. The basis for the relationship with the customer is a high level of knowledge about a customer's travel preferences, which are recorded in a customer profile. As an aside (as this is not part of the scenario classification scope), with its service providers TraXP typically also has semi-dynamic relationships – partnerships can be changed dynamically if market conditions require it.

3.8 Chapter end

We end this chapter on the networked e-business analysis space with a brief summary of the main observations in this chapter and a few questions and exercises to apply the concepts of this chapter.

3.8.1 Chapter summary

E-business scenarios can be classified using a structured, three-dimensional framework. The three dimensions specify the *parties* that collaborate in networked e-business, the *objects* that are traded or handled in networked e-business and the *time scopes* of networked e-business. An e-business scenario has a value in each dimension. The combination of the three values is the classification of the e-business scenario.

In the *parties* dimension we find combinations of business (B), consumer (C) and government (G) parties. These combinations make for $3 \times 3 = 9$ possible values, of which B2B, B2C, C2C and G2C/G2B are the most important.

In the *objects* dimension we find physical goods, digital goods, services, financial goods and hybrid objects. The physical object class is subdivided into discrete goods, bulk goods and immovable goods. The digital object class is subdivided into digital content, digital information and software. The service class is subdivided into physical services and digital services.

The *time scope* dimension ranges from static to semi-dynamic and dynamic to ultra-dynamic. Values in the time scope dimension depend on the relationship of e-business collaborations to e-business orders – not on absolute time periods.

These three dimensions are summarized in Figure 3.9.

3.8.2 Questions and exercises

1 Are *all* combinations of values in the three classification dimensions (as shown in Figure 3.9) practical? Explain your answer. If your answer is 'yes',

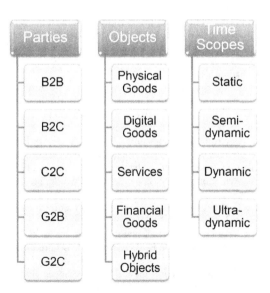

FIGURE 3.9 Overview of e-business classification dimensions.

provide examples of a few less likely combinations. If your answer is 'no', indicate at least one combination that is not practical.

2   We have shown a number of networked e-business examples in this chapter. Try to find a competitor in the networked e-business domain for each example shown.

3   Try to find practical examples of each of the four values in the parties dimension of networked e-business that have not been discussed in detail in this chapter: C2B, B2G, C2G and G2G (see Table 3.1).

4   Find examples of objects traded in networked e-business that are hybrid objects consisting of physical good(s), digital good(s) and service(s). Establish for each example whether the object needs to be traded by one single party or whether each of the components might be traded by separate parties.

5   Find examples of business scenarios that have moved from a static time scope in the 'traditional' business days (i.e., non-e-business in the past) to a dynamic time scope in the networked e-business days (i.e., in the present). In other words, find example scenarios where the introduction of networked e-business has dramatically changed the time scope towards the dynamic end of the dimension.

Notes

1   Structuring an area to be analyzed by the use of interrogatives is a usual approach. It has been used, for example, for the design of the well-known Zachman framework for enterprise architecture [Zach02] and in the description of the architecture of the CrossWork system [Gref09].

2   On the one hand, time gets more important as business relations get more dynamic (see the extended definition of e-business that we developed in section 1.2) and business transactions are performed faster. On the other hand, we see that e-business erases the importance of time when it comes to availability of business possibilities (we discuss this in more detail in chapter 5).

3   By 'orthogonal' we mean that values in different dimensions are independent from each other; that is, a specific choice in one dimension does not influence possible choices in the other dimensions. Compare Figure 3.2 to a set of axes in geometry, in which x, y and z values of a point can be chosen independently.

4   Bartering through electronic markets seemed like a way to avoid the tax system (as no money is transferred). But nowadays, tax offices often have regulations for this – see, for example, the regulations about Barter Exchanges on www.irs.gov. The existence of virtual worlds with their own monetary systems (like Second Life, see www.secondlife.com) gives raise to similar issues.

5   Sometimes also referred to as *government-to-citizen*, which conveniently also can be abbreviated as G2C.

6   One may draw the analogy here that all physical goods consist of atoms and molecules, but there are important differences to be considered when thinking about trading different kinds of physical goods.

7   Note that digital goods are replacing physical goods that are information carriers; for example, online music in MP3 format from commercial music sites is replacing physical CD's containing the same music.

4

THE BOAT FRAMEWORK

Learning goals

- *Understand the fact that an e-business scenario has multiple aspects that describe its internal characteristics.*
- *Know the aspects of the BOAT framework and the possible ways in which they are related to each other.*
- *Understand the relation between the classification dimensions of chapter 3 and the BOAT framework.*

4.1 Introduction

In the previous chapter we have introduced a three-dimensional space for the classification of e-business scenarios. Of this space, the three classification dimensions (*parties*, *objects* and *time scopes*) have been explored. In this chapter we investigate the additional dimension that we use for the analysis and design of the 'internals' of e-business scenarios: that of *aspects* of e-business.

In section 4.2 we describe the four e-business aspects that we find along this analysis dimension, making up the BOAT framework: business, organization, architecture and technology. We continue in section 4.3 with explaining how the BOAT dimension relates to the three classification dimensions of the previous chapter. In section 4.4 we discuss how we can organize the BOAT aspects with respect to each other. As usual, we end the chapter with our three running case studies, summary and questions and exercises.

In the rest of this book we use the BOAT framework as the main structure for the further exploration of the networked e-business domain: chapters 5 to 8 discuss each of the four BOAT aspects in detail.

4.2 BOAT: aspects of networked e-business

Networked e-business is always a mix of business-oriented elements and technology-oriented elements for the simple reason that e-business is IT-enabled business (as we have seen in chapter 1). When we want to perform a good analysis of an existing e-business scenario or a well-structured design of a new e-business scenario, we need to make a clear separation between different elements of a scenario to arrive at clear and well-founded choices: the *what* and the *how* of a scenario are not the same thing and can be seen from different perspectives. For this reason, we introduce the *aspects* dimension of networked e-business to separate these elements in an e-business scenario. In the following sections we first discuss the structure of this aspects dimension. Then we pay attention to the individual values along this dimension.

4.2.1 The structure of the aspect dimension

The *aspects* dimension of networked e-business is the dimension that covers the spectrum from very business-oriented to very technology-oriented aspects. The goal of this dimension is to have a number of clearly delineated aspects of networked e-business that are the basis for separation of concerns in addressing the complexity of the field.

Because the field of networked e-business entails a broad spectrum of elements – including business goals and models, people and other resources, organizational functions and processes, software system structures and diverse concrete information technologies – we need more than just the two aspects *business* and *technology*. Alternatively, we don't want a dimension with too many aspects, because this may bring a separation of concerns but also a lack of structure and cohesion. For these reasons, we decide to operationalize the *business aspect* into a complementary *organization aspect*. Having these two aspects allows us to separate the more abstract elements

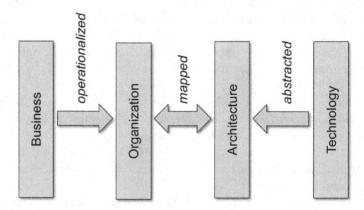

FIGURE 4.1 Four aspects to describe e-business scenarios.

from the more concrete on the business side of the networked e-business spectrum. Likewise, we decide to abstract the *technology aspect* into a complementary *architecture aspect*. These two aspects enable the separation of concrete technology elements from more abstract structural elements on the technology side of the networked e-business spectrum. The *organization* and *architecture aspects* can next be related to each other in a mapping. This line of reasoning leads to four related aspects as illustrated in Figure 4.1.

4.2.2 The values of the aspect dimension: BOAT

As a consequence of the discussion in the previous section, we distinguish four values (aspects) in the aspect dimension of networked e-business that together form the BOAT framework:[1]

Business (B): the business aspect describes the business goals of networked e-business. As such it answers the question *why* a specific e-business scenario exists or should exist or *what* should be reached by the collaboration in a scenario. Topics can be access to new markets, new conceptual ways of collaboration in networks, reorientation of interaction with customers, leverage of efficiency levels, business directions and structures, business model concepts, et cetera. *How* things are done is not of interest in this aspect. The B aspect is treated in detail in chapter 5.

Organization (O): the organization aspect describes *how* organizations are structured and connected to achieve the goals defined in the B aspect. Organization structures at the organization and the business network level, business processes within organizations and across organizations in a business network, business functions and business services are the main ingredients here, complemented by considerations of how to manage and change business operation. Automated e-business systems to support these structures, processes and functions are not within the scope of this aspect. The O aspect is elaborated in chapter 6.

Architecture (A): the architecture aspect covers the conceptual structure or blueprint (i.e., the architecture) of automated information systems required to make the organizations defined in the O aspect work. As such, the A aspect describes *how* automated systems support the involved organizations in a conceptual, high-level fashion. Specific information technology elements are not within the scope of the A aspect. The A aspect is discussed in chapter 7.

Technology (T): the technology aspect describes the technological realization (also called the embodiment) of the systems for which the architecture is specified in the A aspect. In other words, the T aspect describes *from what ingredients* a networked e-business system is built. The T aspect covers the concrete ingredients from information and communication technology, including software, languages, communication protocols and hardware where relevant. This aspect has a strong relation to the *Big Five* developments as discussed in chapter 2. The T aspect is treated in detail in chapter 8.

Before we go further, we need to add a small explanation. The term *architecture* in general relates to the *structure* of arbitrary things. As such, it is in principle applicable to all four BOAT aspects. One may, for example, speak about *business architecture*. In the BOAT framework, however, the A aspect is dedicated to the structure of automated e-business systems. As such, it coincides with the concept of *information system architecture* applied in a context of networked e-business.

4.3 Aspect dimension and classification dimensions

In the previous chapter we have seen three classification dimensions for networked e-business: the *parties*, *objects* and *time scopes* dimensions. As shown in Figure 3.2 each e-business scenario can be positioned in the three-dimensional space created by these three dimensions. In other words, each e-business scenario has in principle *one* value in each of the classification dimensions (although sometimes a combination of values is possible to indicate a hybrid situation – for example, a scenario can be both B2C and B2B).

In the BOAT aspects dimension, each e-business scenario can be described with respect to four aspects: business, organization, architecture, and technology. The aspect descriptions combined constitute the full description of that e-business scenario. In other words, each e-business scenario has in principle *all* 'values' in the aspects dimension. As we will see in the next chapters, the four BOAT aspects do not contain simple values of characteristics (like in the classification dimensions), but complex sets of elements (such as models) describing e-business scenarios.

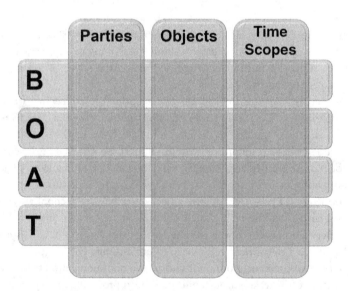

FIGURE 4.2 Classification and aspect dimensions.

The classification dimensions and the BOAT aspect dimension are orthogonal with respect to the e-business characteristics they describe, because each value in a classification dimension can be linked to all four BOAT aspects. This orthogonality of classification dimensions on the one hand and aspect dimension on the other hand is illustrated in Figure 4.2.

Note that the classification dimensions describe the 'outside' of an e-business scenario (i.e., they describe the scenario as a whole), whereas the BOAT aspects describe the 'inside' of a scenario (i.e., they describe the internal organization of a scenario).

4.4 Stack or wheel BOAT model?

In the previous sections we have introduced the four aspects of the BOAT framework, which reach from the business side to the technology side of e-business scenarios. Given this framework as a tool we can analyze a scenario or design a scenario. To do so, we have to decide, however, how we will traverse the BOAT framework. In other words, we have to decide in which order we will treat the BOAT aspects in analyzing or designing a scenario.

In traditional information system design practice, analysis and development of systems proceeds in a linear way from the business to the technology side. This is the order from requirements analysis via system specification and system design to system implementation (or variations on this list), which is commonly referred to as the *waterfall model* of information system design [Wik14h]. A simple waterfall model with four *stages* (also called *phases*) [Denn12] is shown in Figure 4.3.[2]

Using a waterfall approach with the BOAT framework would mean starting from the business (B) aspect and working stepwise to the technology (T) aspect, where the description of each preceding aspect defines the requirements that must be fulfilled in the succeeding aspect.[3] This leads to a design process as depicted

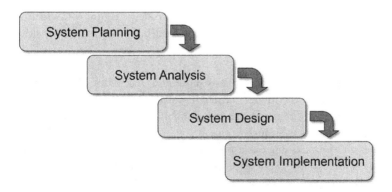

FIGURE 4.3   A simple waterfall model for information system development.

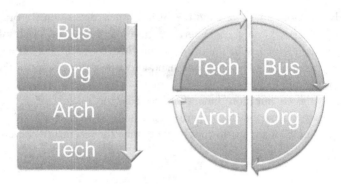

FIGURE 4.4 BOAT – stack or wheel model?

in the left side of Figure 4.4, which we call the *stack model* for BOAT: the aspects are stacked on top of each other (like in the waterfall model), defining a linear ordering.

But in the networked e-business field, the relationship between business and technology is not so linear. As we have seen in section 1.5, business 'pulls' technology development by stating new requirements, but technology also 'pushes' business by offering new opportunities (see Figure 1.5). In other words, sometimes the business aspect is the starting point of analysis or design, and sometimes it is the technology aspect. Likewise, the organization or architecture aspect can be the starting point – this is the case if organizational elements, respectively architecture elements, determine the essential nature of an e-business scenario. The choice of starting point can also depend on changes in the context related to a specific aspect, which trigger new possibilities for networked e-business. For example, if new business process standards are imposed by new regulations in an e-business domain, this may be a good reason to start a BOAT analysis and design from the organization aspect.

To model the fact that we can start at each BOAT aspect, we need to organize the BOAT aspects such that we get a more cyclical dependency among the aspects. This results in the picture as shown in the right side of Figure 4.4, which we call the *wheel model* of BOAT. With the wheel model, we can make two important observations:

1. An analysis or design process of an e-business scenario can – in principle – start at each aspect of the model (although the B and T aspects may be most common). A new organization structure in the O aspect, for example, may be the trigger for a new e-business scenario.
2. The wheel model suggests a non-ending cyclical analysis and design process. An e-business development process does not end after one cycle around the wheel, but keeps 'spinning'. It is a continuous process of adjustment to new business and technology contexts. As we have observed, these contexts change fast and often in the networked e-business world.

Given the multi-aspect, cyclical nature of networked e-business, we use the wheel model of BOAT as a basis throughout this book.

4.5 Running cases

In this section we apply the concepts of the BOAT framework to the three running cases of this book: POSH, TTU and TraXP.

4.5.1 POSH

The e-business designers of POSH recognize that getting into networked e-business is not a one-time affair, but requires constant evolution. Although the office-supply market may – objects-wise – not be the most dynamic market, the market is relatively new to the e-business field and will therefore require proper attention to changes.

Because POSH realizes that their e-business design will have to evolve in the future, the organization embraces the wheel model of BOAT. In the POSH case, e-business development is clearly driven by the quest for new business opportunities. The elements in the other BOAT aspects follow from business requirements. New information technology is certainly not a driver for new opportunities for POSH – existing technology offers more than they need. Hence, the B aspect is the trigger for e-business developments (as shown in Figure 4.5).

4.5.2 TTU

TTU realizes that moving into networked e-business implies constant innovation. The online translation business is a new business domain, requiring

FIGURE 4.5 BOAT wheel model for POSH.

FIGURE 4.6   BOAT wheel model for TTU.

adaptations to follow the market – both where it comes to emerging demands from customers and to developments by competing parties. Also, the business model relies on advanced communication technology when it comes to real-time interpretation (certainly when video or even telepresence is required – we discuss this technology in chapter 8). Because this technology is developing fast, it induces possible changes to the business model or the way TTU is organized. In other words, TTU's business domain is influenced by strong technology push forces.

Hence, TTU uses the wheel model of BOAT. In their application of the wheel model, the T aspect is the trigger for e-business developments (as illustrated in Figure 4.6): the technical possibility to provide online interpretation and translation services leads to the identification of new business opportunities. New communication technologies will heavily influence the nature and way of delivery of services. In other words, new business opportunities and business goals are defined on the basis of the availability of new technologies.

4.5.3 TraXP

TraXP is a spin-off of a major player in the international travel business world. It is positioned as an autonomous organization to allow for swift, agile development outside the existing structures of the organization that created it. The fact that cyclical thinking with short cycles is required is a no-brainer to TraXP management.

Given the fierce competition in the travel world, TraXP realizes it must have a strong competitive edge – just providing common e-business booking services will not have it stand out in the market. TraXP creates its competitive edge in two ways.

FIGURE 4.7   BOAT wheel model for TraXP.

First, it offers a highly integrated travel solution that enables a seamless travel experience. Its aim is to offer this at such a level, that this creates a clearly distinctive offering to the travel market. To achieve this, TraXP needs to create a business network of organizations that can provide elements in the seamless travel experience. This is clearly an ingredient of the business aspect.

Second, TraXP needs to design its organization such that it can actually manage the provisioning of a seamless travel experience. This entails the real-time orchestration of the business network, consisting of the organizations that provide the elements in the experience. These networks will be different for different types of experience (depending on customer groups or profiles). Also, each network will evolve over time as customer expectations change. This requires complex business process management and service management, which is an ingredient of the organization aspect.

TraXP has decided that the organization aspect will be the discriminating factor in the longer run: in a competitive field, a complex organization model will be harder to copy than a business model. Hence, they choose the O aspect of BOAT as their starting point for innovation (as shown in Figure 4.7). TraXP's organization of innovation processes is such that it can make a BOAT cycle at least twice a year.

4.6 Chapter end

We end this chapter with the chapter summary and a set of questions and exercises to put the theory of the basics of the BOAT framework to the test.

4.6.1 Chapter summary

E-business scenarios should be analyzed (or designed) with a clear and structured separation of concerns by distinguishing aspects of those scenarios. The *BOAT framework* provides a set of four aspects for the networked e-business field: *business, organization, architecture* and *technology*. The *business* aspect deals with the *what* and *why* of e-business. The *organization* aspect deals with the *how* from an organizational perspective; that is, without taking automated systems into account. The *architecture* aspect deals with the *how* from an abstract automation perspective, painting the blueprint of networked e-business systems. The *technology* aspect finally provides the technological details for the realization of concrete e-business systems.

The four BOAT aspects have important interrelationships. These can be placed in a linear *stack model* or a cyclical *wheel model*. The stack model represents a one-shot approach from business requirements to technological implementation. The wheel model represents a cyclical approach, where the trigger can be in any of the four BOAT aspects. For most e-business scenarios, the wheel model is preferable over the stack model.

4.6.2 Questions and exercises

1   Take the wheel model of BOAT. For each of the four BOAT aspects, find an existing, real-world e-business example scenario for which that aspect was indeed the trigger for the development of the scenario.

2   Do networked e-business situations exist where the stack model of BOAT may be preferable over the wheel model? If your answer is *yes*, give a convincing example of such a situation. If your answer is *no*, explain why the wheel model is *always* preferable to the stack model.

3   The wheel model of BOAT implies a cyclical development approach to e-business scenarios in which the four BOAT aspects are traversed over and over again. The question is what determines the frequency of 'cycling' through the BOAT aspects. In other words, one may ask what determines how long one cycle lasts (we have seen a period of six months in the TraXP case study, for example). To investigate this, take a few concrete e-business scenarios and discuss for each scenario which main factors may influence the cycle time. Take into account that there is a likely relationship between development triggers in the BOAT model and the factors that influence the cycle time.

4   Find information on the Zachman framework for enterprise architecture [Zach02]. This framework provides structures for the design of information systems in an enterprise engineering context (without an e-business connotation). Try to relate the elements in the Zachman framework to the aspects of the BOAT framework.

Notes

1 More frameworks exist that model a complex environment. A well-known example is the Zachman framework for enterprise architecture [Zach02]. This framework describes corporate information system development in the context of an organization, using a set of six system aspects (formulated as interrogatives) and a set of six groups of stakeholders. The Zachman framework can be related to the BOAT framework, but the mapping is not straightforward.

2 In practice, more elaborate waterfall models are used, possibly including a planning phase, several design and implementation subphases, a testing phase and a system introduction phase.

3 Note that *aspects* in this linear approach are effectively *levels*.

5

BUSINESS ASPECT

Learning goals

- *Understand the set of main business ingredient concepts of networked e-business and their relation to each other.*
- *Know and understand the main business drivers for networked e-business.*
- *Understand business directions for networked e-business that guide business innovation.*
- *Know and understand the main business network operations related to networked e-business.*
- *Understand business structures for e-business that guide the design of e-business networks.*
- *Understand business models for networked e-business and be able to analyze and classify them in a structured way.*

5.1 Introduction

In the previous chapter we have introduced the BOAT framework as the basis for structuring the discussion of networked e-business in this book. In this chapter we explore the main elements of the first aspect of the BOAT framework: the *business aspect*. The business (B) aspect contains those elements of networked e-business that describe the nature of e-business networks at a high level from a business-oriented point of view. As such, it focuses on the *what* and *why* of e-business networks.

The exploration in this chapter is performed in a structured setting following the integrative character of this book. We do this by starting from elementary characteristics of business in the networked e-business domain and working our way to typical networked e-business models. The business models are the basis for the achievement of an organization's business goals. We take four steps in consecutive sections before arriving at business models:

1   We first take a look at main business characteristics that are redefined through the use of networked e-business – the *business drivers* for the e-business case from the viewpoint of a business organization.
2   Next, using the discussed business drivers, we identify a number of new *business directions* that an organization can take into networked e-business.
3   Then, we see how e-business concepts can be used to change *business networks* that contain collaborations between organizations.
4   The new directions and network structures enable new *business structures* between organizations in networked e-business.

As such, we move from the single organization view (in steps 1 and 2) to the business collaboration and network view (in steps 3 and 4). Finally, the characteristics, directions, restructuring possibilities and business structures are used as the ingredients for new business models for networked e-business (illustrated in Figure 5.1), which are discussed in section 5.6. We end the chapter as usual with our running case studies, summary and questions.

Obviously, not all imaginable business topics can be discussed in full detail in one chapter. One topic that we do not discuss, for example, is the set of legal implications of e-business. Further topics and details can be found in other publications that focus on business aspects of e-business; for example, the emergence of new business strategies and models [Evan99, Perk99], e-business cases [Piep01, Jela08], the managerial perspective [Turb02, Chaf11], the economic perspective [VanH03] or the practical perspective [Hold08, Dani11].

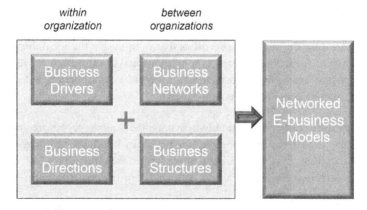

FIGURE 5.1   Business aspect ingredients as input for networked e-business models.

Note that we do not discuss generic business models or the way they are con-
ceived in general in this chapter – there are other publications that have this as an
objective (e.g., [Mitc03, Ches06, Oste10]). In this book we focus on the impact of
e-business elements on networked business models.

5.2 Business drivers

As discussed in section 1.2, business is e-business if it is different from other types
of business through the essential use of information and communication technology. Using this technology, there are two important elements in which e-business
can be different from traditional business in achieving its business goals: *reach* and
richness [Evan99]. Very briefly stated, *reach* describes with whom you can collaborate in an e-business scenario; *richness* describes what you can do with them. These
elements are *drivers* for the development of networked e-business. They are essentials for contacting (potential) business parties, engaging in business with them and
retaining them as business partners. As such, they are major parameters in the way
an organization creates value.[1] In the following sections we first discuss reach and
richness individually. Then, we combine them into a two-dimensional space in
section 5.2.3.

The drivers *reach* and *richness* are related to business functionality that influences
the *effectivity* of e-business scenarios via the deployment of advanced IT. Another
major reason to use IT in general is the *efficiency* of business operation. Obviously, this also holds for networked e-business. But to conform to our definition of
e-business as *IT-enabled* business (see chapter 1), a small efficiency increase does not
create e-business – so we concentrate on situations where the use of IT brings an
essential increase in business efficiency. We discuss efficiency as a business driver in
the context of this discussion in section 5.2.4.

5.2.1 Reach

The *reach* of an e-business scenario defines which set of business parties can be included
in that scenario. The aim of the use of information and communication technology
can be to increase the reach of a scenario; that is, to enable the inclusion of more
potential parties. A party can be any type of individual or organization with whom
business activities can be conducted: customers, providers, collaborators and so on.

We distinguish among three types of reach:

Geographic reach determines where potential business parties are geograph-
ically located; that is, where they are physically based. Increasing geographic
reach means attracting parties that are further away. Reach may, for instance,
be increased from regional to national, from national to continental and
from continental to global.
Temporal reach determines during what times potential parties can be active
in a scenario. Increasing temporal reach means opening up business more

hours a day and/or more days a week. Very often, e-business scenarios are active continuously, typically indicated as *24/7* (all hours of the day, all days of the week).

Modal reach determines through which channels business parties can collaborate; that is, what communication means can be used between partners. Increasing modal reach means opening new channels in an e-business scenario. New channels can be the web, email, instant messaging, text messaging, virtual environments and so on.

Obviously, in a specific e-business scenario, the aim can be (and often is) to address more than one type of reach; for example, the aim can be to reach more parties at more moments. Note that changing one type of reach can imply the necessity to consider another type of reach as well. Increasing the geographic reach from national to global, for instance, can imply the necessity of increasing the temporal reach to deal with parties in different time zones around the globe.

5.2.2 Richness

The *richness* of an e-business scenario is determined by the intensity of the communication between parties that engage in business using the main business communication channels. Intensity of communication can be interpreted both in a quantitative and a qualitative sense (as we discuss further on). We refer to the main communication channels (such as a website in e-business) because in traditional business extended richness in communication is often realized outside the main communication channels. For example, the main channel can be paper-based mail, whereas extended richness is realized through personal contact by phone. Information and communication technology can be used to increase richness by allowing more intense communication without having a substantial efficiency or cost penalty.

Richness has a number of sub-aspects:

Frequency of communication determines how often parties have contact. In traditional business scenarios, frequency may be low because of the cost of communication (in terms of material but certainly also in terms of personnel time) or lack of speed of used channels (like physical mail). In e-business, more frequent communication can often easily be established.

Level of interactivity in communication determines how much interaction is supported in communication sessions. Where traditional, paper-based communication allows very little interaction, internet-based communication allows for much more interaction by having the possibility of instantaneous action-response coupling (e.g., in interactive web forms or by using direct chat).

Level of detail in communication determines how many details about the manipulated objects (as discussed in section 3.5) or the manipulating business processes (as discussed in the next chapter) are communicated between parties. Using higher levels of interactivity allows for providing higher levels of details about traded objects without flooding a party (the receiver can decide to drill down into details). Higher frequencies of communication allow higher levels of details about processes (such as real-time status reports).

Used media in communication determine which media types are used in communication between business parties. In e-business, a richer medium selection can be used than in traditional business without getting into excessive costs. Media types used in e-business range from traditional types, such as text, graphics and photos, to more advanced types, such as animations, audio and video. Recent developments even enable the use of virtual 3D environments[2]: business activities are common in a virtual world such as Second Life [Terd07, Spea14]. Figure 5.2 shows an example of the use of video media in a web shop to provide customers with a 'live' demonstration and explanation of electronics.

Adaptation to party determines how much the communication is adapted towards specific individual business parties or specific groups of them. Adaptation means tuning the content of communication (and possibly the delivery process) such that it best fits the specific characteristics of a party. The presentation of a catalog of a web shop may, for instance, be tuned to

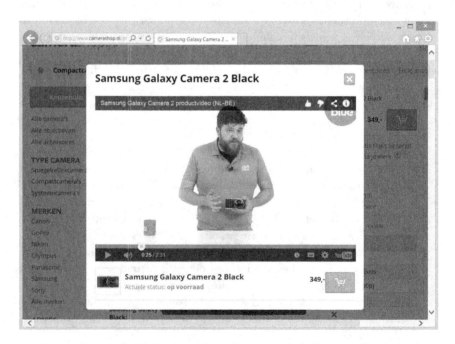

FIGURE 5.2   Increased richness through media use in a web shop.

individual customers based on prior shopping behavior. This is commonly referred to as *customization* or *mass customization*. In B2C scenarios, the term *personalization* is also used.

Note that *modal reach* and *used media* have a strong connection: the characteristics of available communication channels heavily determine which media types can be used. Although related, the two concepts are different: *modal reach* is about communication infrastructures whereas *used media* is about communication content.

5.2.3 Increasing reach and richness

Designing new e-business scenarios is often based on increasing reach, increasing richness or increasing both. Put into other words, an e-business transformation often implies moving a business scenario further into the reach and/or richness dimensions. Reach is increased to address new customer groups. Richness is increased to make business more attractive to existing or projected customer groups.

Increasing reach and richness is illustrated in Figure 5.3, where we show both drivers in a two-dimensional grid. The arrow in the figure indicates an example increase in reach and richness from a traditional business scenario (at the tail of the arrow with low levels of reach and richness) to a networked e-business scenario (at the head of the arrow with higher levels of reach and richness).

Clearly, when designing a concrete e-business scenario a simple sketch like the one in Figure 5.3 does not suffice. Intended increases in reach and/or richness have to be well specified, as realizing these increases is usually not without costs. Each e-business scenario has its own combination of reach and richness characteristics. Changes in reach and richness have to be carefully operationalized; that is, designed concretely in operational terms such as customer groups to address,

FIGURE 5.3 Increasing reach and richness.

channels to be used, time frames for realization and so on. In doing so, the types of reach and the sub-aspects of richness discussed in this section provide a basis for operationalization.

5.2.4 Efficiency

A desired increase of the efficiency of conducting business is often a reason for the use of information and communication technology (both in traditional and electronic business). If the increase of efficiency is used only to reduce the costs related to existing business models without altering the essence of these models, we do not consider this e-business: in this case, technology is supporting business, not enabling business (remember our definition of e-business in chapter 1). Replacing a paper-based personnel administration with an automated system is not e-business according to our definition (although some authors may not share this vision).

When efficiency of conducting business is increased dramatically, however, this may induce the possibility of new business models. An example is enabling the cost-effective handling of far smaller transactions (micro-transactions) than possible in traditional business, thereby moving to entirely different sales models (think, for example, of the music industry selling individual songs in digital format). If this is the case, we do speak of e-business, because information technology is indeed an enabler of new ways of doing business and, hence, of new business models. In other words, efficiency alone is an e-business characteristic in extreme cases only – otherwise, it can be a 'nice extra' to the other e-business drivers (i.e., increased reach and richness).

A business control view on increasing efficiency

We can take a closer look at increasing efficiency by viewing a business organization as a three-level control structure:

- the *operational level* performs the primary business process, making transaction scale decisions;
- the *tactical level* controls the operational level, making medium-term, medium-scale decisions; and
- the *strategic level* controls the tactical level, making long-term, large-scale decisions.

In a traditional business organization, the sizes of the levels in terms of personnel (or effort) count are as shown in the left side of Figure 5.4: the operational level is the largest and the strategic level the smallest, accounting for the pyramid shape. Increasing efficiency in a dramatic way often boils down to highly automating business functionality at the operational level: routine tasks are fully automated and human effort mainly goes into exception handling. As a consequence, the size of

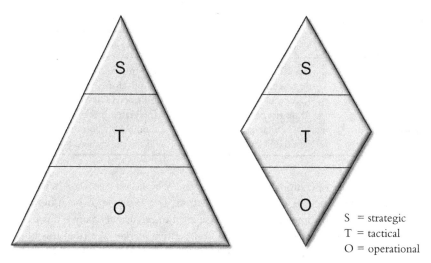

FIGURE 5.4   Pyramid and diamond business control structures.

the operational layer is strongly reduced. This can change the pyramid shape into a diamond shape as shown in the right side of the figure, making the tactical layer the largest. In this case, an important task of the tactical layer is to continuously set the parameters for the automated systems that perform the operational processes such that these can perform the operational processes as autonomously as possible.

5.3 Business directions

Based on business drivers and redefined business characteristics as discussed in the previous section, various new business directions can be distinguished in the networked e-business domain. In this section we discuss several important directions. We don't aim at being complete here (as new directions can always be found in the dynamic domain of e-business); rather, our goal is to identify major directions in a structured way. To identify these directions, we start with the three business drivers that we have discussed in the previous section: *reach*, *richness* and *efficiency*. Next, we operationalize each driver in two ways to become more concrete in terms of business directions.

To operationalize *reach* we can increase the *availability* of e-business applications and we can increase the *accessibility* of applications. Availability in an e-business setting means not only being *online* at the required times (this often means always) but also having the right resources (including required information) available; that is, being *on time*. This leads to a business direction that we label *on time and online business*. Accessibility in an e-business setting means allowing the right channels to be used in the right circumstances; that is, having multiple collaboration channels available for multiple circumstances. This we label the *multi-channel business* direction.

TABLE 5.1 Overview of business directions

Business driver	Operationalized driver	Business direction
Reach	Availability	On time and online business
	Accessibility	Multi-channel business
Richness	Customer intimacy	Enhanced CRM
	Transitionality	Integrated bricks and clicks
Efficiency	Cost efficiency	Completely automated business
	Time efficiency	Time-compressed business

Richness can be operationalized in many ways. We choose two ways here with high practical relevance in networked e-business. The first way is by using rich information about customers to create a high level of *customer intimacy* – this binds a customer to an e-business scenario in a competitive market. We label this business direction *enhanced customer relationship management* (enhanced CRM). The second way to operationalize richness is to provide a customer with a fluent transition between the physical part and digital part of business (either in the course of individual e-business transactions or in a sequence of e-business transactions over time) – we call this *transitionality*. To obtain transitionality, an e-business organization needs to tightly integrate its physical and digital operations, often labeled as *integrated bricks and clicks* (which we choose as the label for the business direction).

Efficiency – as the third business driver – can be operationalized along two dimensions: *cost* and *time*. We relate the operationalized driver *cost efficiency* to a business direction that aims at minimal business operation costs by applying automation at the highest possible level: the *completely automated business*. The operationalized driver *time efficiency* is related to a business direction that aims at reducing throughput times for business operation (transaction execution): the *time-compresses business* direction.

We show an overview of all six identified business directions in Table 5.1. We discuss each individual business direction in a more detailed way in the following sections. For some of the business directions we will see that the networked character of modern e-business has a strong impact on the way that direction can be realized: the scope of a business direction can go beyond a single organization in networked e-business.

5.3.1 On time and online business

The 'old economy' relies heavily on slow and asynchronous communication channels, such as the traditional postal service. This means that direct interaction between business parties is very limited and 'time margins' are built into business processes to accommodate this. In networked e-business, we can have direct interaction between partners using electronic channels such as the internet. This paves the way for *online business*; that is, business where parties interact directly using digital means. Online business allows much tighter synchronization between partners, which enables *on-time processes* – also referred to as *real-time* business processes. In various business domains, this real-time character is very important; for example, in the stock exchange domain. As a consequence, business structures can be built with much tighter coupling (leading to *just-in-time* business operation) or scenarios are enabled with smaller values in the time scopes dimension (see section 3.6).

In the early days of e-business (the end of the twentieth century), being 'truly on time and online' was a major goal to be achieved and sometimes a major selling point for a scenario. The use of a web interface did not necessarily imply full online transaction handling behind it: often, the web interface was only a facade to the manual handling behind it. This means that 'true online' was not achieved, and if manual handling followed typical office hours, neither was 'true on time'. Nowadays, it is more and more taken as a default setting for e-business scenarios that transactions are completely performed in an online and real-time fashion. An example is the travel industry, where actual bookings for air travel and hotels are usually made completely interactively and automatically.

In the transition from 'traditional', non-networked e-business to networked e-business, being on time and online has a new challenge: it is not determined by a single focal organization but by the complete network that delivers a complex e-business object to a customer. If one party in such a network is not on time and online the entire network isn't, from the perspective of the customer (as the object cannot be delivered). In other words, for this business direction a business network is as strong as its weakest member.

5.3.2 Multi-channel business

The introduction of e-business often means that multiple communication channels come into existence through which parties in an e-business scenario can communicate and collaborate. This is certainly the case with integrated bricks and clicks approaches (which we discuss in detail a bit later in this section), where traditional communication channels (e.g., physical post, telephone) are operated alongside digital communication channels (e.g., a website). But in pure e-business more than one channel may exist; for example, e-mail, web-based forms, digital voice response systems and so on.

From a business point of view, two aspects are of paramount importance when using multiple channels in parallel: flexibility and synchronization. Flexibility should allow business partners to change channels without disturbing tactical business relations or even change channels within the scope of a single business order without disturbing operational business processes. Synchronization must be taken into account in the business design to make sure that transactions conducted over more than one channel in parallel still provide consistent results.[3] We refer to e-business setup taking this into proper account as *multi-channel business design*.

A multi-channel business design may be necessary for several reasons. An important reason is the existence of different customer groups, each of which prefers a different primary channel. We see this, for example, with general mail order companies, where older customers may prefer traditional channels and younger customers may prefer digital channels. Another reason is the use of different kinds of communication devices. We see this, for example, in m-business settings, where different kinds of mobile devices are used depending on the actual physical context of a user, and a user may change channels on the fly when this context changes.

5.3.3 Enriched customer relationship management

In the 'old economy' the nature of communication media typically enforces infrequent, coarse-grained communication between partners. The cost of offline, manual communication and data processing prevents the management of detailed, up-to-date partner information. This makes customer relationship management (CRM) limited. In e-business scenarios, interaction between partners can be cheap, fast and frequent. Online data gathering allows the management and use of very detailed and up-to-date information about partners. This holds both for individual partners and for groups or classes of partners. This kind of customer data processing relies on big data technologies such as those we have seen in section 2.2. These developments open the door to complete new forms of CRM and thereby to new forms of business that rely on a high level of customer intimacy.

Examples can be found in electronic retail applications that dynamically compose offers for customers based on their current and past behaviors. Note that in traditional retail typically only transactions (sales) are recorded, leading to coarse pictures of client behavior. In electronic retail the complete behavior of customers can be recorded in great detail (e.g., their catalog browsing history) even when this does not lead to any transactions. Behavior of customers can be matched against behavior of comparable customers to suggest or even predict future behavior. Obviously, privacy of B2C customers in a digital environment [Acqu08] is an important issue in this context.

5.3.4 Integrated bricks and clicks

Many business organizations already have an established footprint in the 'old economy'. Recognizing that networked e-business offers new possibilities does not necessarily mean doing away completely with this established presence, because this might imply a substantial loss of customer base. In this context the 'old' business is often referred to as *bricks* and the 'new' business as *clicks* [Lind01]. An integration of 'old' and 'new' business is necessary, referred to as *integrated bricks and clicks*.[4]

In this integration two aspects are of utmost importance. First, there should be synergy between the bricks and the clicks such that the one offers added value to the other (e.g., by offering additional services to business partners). Second, the demarcation between bricks and clicks should be flexible such that both customers and business activities can be moved from the one to the other without disturbing business operation. Usually the move is from bricks to clicks, but not necessarily so (if a clicks scenario fails, a bricks backup should be available in some business segments).

An integrated bricks and clicks business direction is – obviously – often coupled to a multi-channel business design as discussed before. In this case, part of the channels addresses the bricks part of the business and part addresses the clicks part.

A business domain in which integrated bricks and clicks has been of major importance is that of mail-order companies. These companies started in a completely bricks world with communication based on paper catalogs and order forms. They have moved into the clicks domain by introducing web shops with electronic catalogs and ordering. Given the fact that they often address various customer segments with different internet adoption rates, parallel operation of bricks and clicks is essential. Some parts of business, like the return of goods [Kost05], retain bricks elements and therefore will require proper integration towards the future.

5.3.5 Completely automated business

In e-business in general, information technology is used to automate business functions that are performed by humans in traditional business settings. As such, the amount of human intervention in business processes is reduced – typically to reduce costs. In an extreme case of networked e-business, one may strive for business operation (at the operational level) without human intervention at all – thus, human effort is only required for management tasks (at the tactic and strategic levels). We call this business direction the *completely automated business*. This business direction is an extreme version of the efficiency increase as discussed in section 5.2.4, actually 'erasing' the operational business control level as shown in Figure 5.4.

Complete automation in an e-business scenario is typically only achievable if there is no manipulation of physical objects (see section 3.5). This implies that only digital objects or services are manipulated *or* physical handling is completely outsourced to external service providers that are not considered part of the e-business scenario.

Often, however, automation of operational business processes cannot be pursued in its full completeness: humans may be needed to deal with exception handling; that is, dealing with non-programmed cases. But for highly standardized digital objects or services, complete automation is *in principle* achievable. Note that even the operation and maintenance of the required computing infrastructure can be outsourced (e.g., using cloud computing, as discussed in section 2.2.3) such that a business organization can completely focus on tactical and strategic activities.

5.3.6 Time-compressed business

By integrating elements of the *true on-time and online* business and *completely automated* business directions, one can obtain the *time-compressed business* direction. This means that e-business models can be used that are based on business transactions that are executed in a fraction of the time compared to traditional business models. For example, traditional transactions that take days are compressed into e-business transactions that are completed in seconds. The same goes for multi-transaction business processes.

Time compression is enabled by the fact that reactions of business partners in transaction execution can always be almost instantaneous (as they are always online and they can automate operational decision-making tasks). This business direction enables business models with high levels of just-in-time behavior and short-lived partnerships. Note that the latter is related to the *time scopes* dimension that we have discussed in section 3.6: moving towards time-compressed business may mean moving business models to the 'short-lived' end of the *time scopes* dimension.

Practical examples of e-business scenarios with extreme time compression can be found in stock and currency markets, where fast-moving players obviously have advantages over slow-moving players. Extreme examples of time-compressed business are often found in e-business scenarios with digital objects only (see section 3.5). This is caused by the fact that handling physical objects requires time as dictated by physical constraints. For instance, goods have to be transported over physical distances, which takes time that can only be compressed to a certain degree.

The directions of *time compression* and *complete automation* can be found simultaneously in an e-business scenario. However, they are not the same, because *time compression* aims at business execution time reduction whereas *complete automation* aims at business costs reduction (see Table 5.1).

As with the *on time and online* business direction, the network aspect is very important for the *time-compressed business* direction: it usually does not make much sense to compress the execution time of one single organization in an e-business network if the other organizations remain at their old execution speed (unless that one organization was a bottleneck, of course).

An automotive case of time compression. In the automotive industry, complex business networks are required for the production of cars and trucks. These networks consist of organizations that produce automotive parts and subsystems, organizations that handle logistics and organizations that assemble subsystems and complete cars. Launching a new car or truck model typically requires the setup of a new network. Traditionally, setting up a network is a manual process that is performed by intensive communication between possible network partners to discuss involved technical, organizational and business issues. This process can easily cause several months of lead time before the automotive production process can actually start. In the European CrossWork project [Meha10, Gref09] a networked e-business approach with supporting information technology has been proposed to compress the time of the setup process from several months to several weeks, or even several days in an optimal setting. This time reduction increases the agility of the business network to a large extent.

5.4 Changing e-business networks

In section 5.2 we have seen that business characteristics such as reach and richness can be changed by the use of networked e-business. These new characteristics are implemented in business models (which we will see later in this chapter) that are based on new forms of business collaboration enabled by the use of information and communication technology. In other words, e-business changes business relationships by restructuring business collaborations.

These business collaborations take place in e-business networks. These networks can have linear structures; for example, production chains, service chains and supply chains. They can also have different topologies; for example; hub-and-spoke service networks (we have seen an example of this in Figure 2.5). A network consists of a number of *nodes*, which are also referred to as *links* in linear chains. Each node is a business organization that provides a specific part of the functionality of the overall network. In this section we show simple chains with a linear structure for the sake of simplicity. The principles discussed apply similarly to networks with a more complex structure.

In business networks restructuring a collaboration topology from a functionality point of view is implemented through the two basic forms of *disintermediation* and *reintermediation*. We discuss these two 'operations' on e-business networks in the first two following subsections. When we take functional restructuring of a business network to the extreme, we get the forms of *deconstruction* and *reconstruction*. We discuss these in section 5.4.3. Finally, an e-business network can be changed without changing the functional topology but by substituting a node by a functionally similar node – this *substitution* operation on business networks is discussed at the end of this section.

5.4.1 Disintermediation

In typical 'traditional' business networks nodes often exist that have a function between other nodes that is heavily based on 'traditional' collaboration or communication patterns. *Disintermediation* is the removal of such a node from a business network (as illustrated in Figure 5.5 for a link in a simple business chain) because it has become 'superfluous' through the use of e-business technology that allows increase of reach (and sometimes richness) [Evan99, Turb02].

FIGURE 5.5   Disintermediation in a simple chain.

Typically, disintermediation applies to a node in a network that has some kind of intermediary function between other nodes in the network. A typical B2C example is disintermediation in supply chains for consumer products where the retailer is removed because the producer (or distributor) of the goods has direct contact with the individual consumers through digital channels (typically, websites). In the B2B world we can find comparable examples, where suppliers of professional products (e.g., office or computing equipment) sell directly to user organizations.

5.4.2 Reintermediation

Reintermediation is the insertion of a new node in an existing business network [Turb02], as illustrated in Figure 5.6 for a simple chain network topology. The new node provides new functionality (i.e., new added value) to the network that is enabled by the use of information and communication technology. As such, reintermediation can be seen as the opposite of disintermediation.

Reintermediation often applies to organizations with a new kind of intermediary function that is enabled by e-business technology. Common B2C examples can be found in the electronic retail world, where product comparison or integration sites take a new place as a broker in a supply chain between producers and consumers. An interesting playing field emerges when large social media operators (as discussed in section 2.2.1) reintermediate themselves into existing e-business networks, using the 'power' of their large user base. A B2B example of reintermediation is the creation of electronic marketplaces where products (or services) are traded within communities of suppliers and consumers instead of between fixed pairs of business partners.

5.4.3 Deconstruction and reconstruction

In disintermediation and reintermediation a business network is modified by manipulating one single node (as shown in Figure 5.5 and Figure 5.6). If we take

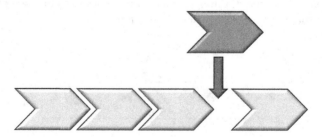

FIGURE 5.6 Reintermediation in a simple chain.

the approach to the extreme, we deconstruct a complete network into its constituent pieces (nodes). Next, we evaluate the added value of each piece, perhaps throw away a few, combine a few and add a few. From the results of this we finally reconstruct a completely new network [Evan99]. This new network may follow a completely different business model from the old network, yet provide a similar functionality to a market. We call this approach *deconstruction and reconstruction*. This is illustrated for a simple business chain in Figure 5.7.

Clearly, deconstruction and reconstruction can most easily be applied to networks that are not so 'physical' in nature; for example, information-intensive networks. A typical example is the travel world, in which the service chains between providers (airlines, hotels and so on) and consumers (the travelers) have been completely changed by the introduction of e-business. In the traditional economy most transactions were channeled through large travel organizations with many travel agencies close to the consumers (both private and professional travelers). In the digital economy we see that the role of travel offices is decreasing, that providers sell directly to consumers (some low-fare airlines even only use direct sales), that product integration and product comparison services have emerged, that physical travel documents (tickets, vouchers) are disappearing and hence the role of postal services is fading and so on.

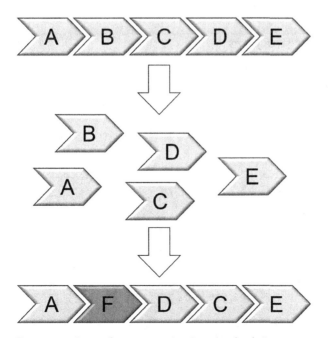

FIGURE 5.7 Deconstruction and reconstruction in a simple chain.

5.4.4 Substitution

The operations on e-business networks that we have discussed so far in this section change the functional topology of a network; that is, they change the structure of the collaboration in the network. It is also possible to modify a network without changing the functional topology. In this case we replace a node in a network by a functionally similar node such that the overall functional structure remains the same. We call this operation *substitution*. Substitution is applied in a network to include a new node that has better non-functional characteristics than the node to be replaced. Non-functional characteristics may pertain to cost efficiency or time efficiency (as discussed in section 5.2.4), but they may also pertain to other aspects such as trustworthiness or level of offered transaction security. Substitution in a simple e-business chain is illustrated in Figure 5.8.

Substitution in e-business networks is related to increased reach and richness between possible partners in business domains (note that this is different from increased reach and richness towards customers, although similar thoughts apply). Increased reach leads to the availability of more alternative nodes for a network. Increased richness leads to easier replacement of nodes, because more aspects of connecting a new node in a network can be handled via e-business means (thereby lowering the so-called switching costs). The use of electronic certificates, formalized service-level agreements and electronic contracts can play an important role here (we discuss these technology elements when we get to the technology aspect of the BOAT framework in chapter 8).

5.5 Business structures

Inspired by the business network operations discussed in the previous section, new business structures for e-business networks can be defined. These structures can be seen as collaboration patterns that are used in the design of business models for networked e-business.

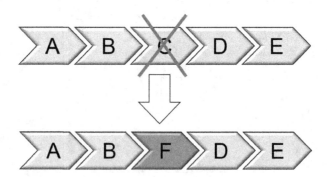

FIGURE 5.8 Substitution in a simple chain.

In this section we introduce a number of important classes of such business structures that are used as a basis (or inspiration) for new business models in networked e-business (discussed in the next section). These business structures can be rather diverse (and new ones can emerge). Therefore, we do not attempt to give a highly structured, exhaustive overview here; rather, we discuss an illustrative set. The structures that we discuss are listed in Table 5.2 together with their related business network operations as discussed in the previous section.

5.5.1 Dynamic partnering

The flexibility and efficiency of e-business technology allows the 'on-the-fly' establishment of peer-to-peer business collaborations between autonomous business organizations. With peer-to-peer collaboration we indicate the form of collaboration where there is no hierarchical relationship between the collaborators. An example is a door-to-door public transportation service, where one party takes care of the long-haul part of a trip (e.g., a railroad operator) and another party takes care of the 'head and tail' of a trip (e.g., a local bus or taxi operator).

With *on-the-fly* establishment of collaboration we mean the selection of collaboration parties *during* the execution of business operations. This can differ radically from traditional collaboration forms. In traditional forms collaborations are typically set up before the actual business operation starts (e.g., in physical collaboration contracts). Given the cost of such setup, these collaborations are often forged for prolonged time spans (e.g., several years or even indefinitely). In the e-business form of collaboration setup, the partnership is created during business operation at the time that the functionality of a partner is actually needed. We call this *dynamic partnering*. In an extreme form we have *just-in-time* partnering: choosing and binding a partner at the latest possible moment in order to be able to use as much context information (e.g., market conditions or case characteristics) as possible in choosing the best partner.

Clearly, this business structure is related to the *time scopes* classification dimension discussed in section 3.6: long-term traditional partnerships (which are *static* in this dimension) are replaced by dynamically forged short-term relationships in which

TABLE 5.2 Overview of business structures

Business structure	Related business network operation
Dynamic partnering	Substitution
Dynamic outsourcing	Reintermediation and substitution
Dynamic insourcing	Disintermediation and substitution
Crowdsourcing	Reintermediation
Highly dynamic supply chain	Substitution
Demand chain	Deconstruction and reconstruction

parties can be replaced. This possible replacement of parties uses the *substitution* business network operation that we have discussed in the previous section.

5.5.2 Dynamic outsourcing

A business structure that has some similarities with *dynamic partnering* is *dynamic outsourcing*, a business structure in which a business organization dynamically delegates a non-core part of its processes to another organization. Delegation implies a hierarchical relationship between collaborators: one organization instructs another organization to perform a sub-process on its behalf. Dynamic delegation means that these third parties are selected and connected in an on-the-fly way (using the *dynamic* or even *ultra-dynamic* time scope value as discussed in section 3.6) using e-business channels.

Delegation means that an internal sub-process of the outsourcing party is replaced by an external process. This implies the inclusion of a new partner in a business network, which we can consider a specific kind of *reintermediation*. Dynamic delegation implies that delegates can be easily replaced – hence, this business structure uses the *substitution* business network operation as discussed in the previous section. Delegated sub-processes can be service processes or production processes. We concentrate on service processes further on, as these use e-business characteristics best.

When service processes are outsourced we speak of *dynamic service outsourcing* [Strö00]. In this business paradigm an organization chooses parts of its business process that it doesn't consider part of its core competence and outsources these sub-processes to specialist service provider organizations. For these organizations the outsourced sub-processes are core competence, such that they can perform these in a better way than the outsourcer. The decision to select a specific service provider for a specific piece of work is taken dynamically – possibly just-in-time to take current market circumstances into account. Clearly, just-in-time outsourcing requires fast communication channels. Service providers can be selected using electronic markets in which they advertise their services.

Dynamic service outsourcing is schematically illustrated in Figure 5.9. In the middle of the figure we see an organization with five business competences (implemented as business sub-processes). Three are core competences (indicated by stars) and two are non-core (indicated by circles). The non-core competences are dynamically outsourced to external parties, for whom these activities are core competences. For one sub-process there is a choice of three service providers from which to dynamically select; for the other a choice of two. In practical situations these numbers may be (much) greater.

Dynamic service outsourcing can improve the competitiveness of the outsourcer in a number of ways. It can enhance the efficiency of its processes because a provider can perform an outsourced sub-process faster and/or cheaper. It can enhance the effectiveness of its processes because the provider can perform the tasks in which it specializes in a qualitatively better way. Finally, it can greatly enhance the flexibility (also called agility) of the outsourcing organization because the provider

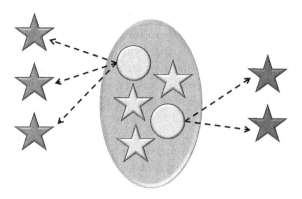

FIGURE 5.9 Dynamic service outsourcing.

can be chosen dynamically, depending on both the case (e.g., customer order) at hand and the current market circumstances.

5.5.3 Dynamic insourcing

Where dynamic outsourcing focuses on delegating secondary tasks from an organization to dynamically selected providers, *dynamic insourcing* is the opposite: here, the focus is on dynamically selecting providers from which to obtain (insource) essential parts of a primary e-business object. This object can either be a physical good, a digital good or a service – as discussed in section 3.5.

In the case of physical goods insourcing often relates to complex products that are composed of components, the providers of which are selected on a dynamic basis. An example can be found in the computer industry, where PCs (desktops and laptops) are assembled from a spectrum of components, such as processors, memory chips, hard drives and displays. The providers of these components can be selected dynamically to make the best use of current market circumstances (such as prices or availability of components). The case for digital goods is quite comparable, although switching providers is often easier because no transportation of physical components is involved.

In the case of services we see that an insourcing service integrator obtains a number of component services from dynamically selected service providers to deliver a complex service to its customer. A good example of dynamic insourcing is TraXP: here, component travel services (such as air transportation) are dynamically insourced based on current market circumstances. We discuss this example in more detail in section 5.9.3.

5.5.4 Crowdsourcing

Crowdsourcing [Howe08] is a business structure in which the 'power of the masses' is used to address business problems. The increase in the reach of an organization enabled by e-business (see section 5.2.1) is used to facilitate outsourcing to a very large number of 'business partners' (which can be individual people), each of which contributes a small element to the overall task. In crowdsourcing the business partners are typically individuals with whom the outsourcing organization has no official relationship (i.e., they are not employees of the organization in any form) but who may be part of some virtual community. As such, crowdsourcing can be considered a *reversed B2C* business model – reversed because the C side provides input to the B side (contrary to typical B2C models such as e-retailing).

Crowdsourcing can have an outsourcing or an insourcing character. In the outsourcing case routine tasks to be performed are offered to the crowd for execution. In this case, members of the crowd pick tasks to be performed (which are removed from the task pool). In the insourcing task the crowd is offered a request for input (i.e., the creation of object components). Here, multiple crowd members may compete to produce the same input element.

All three business drivers (as discussed in section 5.2) are essential here. Reach is essential to be able to be in contact with the crowd – both for disseminating requests and for collecting results. Richness is essential to obtain enough intimacy with the crowd to create some kind of a collaboration community. Extreme efficiency is essential to be able to resourcefully deal with the collaboration of the individuals in a potentially very large crowd.

5.5.5 Highly dynamic supply chain

Traditionally, supply chain structures have limited flexibility with respect to the partners involved in a specific supply chain. An organization in a chain typically obtains a specific type of input object from one or a small set of providers. Similarly, it typically delivers a specific type of output object to a more or less fixed set of consumers. An example is a traditional automotive supply chain, in which a static routing between organizations exists for parts, components and large modules towards complete cars. This inflexibility in traditional supply chains is related to the slowness and cost of traditional communication and collaboration channels. In other words, so-called *switching costs* (the cost to change to a different collaboration partner) are typically high in traditional business scenarios, leading to *switching barriers*.

Networked e-business enables the design of supply chains with much more 'routing flexibility'; that is, the dynamic selection of input and output partners in a chain. Standardized and inexpensive digital communication and collaboration platforms (we discuss these in chapter 8) can lower switching costs considerably. In a highly dynamic chain both types of partners (providers and consumers) may be selected completely on the fly, based on selection processes conducted on real-time electronic market places. This is illustrated in Figure 5.10, where the focus organization is shown in the center and both the input side and output side of this organization are connected to an electronic market (EM), providing connections to many potential business partners.

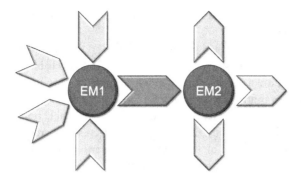

FIGURE 5.10 A highly dynamic supply chain with two electronic markets.

The highly dynamic supply chain business structure can be considered a chain-level specialization of the dynamic partnering business structure discussed in section 5.5.1: partners are chosen dynamically, but for a specific reason – providing goods from or selling goods to. On the input side of an organization the highly dynamic supply chain business structure can be considered a generalization of the dynamic insourcing structure discussed in section 5.5.3. The highly dynamic supply chain structure, however, focuses on the network level of business (i.e., on flexibility at the level of an entire supply chain), whereas the dynamic insourcing structure focuses on bilateral relationships between business parties.

5.5.6 Demand chain

Traditionally, the operation of many supply chains is producer controlled. This means that a producer of goods decides what to produce (and at what point in time) and 'pumps' it into a supply chain. At the end of this supply chain the consumer decides what to buy from the offering predefined by the producer. A supermarket is a typical example of such a supply chain. Disadvantages of this business design are the fact that production may not meet consumer wishes qualitatively or quantitatively. For example,

- Consumers may want products with different characteristics (e.g., with a different color) than available at the purchasing moment.
- There may be too few or too many products on the market at a given moment. The former may lead to loss of market, the latter to substantial waste.

Hence, this business design may be suboptimal in markets where consumer behavior changes quickly and is unpredictable. Traditionally, more direct coupling between consumer behavior and producer activities was hard to realize because the necessary synchronization channels either did not exist or were far too costly or slow to be used in practice.

To cope with the mentioned problems, one may go from a supply chain business design to a *demand chain* business design. In the pure demand chain design a producer only produces a product after a consumer has ordered it; that is, the operation of the chain is consumer-controlled (see Figure 5.11). This is a form of just-in-time business operation, facilitated by the fact that electronic channels enable both fast and cheap synchronization between consumer and producer (even if there are many diverse consumers) and the efficient orchestration of the intermediate links in a chain.

Moving from a supply chain to a demand chain business design may imply moving in the time scopes dimension (see section 3.6): a static time scope is exchanged for a dynamic time scope. This is the case if the characteristics of customer orders determine the optimal provider 'upstream in the chain': depending on what a customer wants, providers are selected. In this case the demand chain business structure also has characteristics of the dynamic insourcing business structure discussed in section 5.5.3.

A demand chain business design allows mass customization, producing large volumes of products, each of which can be customized to meet the requirements of an individual buyer. An example of this business design is Dell (www.dell.com), a computer supplier that produces personal computers per customer orders in a demand chain fashion [Dell06].

In a hybrid supply/demand chain design we have a well-defined *customer order decoupling point*. At the producer side of this point the chain operates in supply mode

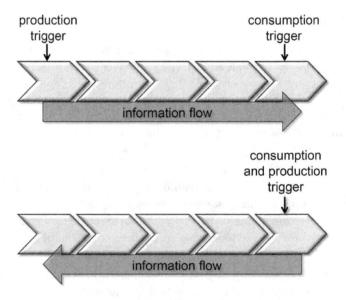

FIGURE 5.11   Supply chain and demand chain.

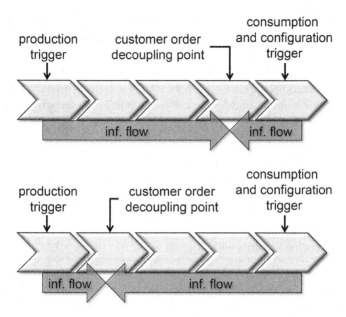

FIGURE 5.12 Traditional and e-business hybrid supply/demand chain.
inf. flow = information flow.

(referred to as *produce to stock*), producing products that can be configured to customer demands. At the consumer side of this point the chain operates in demand
mode (referred to as *produce to order*). At the customer order decoupling point the
configuration of products takes place. This is illustrated in Figure 5.12.

Where traditional business scenarios do allow hybrid chain designs, e-business
allows designs in which the decoupling point is moved much more towards the
producer (i.e., a larger part of the chain is operating in demand mode – illustrated in Figure 5.12). As in the case of pure demand chains, this is enabled by
more efficient and richer communication and synchronization between links in
the chain.

The hybrid supply/demand chain business structure also allows mass customization of products (be it at a lower level than a pure demand chain) – we see this, for
instance, in the automotive domain, where cars are configured to buyer's specifications but start from a standardized basic configuration.

5.6 Business models

In this section we combine all elements of the previous sections of this chapter
to arrive at definitions of prototype business models for networked e-business –
or blueprints for business models of the 'new networked economy'. The business

models we discuss in this section can be considered template business models (or reference business models), which can be instantiated for concrete business cases to arrive at actual e-business scenarios.

Because new business models are 'invented' continuously, obviously we cannot be complete here. Therefore, we rely on a simple taxonomy to arrive at a structured set of prototype business models. The taxonomy is based on three top-level classes of business models:

- models that are based on provisioning products for customers – that is, creating e-business objects (as discussed in section 3.5) with business value;
- models that are based on intermediating between other e-business parties – that is, creating collaborations with business value; and
- models that are based on enabling cooperation between e-business parties – that is, creating activities with business value.

Within each class we distinguish three reference business models. The resulting taxonomy of nine reference business models for networked e-business is shown as a small catalog in Table 5.3.

Each reference business model is discussed further on in this section. After the discussion, each business model is summarized in a table, which combines a classification in the three dimensions of chapter 3 and an identification of the B aspect ingredients as treated in the previous four sections of this chapter. We also pay brief attention to the economical aspect of networked e-business by adding an indication of a typical revenue stream for a business model. This leads to eight rows in a reference business model characteristics table, as illustrated in Table 5.4 (the table indicates where the theory behind each row is discussed).

TABLE 5.3 Reference business model taxonomy

Business model catalog	
Class	*Reference business model*
Object provisioning	e–retailer
	e–producer
	e–integrator
Intermediation	e–marketplace
	e–indexer
	e–comparator
Cooperation	e–facilitator
	e–collaborator
	e–sourcer

TABLE 5.4 Business model summary table ingredients

Business model summary	
Parties	Section 3.4
Objects	Section 3.5
Time scope	Section 3.6
Drivers	Section 5.2
Directions	Section 5.3
Networks	Section 5.4
Structures	Section 5.5
Revenue stream	This section

5.6.1 The e-retailer

Probably the best-known business model in the e-business domain is the *e-retailer*, simply because we as consumers are often confronted with it. E-retailing in its basic form brings traditional consumer shopping to the internet – therefore, it is a very typical B2C model. Objects traded in an e-retailing scenario can in principle be of any kind, but often they are physical goods or digital goods (as discussed in section 3.5.2). In the time scopes dimension, e-retailer scenarios are typically dynamic: a customer chooses an e-retailer to do business with on a per-transaction (purchase) basis.

The business drivers behind e-retailing are typically twofold. First, the use of the internet provides an extreme reach increase when compared to traditional, physical shops – both in geographical and in temporal reach (see section 5.2.1). Second, pure e-retailing may provide a substantial cost reduction because physical shops are not necessary – hence a substantial efficiency increase. Note, however, that e-retailing may imply other costs, such as the maintenance of an elaborate website and to-customer shipping. The richness aspect in e-retailing depends very

---

The Pets.com story. Not all e-business retailer initiatives have worked. A striking example is Pets.com. Pets.com opened for business in August 1998 as an online retailer for pet supplies. It received broad attention as a consequence of an expensive media advertising campaign. Its sock puppet mascot appeared at important occasions – it was even interviewed by *People* magazine. Pets.com closed in November 2000, and $300 million of investment capital was lost with the failure of the company [Wik14j].

As stated in the *New York Times* in November 2000 [Abel00]: 'Not even its popular Sock Puppet, the toy dog that starred in its television commercials, could save Pets.com.'

much on the type of product being traded. On the one hand, customer experience is typically low in a web shop compared to a physical shop, because products cannot be physically examined. The inability of a consumer to physically examine a product can be compensated for in some respects by providing actual user reports for the products offered. On the other hand, web shops allow more elaborate product presentations, both in number of products and in the way these are presented to the customer. For example, electronic catalogs can show many product variants (e.g., many different colors) and can provide usage pictures or discussion videos of offered products (see, for example, Figure 5.2).

In terms of business directions, two are mainly important for e-retailing. The first direction is *on time and online*: one of the added values of e-retailing with respect to traditional retailing is the fact that transactions can be performed at any time of day with direct feedback to the customer. The second dimension is *integrated bricks and clicks*: many e-retailers integrate digital presence with physical presence, which requires explicit attention for synchronization between these forms of presence. For example, customers may order products in a web shop that they collect in a physical shop.

In terms of business chains operations, e-retailing is typically a clear case of disintermediation: compared to traditional retail supply chains, one or more links in the chain have been removed. In terms of business structures, we sometimes find highly dynamic supply chains or demand chains – but often, business structures are traditional.

The revenue stream of an e-business scenario with the e-retailer business model is typically based on a margin on the sales price of objects. As such, this is not much different from traditional retailing. The cost model, however, for an e-retailer is very different from the cost model of a traditional retailer (as mentioned earlier), which makes the cost/benefit trade-off very different, too.

In Table 5.5 we summarize the e-retailer business model in terms of the classification dimensions and in terms of the ingredients introduced in the previous sections of this chapter (corresponding sections are indicated in the table for easy reference), augmented with the typical revenue stream indication (in the format shown in Table 5.4). Note that we show the most common choices for all ingredients – obviously, other choices are possible, too. In the third column we provide additional remarks with respect to the chosen ingredients.

There are many, many practical examples of e-retailing. One of the earliest and best-known examples is Amazon, which started business in 1995 as an online bookstore – it is one of the pioneers of this business model. From a simple e-retailing business, Amazon has now grown to a complex organization that in 2014 had more than 100,000 employees. Not all e-retailing initiatives have been successful, however (see 'The Pets.com story' sidebar).

5.6.2 The e-producer

Where the e-retailer sells objects produced by third parties, the e-producer actually produces e-business objects and sells them. In the context of networked e-business,

TABLE 5.5 Summary of the e-retailer business model

Business model: e-retailer			
Parties	*(3.4)*	B2C	B2B is possible too
Objects	*(3.5)*	Physical goods Digital goods	Services can be offered too, but are less common
Time scope	*(3.6)*	Dynamic	
Drivers	*(5.2)*	Increasing reach Increasing efficiency	Geographic and temporal reach, possibly increasing richness
Directions	*(5.3)*	On time and online Integrated bricks and clicks	If physical goods
Networks	*(5.4)*	Disintermediation	
Structures	*(5.5)*	Highly dynamic supply chains Demand chains	In specific domains In specific domains
Revenue stream		Margin on sales price of objects	

this business model is most interesting when we consider the production of digital objects only. The case of the production of physical objects can be considered a combination of a traditional producer and an e-retailer.

An e-producer can operate in a B2B or in a B2C scenario (although G2B, G2C and C2C scenarios can also be created – we address this in the questions at the end of this chapter). An e-producer can produce digital goods, digital services or hybrid objects as a combination of the two. An example of digital goods e-production is the production of digital reports, such as weather reports or reports forecasting traffic situations in harbors. Examples of the production of digital services are alerting services (e.g., in a stock brokering context) or driving instructions for automotive use. Note that there is a gray area between goods and services here – a report with driving instructions and online driving instructions come quite close, certainly when one considers hybrid solutions. An interesting question is whether platform provisioning (as in the case of cloud computing – see section 2.2.3) can be considered digital service e-production. For the e-producer business model we can find time scopes from static to dynamic.

For business drivers, business directions and business structures we can find various values for the e-producer business model, as shown in Table 5.6. This very much depends on the precise nature of the production. For business network operations the e-producer model is often related to reintermediation: the production of new digital services or new digital goods is inserted into an existing business network.

In terms of revenue streams the e-producer model typically works in one of two modes. The first mode is a price-per-object revenue stream: the customer pays per copy of received objects. The second mode is a subscription revenue stream: the customer subscribes to a stream of objects and pays per time unit (e.g., per month). Note that the customer can be either the actual user of the object (e.g., the recipient of a report) or a third party that pays for the e-production but does not actually

TABLE 5.6 Summary of the e-producer business model

Business model: e-producer

Parties	*(3.4)*	B2B B2C	
Objects	*(3.5)*	Digital goods Digital services	
Time scope	*(3.6)*	Dynamic Semi-dynamic Static	
Drivers	*(5.2)*	Increasing reach Increasing richness Increasing efficiency	
Directions	*(5.3)*	On-time and online business Enriched CRM Completely automated business Time-compressed business	
Networks	*(5.4)*	Reintermediation	
Structures	*(5.5)*	Dynamic outsourcing Demand chain	
Revenue stream		Price per object Subscription per customer	Revenue stream may come from object user or object financier

use the object. The latter case arises, for example, when advertising is included in the e-produced objects (as happens, for example, in free variants of streaming music services).

5.6.3 The e-integrator

An e-integrator organization is an organization that only integrates products of other companies in an e-business network; that is, does not produce product ingredients itself. As such, it either buys product elements from other organizations or forms a virtual organization with other companies that provide product elements to it. As such, an e-integrator has no production facilities (unless you view integrating the same as producing, of course). In terms of e-business network structures, this typically is a clear case of *reintermediation*.

E-integrator organizations typically provide digital goods or digital services (see section 3.5) – integrating physical objects or services implies physical production facilities. The added value of an e-integrator is providing the right combination of digital objects or services to the right customers at the right time. Hence, customer relationship management is often important for this business model – the *enriched CRM* business direction is very relevant here. Using enriched CRM, an e-integrator can perform mass customization towards its customers; that is, integrate object components specific to individual customers. To do so, an e-integrator

TABLE 5.7 Summary of the e-integrator business model

Business model: e-integrator			
Parties	(3.4)	B2C B2B	
Objects	(3.5)	Digital goods Digital services	
Time scope	(3.6)	Static Semi-dynamic Dynamic	Depends on the integrated object and the market
Drivers	(5.2)	Increasing richness	
Directions	(5.3)	Enriched CRM	
Networks	(5.4)	Reintermediation	
Structures	(5.5)	Dynamic supply chain Demand chain	In dynamic markets
Revenue stream		Margin on top of sum of component object prices	Subscription-based models possible in service markets

may build customer profiles such that preferences of customers can be used with-out explicitly asking them for every transaction. This can lead to a higher level of customer intimacy and thereby to higher levels of customer retention. This means that *increasing richness* is a main business driver for the e-integrator business model.

A typical revenue stream model for e-integrators is based on a margin on top of the price of the components they integrate. This is a transaction-based revenue stream model. Subscription-based models are also possible in specific service markets.

The e-integrator business model can, for instance, be applied in the financial domain. Here, an integrator can combine the financial products of other financial service providers to obtain integrated financial products that are tailored to specific customers (either of the business or the consumer type). Ingredients can be banking accounts, savings accounts, mortgages, stock portfolios, insurances and so on, which are combined into highly customized financial packages.

A summary of the e-integrator business model is shown in Table 5.7. When we get to the running case studies at the end of this chapter we will see that TraXP is partly an e-integrator.

5.6.4 The e-marketplace

The three reference business models described so far are all in the category *object provisioning* (see Table 5.3); that is, they are meant to directly provision e-business objects to a customer. The *e-marketplace* business model is not meant to directly provision objects to a customer; rather, it brings object providers and object consumers together. As such, it performs the function of intermediation between these two groups.

In the parties classification dimension the e-marketplace business model exists in B2B, B2C and C2C forms. A very well-known example of the B2C and C2C forms is

TABLE 5.8 Summary of the e-marketplace business model

Business model: e-marketplace			
Parties	*(3.4)*	B2B B2C C2C	
Objects	*(3.5)*	Any	
Time scope	*(3.6)*	Static, semi-dynamic Dynamic	Often in B2B Often in B2C
Drivers	*(5.2)*	Increasing reach	
Directions	*(5.3)*	Enriched CRM	For static and semi-dynamic time scopes
Networks	*(5.4)*	Reintermediation	
Structures	*(5.5)*	Dynamic partnering Dynamic outsourcing Dynamic insourcing	
Revenue stream		Percentage of object price from seller Advertising fees Periodic fees from sellers or buyers	

eBay (shown in Figure 3.5). In principle, any type of e-business object can be traded via an e-marketplace. In the time scope dimension we find values from static (for specialized B2B marketplace scenarios) to dynamic (for many B2C marketplace scenarios).

The main business driver for the e-marketplace business model is increasing reach: parties who want to sell e-business objects use the e-marketplaces to increase their reach towards potential buyers. In terms of business directions, enriched CRM is common: e-marketplaces can store customer profiles to help them search through market offerings and perform buying transactions. The e-marketplace business model is a clear case of reintermediation. We can find various dynamic business structures with this business model.

Several revenue stream models are possible for e-marketplaces. Perhaps the most common ones are charging a percentage of the price of sold objects from the selling party and earning a revenue by placing advertisements on the website of the marketplace. But an e-marketplace may also charge a periodic fee to either its sellers or its buyers.

Currently, social media providers (as discussed in chapter 1) are moving towards taking roles as (more or less implicit) e-marketplaces in the B2C segment, offering access to e-business objects provided by third parties. An example is the support for direct-buy facilities (e.g., a 'buy button') that are integrated with advertisements channeled through social media.

A special subclass of e-marketplaces is formed by dating and relationship-matching sites, such as Match.com (and its regionalized brands). Obviously, there are no 'products' sold here, unless contact details are considered products. The typical revenue stream for dating and matching sites is based on periodic fees.

5.6.5 The e-indexer

In the e-marketplace business model, providers of e-business objects make themselves actively known to potential buyers of these object with the e-marketplace as a passive intermediating party. The *e-indexer* business model also relies on intermediation, but here it is the intermediating party that actively identifies potential sellers of e-business objects and structures them in predefined indexes. These indexes are next used by potential buyers to initiate e-business transactions with the sellers. Obviously, completeness of its indexes is of paramount importance for the success of an e-indexer. A second difference is the fact that with the e-marketplace model, actual buy transactions can typically be initiated from the market, whereas the e-indexer often refers buyers to (websites of) sellers to initiate actual transactions. As such, the *e-indexer* business model operates like a digital yellow pages. In short, we can say that the e-indexer primarily operates on behalf of buyers of e-business objects, where the e-marketplace primarily operates on behalf of sellers.

In terms of classification dimensions, the e-indexer business model is similar to the e-marketplace model. In terms of business drivers, directions, networks and structures, the e-indexer model is also much like the e-marketplace model.

In terms of revenue streams, the e-indexer model often relies on advertisements. As transactions are often not initiated by the e-indexer itself, it is not easy to generate a revenue stream based on executed sales transactions.

In principle, search engine providers (such as Google) can be seen as general-purpose e-indexers.

TABLE 5.9 Summary of the e-indexer business model

Business model: e-indexer			
Parties	*(3.4)*	B2B B2C	
Objects	*(3.5)*	Any	
Time scope	*(3.6)*	Static, semi-dynamic Dynamic	Often in B2B Often in B2C
Drivers	*(5.2)*	Increasing reach	
Directions	*(5.3)*	Enriched CRM	For static and semi-dynamic time scopes
Networks	*(5.4)*	Reintermediation	
Structures	*(5.5)*	Dynamic partnering Dynamic outsourcing Dynamic insourcing	
Revenue stream		Advertisements	

TABLE 5.10 Summary of the e-comparator business model

Business model: e-comparator			
Parties	(3.4)	B2B	
		B2C	
Objects	(3.5)	Any	
Time scope	(3.6)	Static, semi-dynamic	Often in B2B
		Dynamic	Often in B2C
Drivers	(5.2)	Increasing reach	
		Increasing richness	
Directions	(5.3)	On time and online	For static and semi-dynamic
		Enriched CRM	time scopes
Networks	(5.4)	Reintermediation	
Structures	(5.5)	Dynamic partnering	
		Dynamic outsourcing	
		Dynamic insourcing	
Revenue stream		Advertisements	

5.6.6 The e-comparator

With the e-indexer business model, sellers of e-business objects are only indexed. This business model can be augmented by adding an active comparison of offers by sellers in markets, leading to the *e-comparator* business model. Comparisons may be made on the basis of object price, object availability or object evaluations (e.g., by prior buyers). A well-known e-comparator is Yelp (www.yelp.com).

As shown in Table 5.10 the e-comparator model is much like the e-indexer model. However, it adds two important elements. In terms of business drivers, it adds increasing richness: the comparison of offers provides additional, enriched information to buyers. In terms of business directions, the on-time and online element is added: it is extremely important for an e-comparator to be actual (i.e., completely up to date) with its comparisons.

5.6.7 The e-facilitator

With the *e-facilitator* business model we move to a new main class of reference business models (see the taxonomy in Table 5.3): those that are aimed at parties supporting the actual cooperation between other parties (sometimes after parties with intermediation models, as discussed before, have been in play).

A networked e-business organization using the *e-facilitator* model provides an e-business platform that is used by a set of other parties to collaborate using their own e-business models. An e-facilitator platform can offer functionality such as secure business message exchange, business process execution, business service execution or electronic contract establishment. Such a platform is often offered in the form of a cloud computing solution (as discussed in section 2.2.3).

TABLE 5.11 Summary of the e-facilitator business model

Business model: e-facilitator			
Parties	*(3.4)*	B2B	B2G/G2B possible, too
Objects	*(3.5)*	Digital services	
Time scope	*(3.6)*	Static Semi-dynamic	
Drivers	*(5.2)*	All	Depends on type of platform
Directions	*(5.3)*	On time and online Completely automated business	
Networks	*(5.4)*	Reintermediation	
Structures	*(5.5)*	Dynamic outsourcing	With limited dynamism
Revenue stream		Transaction fees Subscription fees	

The e-facilitator model can be positioned in the classification dimensions as follows. The model is typically used in B2B settings (although B2G and G2B settings are possible). The e-business objects exchanged are digital services. The time scope is static or semi-dynamic: a user of an e-business platform typically does not switch to another platform very frequently, as this may imply a different way of working.

The business drivers behind an e-facilitator scenario can be very diverse. The driver can be increased cost efficiency (a platform with many users can use the principle of economies of scale), increased reach (in any of the three sub-dimensions as discussed in section 5.2.1) towards the users of the platform or increased richness towards the users in terms of a platform with a broad spectrum of functionality.

Being on time and online is obviously of paramount importance in facilitating e-business platforms. Platform facilitation should be as efficient as possible; hence, the direction of completely automated business applies here, too. In terms of business network operations, the e-facilitator model is a case of reintermediation. In terms of business structures, we find the dynamic outsourcing structure, with the remark that dynamism is typically limited here (related to the time scope issues discussed before).

The e-facilitator business model typically relies on transaction fees or subscription fees to realize its revenue stream.

E-facilitators can be found as the connecting business platform in specific trading communities. An example is a *port community system (PCS) operator* that supports the execution of B2B and B2G logistics transactions around a sea port. In the ports of Rotterdam and Amsterdam, Portbase fulfills this role.[5]

5.6.8 The e-collaborator

The *e-collaborator* reference business model is a model in which a party closely engages with one or more other parties to form a virtual collaboration business entity that aims at a common goal. Using networked e-business concepts and tech-nologies, such a virtual collaboration entity can be formed much more dynamically than in traditional business settings. To put things more concretely, dynamic part-nering, dynamic outsourcing and dynamic insourcing as discussed in section 5.5 can lead to the establishment of *dynamic virtual enterprises*. Virtual enterprises are business collaborations that have a formal character (typically based on a contractual agreement) and that present themselves to third parties as a single business entity. Dynamic virtual enterprises are virtual enterprises that have a dynamic character; that is, they are established on the fly when opportunities arise and are dismantled again when the opportunity disappears.

Whereas the life cycle of a traditional virtual enterprise usually spans multiple years, the life cycle of a dynamic virtual enterprise may in principle be as short as several days or even less. Also the business scope of a dynamic virtual enterprise may be small; that is, it may be set up to accomplish a very specific, relatively small business goal. In the CrossFlow project [Gref00], for example, extreme collabora-tive prototype scenarios have been developed where a dynamic virtual enterprise is established for the fulfillment of an individual customer order. In the telecom and logistics domain, a scenario has been developed in which a telecom opera-tor and a logistics provider can form a dynamic virtual enterprise for the sale and delivery of one single mobile phone. In the car insurance domain, a scenario has been developed for the handling of a single insurance claim, where the dynamic virtual enterprise is formed between an insurance company and a damage assess-ment bureau.

Clearly, such short life cycles and small scopes require extremely efficient sup-port for the setup and management of the collaboration to deal with time and cost conditions – hence the full entrance of e-business. In some domains, so-called *breed-ing environments* are created, which provide the infrastructure for setting up virtual environments. These environments offer, for instance, electronic marketplaces in which potential partners can find each other and platforms for the operation of vir-tual enterprises. Electronic contracting and automated business process support are typical ingredients for the support of dynamic virtual enterprises [Hof01a, Gref00]. These mechanisms deal with the formal character and the required efficiency of collaboration, respectively.

The revenue stream for the e-collaborator model depends strongly on the type and aim of collaboration supported, so we cannot be specific here.

We summarize the e-collaborator reference business model in Table 5.12.

The term *instant virtual enterprise* is also used to indicate a virtual enterprise that is created dynamically. For example, in the CrossWork project [Gref09, Meha10] an approach has been developed to create instant virtual enterprises semi-automatically based on explicitly specified business goals. The approach was prototyped in the automotive industry to massively reduce time and effort in setting up and man-aging virtual enterprises for car production. The time scope for this scenario is semi-dynamic, dictated by the 'physical' nature of the automotive industry (a strong *bricks and clicks* combination).

TABLE 5.12 Summary of the e-collaborator business model

Business model: e-collaborator

Parties	*(3.4)*	B2B	
Objects	*(3.5)*	All	Typically of a complex nature
Time Scope	*(3.6)*	Semi-dynamic Dynamic	
Drivers	*(5.2)*	Increasing richness	In collaboration
Directions	*(5.3)*	Time-compressed business	In set-up and execution of the dynamic virtual enterprise
Networks	*(5.4)*	Reintermediation	If a controller party is used for the dynamic virtual enterprise
Structures	*(5.5)*	Dynamic partnering Dynamic outsourcing Dynamic insourcing	
Revenue stream		Various	Depends on details of the e-business scenario

5.6.9 The e-sourcer

The last reference business model we discuss is the *e-sourcer*. This business model relies on the crowdsourcing business structure that we have seen in section 5.5.4. The e-sourcer business model has a number of variations depending on the kind of task sourced to the 'crowd'. Following, we discuss three important variations.

Crowdcasting

Crowdcasting[6] is a business model in which the crowd is used to generate ideas that answer specific questions; for example, ideas for new products or product variations. An example of a company employing crowdcasting is InnoCentive (www.innocentive.com), which uses a crowd of researchers to try and solve companies' problems. Crowdstorming is a variation on crowdcasting in which the crowd forms a brainstorming power to generate completely new ideas without very clear questions as a foundation.

Crowdproduction

Crowdproduction is a business model in which the crowd is used to actually produce a product or a collection of products. Often, these products are of a digital nature (see section 3.5). A well-known example where a crowd produces one product is Wikipedia (www.wikipedia.org), where large numbers of people collaboratively build a digital encyclopedia (we actually use Wikipedia as a reference source in this book). An example where a set of products is produced is iStockPhoto (www.istockphoto.com), where individual photographers offer their photos to media users.

Crowdfunding

Crowdfunding is aimed at having a crowd fund a venture for which 'regular' funding channels are not available. Typically, a crowdfunding platform allows ventures to advertise themselves to try and attract many small investors. A well-known crowdfunding application for creative projects is Kickstarter (www.kickstarter.com).

Another good example of crowdfunding is Sellaband (www.sellaband.com), which operates as an alternative business model in the music industry (see Figure 5.13). In the Sellaband model, bands (and individual artists) in the music scene advertise their work on the Sellaband website and try to sell 'parts' to people who believe the band has potential. When a band has sold a specific number of parts,[7] it has funding to record and publish a music album in a professional way. Buying a part gives specific rights to the part owner (called a 'believer' in the Sellaband model), such as a copy of an album by the artist and a share in any profits.

A number of issues have to be taken into account to use crowdsourcing effectively. One important issue is handling the crowd efficiently. In crowdcasting, for example, an efficient filtering mechanism must be employed to separate the few usable ideas from the many unusable ones. Another important issue is the reimbursement of the crowd; that is, the way the individuals in the crowd get something in return for

FIGURE 5.13 Sellaband as an example of the crowdfunding business model.

TABLE 5.13 Summary of the e-sourcer business model

Business model: e-sourcer

Parties	*(3.4)*	B2C	Reversed object flow
Objects	*(3.5)*	Digital goods	Can include money
Time scope	*(3.6)*	Dynamic Ultra-dynamic	
Drivers	*(5.2)*	Increasing reach Increasing efficiency	Reach on 'input side'
Directions	*(5.3)*	On time and on-line	
Networks	*(5.4)*	Reconstruction	
Structures	*(5.5)*	Dynamic service outsourcing	Extreme B2C scenario
Revenue stream		Price per output object	

their contribution and thus stay motivated to continue contributing (this is related to the exchange of e-business objects as discussed in section 3.5). In a crowdfunding scenario, this may be easier, but in a crowdcasting scenario, it is not always obvious.

In Table 5.13 we show the summary of the e-sourcer business model. Depending on the type of crowdsourcing – as discussed earlier – the table can be further specialized. We leave this as an exercise to the reader. We have included the ultra-dynamic value in the time scope classification dimension because a crowd can be changed during the execution of a crowdsourcing task, which means that the parties in the e-business scenario change during the execution of a single customer order. In terms of network operations, we have listed reconstruction as an element. The reason for this is the fact that crowdsourcing scenarios often (re)construct completely new e-business scenarios.

5.7 Relating B aspect elements

So far in this chapter we have analyzed the B aspect element classes of networked e-business, following a path from basic ingredients to business models. These element classes can be used for B aspect design or analysis by relating them in a structured way. This can be done in several ways.

The most obvious way is the one illustrated in Figure 5.14. One starts characterizing an e-business scenario using the reach and richness business drivers (and, if applicable, the extreme efficiency characteristic). Based on the business drivers, one can find new business directions. Also based on the business drivers, the disintermediation and reintermediation principles (deconstruction and reconstruction in the extreme cases) and the substitution principle can be used to see how business networks are affected. The combination of business directions and choices with respect to business networks leads to the identification (or definition) of business structures. All these elements combined lead to the definition of concrete networked e-business models.

The four business element classes can be analyzed in different orders, too. For example, one may use a linear order from drivers to directions, to networks and on to structures, as illustrated in Figure 5.15. One may even work back starting from structures and analyze how a specific structure in a specific situation affects the choice of the other three element classes. The element classes and their ordering are intended to be a thinking structure, not a rigid recipe.

As shown in Figures 5.14 and 5.15 combinations of the elements in the four classes lead to the definition of new business models (or the application of existing reference models in a new context). We have seen a number of reference business models in this chapter, organized into a simple taxonomy. As we have stated before, this taxonomy is by no means exhaustive: new business models are designed continuously – networked e-business is a dynamic domain.

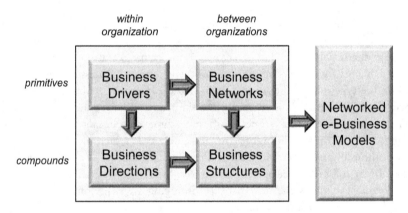

FIGURE 5.14   Common relationships between B aspect elements.

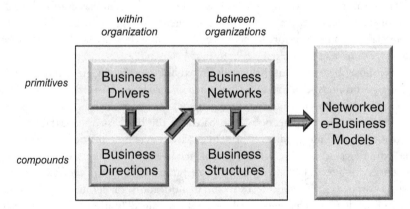

FIGURE 5.15   Alternative relationships between B aspect elements.

5.8 The service-dominant view

Our discussion so far of elements in the business aspect of the BOAT model has concentrated around 'business by exchange of e-business objects', where e-business objects can have many different forms, as outlined in section 3.5. Discussed reference business models are built around an exchange of objects (like the *e-retailer*), facilitate the exchange of objects (like the *e-marketplace*) or foster collaboration for the creation of objects (like the *e-collaborator*). A relatively new way of business thinking that takes a different approach in some respects is *service-dominant logic*.

5.8.1 Service-dominant logic

Service-dominant (SD) logic is an approach that has emerged from the marketing domain. It puts the customer experience at the center of business thinking. Briefly stated, the SD point of departure is the observation that services are the fundamental basis for business exchange [Varg08]. Services define a *value-in-use* for a customer; that is, an added value for the customer by generating a user experience. Goods (either physical or digital) are considered merely distribution mechanisms for service provisioning. Service-dominant logic is currently applied in a wide range of business domains, ranging even into high-tech manufacturing [Ng12].

As an example from the B2C music industry, SD logic states that the essence of the industry is not the sale of music objects (either physical CDs or digital tracks) but the music-listening experience, which is enabled by music services. In other words, a music lover is not interested in *owning* music but in *enjoying* it in the right way. In the B2B mobility industry, SD logic states that the essence is not the provisioning of cars (either through sales or leasing) but in mobility services that provide the experience of seamless transportation [Lüft14].

Another important starting point of SD logic is the view that a customer is always a co-creator of value. A business organization cannot deliver value; it can only offer value propositions to a customer [Varg08]. In other words, a customer creates part of the experience that results from the value-in-use. For our music industry example, it means that a customer creates part of the music-listening experience, for example, by creating playlists of music (for him- or herself and possibly for a music-listening community). A concrete value-in-use is only fully determined at the moment of the delivery to the specific customer. This can give rise to forms of mass customization, as a service may have to be tuned towards the characteristics of specific customers and the specific time of delivery.

5.8.2 Implications for networked e-business

Service-dominant logic is a way of thinking that has generated ample attention. It does not invalidate business aspect elements as we have discussed them in this chapter. It does, however, emphasize certain elements and deemphasize others.

The fact that SD business takes services as the basis of business exchange means that e-business scenarios that are formulated in terms of goods exchanges must be re-formulated to fit into SD logic. In other words, SD logic focuses on the service value of the object's classification dimension from section 3.5 and sees the physical and digital goods values merely as enabling values for the services value.

The fact that SD logic takes co-creation with a customer as a fundamental premise implies that customers have to be treated partly as producers. In some scenarios it may even mean that the boundary between customer and collaborator blurs to some extent. The use of mass customization can put strong requirements on the flexibility of service providers, and in the context of networked e-business on the flexibility of the used business structures (such as the dynamic outsourcing structure that we have seen in section 5.5).

We see an operationalization of SD logic ideas in the discussion of the TraXP case study in the next section, because TraXP has adopted the SD view to a large extent.

5.9 Running cases

In this section we turn again to our three running cases – POSH, TTU and TraXP – and discuss their business aspect elements.

5.9.1 POSH

We have introduced the POSH case in chapter 2. As we have seen in that chapter, POSH has embraced two new business goals:

1 Sell to all customers in the country directly, without the intervention of third-party retailers.
2 Offer a broader spectrum of advisory services to customers.

These business goals can be related to business drivers, as we have discussed in section 5.2. Business goal 1 is a case of increasing geographical reach. When thinking about increasing reach, POSH realizes that they should also increase temporal reach, as owners of smaller companies may want to do business with POSH outside regular business hours. Business goal 2 is a case of increasing richness: POSH wants to have more interaction with its customers to bind them more strongly to the company.

In terms of new business directions, enriched CRM is most applicable to the POSH scenario: POSH wants to increase its customer intimacy. Apart from this, being on time and online is a business direction for POSH, too (as a consequence of increased temporal reach). Removing the intervention of third-party retailers from the supply chain (as stated in their business goal 1) is a typical case of disintermediation. Of the business structures discussed in this chapter, none applies directly to the POSH scenario. This may indicate that POSH still uses traditional business thinking in its approach to networked e-business. In terms of business models, POSH uses a combined B2C and B2B e-retailer model (as discussed in section 5.6.1).

The earlier discussion can be summarized in a table similar to what we have used to describe the reference business models in section 5.6 but augmented with a *business model* row. The result for POSH is shown in Table 5.14.

5.9.2 TTU

In chapter 2 we have introduced TTU as a new entrant to the market of translation and interpretation services. TTU has a vision that is strongly based on networked e-business principles.

The main business driver for TTU is increasing reach: through e-business channels it can reach more potential customers than a traditional translation service can (offering either document translation or 'physical' interpretation services). TTU aims to increase reach in the geographical, the temporal and the modal sense. The modal sense pertains most clearly to providing online, real-time interpretation services in videoconferencing sessions. Increasing richness is not a major point for TTU, although they will use any opportunities 'on the side' here. We can thus modify the e-business transformation shown in Figure 5.3 for TTU into the transformation shown in Figure 5.16.

There are two main e-business directions for TTU. The first is *on-time and online business*: the strength of the TTU approach is the fact that they can be contacted through the internet at the time when their services are needed. The second direction is *time-compressed business*: by having all communication and (most of) document transfer proceed through electronic channels, throughput times for business processes requiring translation or interpretation can be substantially shortened.

In terms of business network restructuring, the TTU case belongs in the reintermediation category: they provide services that did not exist in the TTU form in the 'traditional economy'. In terms of e-business structures, the TTU case is a form of

TABLE 5.14 Summary of the business model ingredients of the POSH case study

Case study: POSH			
Parties	*(3.4)*	B2B B2C	
Objects	*(3.5)*	Physical objects	
Time scope	*(3.6)*	Semi-dynamic Dynamic	
Drivers	*(5.2)*	Increasing reach	Mainly geographical, temporal secondary
Directions	*(5.3)*	Enriched CRM On time and online	
Networks	*(5.4)*	Disintermediation	
Structures	*(5.5)*	None as described	
Model	*(5.6)*	E-retailer	
Revenue stream		Margin on sales price of objects	

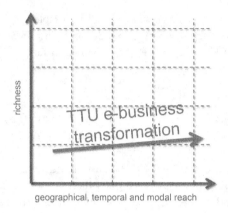

FIGURE 5.16 Increasing reach for TTU.

dynamic service outsourcing: a party needing a translation service in its business process outsources this part of the process to TTU instead of getting a translator 'on board'.

The TTU business model is a case of an e-facilitator: the services offered by TTU enable other business scenarios; that is, international business scenarios that require dealing with language barriers. The revenue stream for TTU is based on a fee-per-service basis.

Like we did for the POSH case study, the previous discussion about business aspect elements of TTU is summarized in Table 5.15.

5.9.3 TraXP

As we have seen in chapter 2, TraXP is a new entrant to a heavily populated business domain: travel services. By providing a new kind of integrated business concept, they intend to emerge as a major new player in this market. This concept is strongly rooted in service-dominant logic, which we have discussed in section 5.8.

In terms of business drivers, the business concept of TraXP is heavily based on increasing richness in their business offering. Increasing reach or efficiency is not a basis for a new competitive business operation, because these drivers are already adequately addressed by existing parties in the travel services domain. Consequently, this is a case where networked e-business explicitly has to move beyond traditional e-business (which would concentrate on increasing reach and efficiency in this domain). In terms of business directions, TraXP puts *enriched CRM* at the center of their attention – this is the basis for achieving increased richness. This direction is operationalized by extensive customer profiling on the one hand and use of these profiles in travel selection and execution on the other hand. The *on-time and online* business direction is an important direction, too, but with an important observation. For the process of booking travel by customers, this will not be a great discriminating factor in the competitive online travel services domain. In the process of travel

TABLE 5.15 Summary of the business model ingredients of the TTU case study

Case study: TTU			
Parties	*(3.4)*	B2B	B2C possible too, but not main aim
Objects	*(3.5)*	Digital services	
Time scope	*(3.6)*	Dynamic	
Drivers	*(5.2)*	Increasing reach	Geographical + temporal + modal
Directions	*(5.3)*	On time and online Time-compressed business	
Networks	*(5.4)*	Reintermediation	
Structures	*(5.5)*	Dynamic service outsourcing	
Model	*(5.6)*	E-facilitator	
Revenue stream		Fee per service	

execution (i.e., during the time customers are traveling), TraXP wants to make a difference in being *on time and online*.

The TraXP model is a clear case of reintermediation: TraXP takes a new position between basic travel service providers and travelers. The main business structure it uses is *dynamic service insourcing*: it obtains essential elements in its service offering from dynamically selected providers.

In terms of business models, TraXP uses a hybrid form of the *e-producer* and the *e-integrator* reference models. It integrates existing e-business objects, but also adds objects that it produces itself. Note that from the service-dominant point of view, TraXP does not sell e-business objects; rather, it sells a value-in-use materialized in a traveler's seamless travel experience.

TraXP uses various revenue stream models based on specializations of their offering of a seamless travel experience [Gre13a]. Each specialization targets a specific customer segment, has its own combination of basic travel services and its own revenue stream model. At one end of the spectrum, TraXP has a B2C free model that targets student travelers with small budgets. In this model the revenue stream is mainly based on kick-back fees from providers of elementary travel services (such as airlines or hotel chains). At the other end of the spectrum, it has a B2B executive model that targets high-profile business executives. The revenue stream in this model is based on a monthly subscription fee. In between, it has a B2C revenue stream model for luxury leisure travelers and a B2B model for standard corporate travelers.

As mentioned earlier, the travel services offered to customers vary per revenue model. A new service that TraXP is currently integrating into its B2B models is a language service. This service is becoming important, because more and more of their business customers travel to new economies such as China and Brazil, where the difference in languages can be an issue. TraXP chooses TTU as their language

TABLE 5.16 Summary of the business model ingredients of the TraXP case study

Case study: TraXP			
Parties	(3.4)	B2C B2B	
Objects	(3.5)	Digital services	
Time scope	(3.6)	Dynamic	
Drivers	(5.2)	Increasing richness	
Directions	(5.3)	Enriched CRM On time and online	On time and online, mainly for *in-travel* services
Networks	(5.4)	Reintermediation	
Structures	(5.5)	Dynamic insourcing	
Model	(5.6)	E-producer E-integrator	
Revenue stream		Kick-back fees Service fees Subscriptions	Combinations depend on specialized offering per customer segment

FIGURE 5.17 Extended (part of) TraXP e-business network.

services provider (LSP) because of TTU's flexible service offering. This means that we can extend the TraXP business network with TTU, as shown in Figure 5.17 (as an extension of Figure 2.5). This extension shows the flexibility of truly networked e-business: complex services are provided by dynamically changing business networks to cater for changing customer needs.

5.10 Chapter end

This section concludes the discussion of the business aspect of the BOAT frame-work. We first provide a summary of the most important elements of this aspect as they were discussed in this chapter. Then, we provide a few questions and exercises to apply the contents of this chapter.

5.10.1 Chapter summary

In this chapter we have seen the basic business aspect ingredients of networked e-business in four element classes and one resulting class:

E-business drivers are the basic reasons to engage in networked e-business. Important drivers are increasing *reach* and increasing *richness*. A third driver is increasing *efficiency* – we consider this an e-business driver only when efficiency is dramatically increased.

E-business directions are the directions in which a business scenario can be developed to facilitate the operationalization of e-business drivers. Example directions are *multi-channel business, integrated bricks and clicks, completely automated business* and *time-compressed business*.

E-business network operations are the basic ways to manipulate an e-business network based on the new opportunities e-business offers. *Disintermediation* and *reintermediation* are the basic operations to remove a link from a chain and insert a new link, respectively. *Deconstruction* and *reconstruction* are the extreme forms in which complete business chains are redesigned. *Substitution* is important to obtain non-functional flexibility in an e-business network.

E-business structures are the 'abstract structures' to form business models – they can be seen as patterns for e-business model development. Example structures are *demand chains, dynamic service outsourcing* and *crowdsourcing*.

E-Business models are the 'complete template structures' for e-business in the business aspect. Example reference business models are *e-retailer, e-integrator* and *e-sourcer*. Reference models can be operationalized into concrete business models.

These ingredients can be related in various ways in analyzing or designing e-business scenarios. An overview of all BOAT business aspect ingredients is presented in Table 5.17.

5.10.2 Questions and exercises

1   Take an existing B2C e-business scenario – preferably a real-world case that is not a standard e-retailing scenario. Analyze its B aspect using the elements of this chapter and describe it in a summary table (as shown for POSH and TraXP

TABLE 5.17 Overview of business aspect ingredients

Business drivers	Business network operations
Reach	Disintermediation
Richness	Reintermediation
Extreme efficiency (cost / time)	Deconstruction and reconstruction
	Substitution

Business directions	Business structures
On time and online	Dynamic partnering
Multi-channel business	Dynamic outsourcing
Enriched CRM	Dynamic insourcing
Integrated bricks and clicks	Crowdsourcing
Completely automated business	Highly dynamic supply chain
Time-compressed business	Demand chain

Reference business models

Object provisioning	Intermediation	Cooperation
e-retailer	e-marketplace	e-facilitator
e-producer	e-indexer	e-collaborator
e-integrator	e-comparator	e-sourcer

in Table 5.14 and Table 5.16). Explicitly choose an approach as discussed in section 5.7.

2   Take an existing B2B e-business scenario. Analyze its B aspect and describe it in a summary table (as shown for TTU in Table 5.15). Explicitly choose an approach to relate elements as discussed in section 5.7.

3   Which of the reference business models discussed in section 5.6 is also applicable to e-government; that is, to G2C or G2B scenarios (see section 3.4.5)? Provide a convincing example for each model chosen.

4   In section 5.5 we have seen the business structures *demand chain* and *highly dynamic supply chain*. Can these two business structures be combined to arrive at a *highly dynamic demand chain* structure? If you think so, give an application example of a highly dynamic demand chain. If you think they cannot be combined, explain why.

5   As noted before, the taxonomy of reference e-business models presented in this chapter is not exhaustive. Find an e-business model that is not discussed in this chapter, analyze it and describe it in a summary table (such as for example done for the e-sourcer business model in Table 5.13).

6   Specialize the summary table for the e-sourcer business model (see Table 5.13) for the crowdfunding business model. Pay special attention to the objects dimension, as discussed in section 3.5.

7   Design a concrete C2C business model based on the e-producer reference business model discussed in section 5.6.2. Clearly describe the model in terms of the classification of traded e-business objects (as discussed in section 3.5).

Notes

1 The concept of *value creation* is essential in the basic notion of a *business model*. For instance, Osterwalder and Pigneur [Oste10] use the following definition: 'A business model describes the rationale of how an organization creates, delivers, and captures value.'
2 Note that virtual environments have also been mentioned as communication *channels*. Modern virtual environments such as Second Life do have both well-elaborated communication (channel) and presentation (media) aspects that are strongly intertwined.
3 This is certainly true when new communication channels are introduced. For example, in the early days of electronic retail, consumers might place orders over the web, then start doubting whether it worked and subsequently place the same order using a traditional channel (like a physical form per postal service), leading to many double deliveries.
4 We use the term *bricks and clicks* to refer to the integration of the principles from the old and the new economy. We also see the term *bricks and mortar* to refer to the old economy and *clicks and mortar* to refer to the integration of new and old (see, e.g., [Jela08]).
5 See http://portbase.com/en/Portbase.aspx.
6 The term 'crowdcasting' is a mix of the terms 'crowdsourcing' and 'broadcasting'.
7 To illustrate: in the 2009 Sellaband business model, a band had to sell 5,000 parts of $10.00 each to obtain a required funding of $50,000 (as listed at www.sellaband.com). In principle, each part can be owned by a different believer. This illustrates that crowdsourcing may indeed involve large crowds.

6

ORGANIZATION ASPECT

Learning goals

- *Understand hierarchically arranged organization structures for networked e-business.*
- *Know a set of business functions for networked e-business and understand its organization based on a business framework and organization structures.*
- *Understand business processes in a networked e-business setting and be able to specify them.*
- *Understand the role of service orientation for the organization aspect of networked e-business.*
- *Understand the role of operations management and change management in a networked e-business setting.*
- *Understand the mapping of business aspect elements as discussed in chapter 5 to organization aspect elements.*

6.1 Introduction

In the previous chapter we have discussed the business aspect of the BOAT framework for networked e-business. In this chapter we continue our discussion with the organization (O) aspect. The aim is to provide a well-structured overview of relevant organizational issues for networked e-business. For more elaborate discussions of organization aspects in a more general context, the reader is referred to more detailed material (e.g., [Mint92, Jest08]).

We start with turning our attention to e-business organization structures. Using a top-down approach, we first discuss structures at the business network level between organizations (called inter-organizational structures) and after that structures within individual organizations (called intra-organizational structures). Then, we focus on the systematic treatment of business functions for networked e-business that appear in these organizational structures. Next, we discuss how business processes can be placed in the context of these organization structures and functions, both at the network and at the organization levels.

Having laid the groundwork of the O aspect, we turn our attention to the service-oriented view on the O aspect – this as a continuation of the discussion on service-dominant business in chapter 5. We continue with an explanation of how operations management is required to keep business processes running and how change management is required to keep organization structures and business processes aligned with new developments. These developments can be changes in the business aspect or in the technology aspect of networked e-business.

In section 6.8 we show how elements in the B aspect (as discussed in chapter 5) can be mapped to elements in the O aspect. This explains the relationship between the two aspects in the wheel model of BOAT (see Figure 4.4). Here, we show how business concepts such as reach, richness, disintermediation and reintermediation can be operationalized in terms of concepts of the organization aspect. We then further develop our running cases with organization aspect elements and conclude the chapter with a summary and a set of questions and exercises.

6.2 Inter-organization structures

A good understanding of organization structures is important for every type of business domain (see, e.g., [Mint92]). In networked e-business this is very strongly the case: we generally deal with complex scenarios in which a clear structure of the business organization is essential for a decent understanding of the scenarios. The dynamic nature of many e-business scenarios further increases the need for clear structure: one needs to understand what is subject to change and what is not.[1]

In this section we explore the structure of e-business collaborations at the network level in a stepwise, top-down manner: we start with a very high-level picture and then refine this in two steps. In section 6.3 we continue the refinement within organization boundaries; that is, at the individual organization level. The network level deals with e-business scenarios, the organization level with individual parties in e-business scenarios.

6.2.1 Parties in an e-business scenario

As we have seen in section 1.2, we focus in this book on inter-organizational e-business scenarios; that is, scenarios in which two or more autonomous business parties are involved that collaborate in an e-business market. So the most trivial structure of an e-business scenario is just the market as a black box, as shown in Figure 6.1. Obviously, this organization structure is not very informative – therefore, we label it *level 0*. It gets more interesting when we open it up – in other words, refine or explode it.[2]

FIGURE 6.1 E-business organization structure (level 0).

When we refine an e-business market, we typically identify three roles of parties collaborating in that market:

- *consumer*[3]: a party that requires an e-business object (a product or service, as discussed in section 3.5);
- *provider*: a party that offers an e-business object (a product or service); and
- *intermediary*: a party that has an auxiliary role in the transfer of e-business objects from provider to consumer.

When we put the three roles of parties and their relationships into a diagram that refines Figure 6.1 we get Figure 6.2. This figure shows an e-business organization structure at *level 1*. Each of the three parties can be of a different type, as discussed in section 3.4.

The organization structure shown in Figure 6.2 contains the collaboration between a single consumer and a single provider. In practice, however, an e-business organization structure at this level of aggregation can be more complex. This follows from the business models that we discussed in section 5.6. If we take, for example, an *e-integrator* business model, we have one provider that provides an integrated e-business object to a customer, but uses a number of providers itself to obtain the e-business object elements that are integrated. This results in a networked e-business organization structure as shown in Figure 6.3.

The structures in the right side of the figure are similar to those on the left side: we have collaboration of a provider and a consumer (in the right side of the figure, the provider is actually a consumer of its own providers). In other words, we find the same organization structure pattern repeatedly in the figure. This means that we can understand more complex networked e-business organization structures if we understand the basic pattern. For this reason, we concentrate on the basic pattern (as in Figure 6.2) in further analyzing organization structures for networked e-business.

Note that *consumer* and *provider* are roles – one organization can be a provider in one e-business relationship but at the same time a consumer in another relationship (as shown in Figure 6.3). Note also that the role of *intermediary* is to some extent relative to an e-business scenario. When analyzing an e-retailing scenario, for example, a credit card organization is an intermediary. In a payment

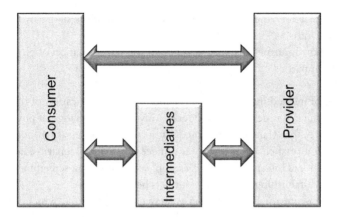

FIGURE 6.2   E-business organization structure (level 1).

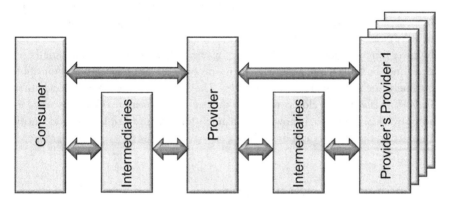

FIGURE 6.3   Network view of e-business organization structure (level 1).

handling scenario, however, the same organization can act as a provider. Typically, an intermediary is characterized by the fact that it does not produce or consume primary objects (as discussed in section 3.5) in an e-business scenario.

The structure in Figure 6.2 may be clear, but it contains too little structure to be of help in a detailed design or analysis of an e-business scenario. Therefore, we further refine this figure in the following section.

6.2.2 Refining intermediaries and channels

In Figure 6.2 there is no distinction among different types of intermediaries. Often, however, an e-business scenario requires more than one type of intermediary. Examples of intermediaries are:

•   a broker that helps parties find and identify each other in an e-business market (e.g., through a mechanism such as electronic yellow pages);

- a financial intermediary that arranges the execution of payments between parties; and
- a transport intermediary that arranges for the transportation of physical objects between parties.

The set of needed intermediaries depends on the classification of the e-business scenario. If the e-business scenario does not involve an exchange of physical objects (see section 3.5), a transport intermediary may be unnecessary. In a pure bartering scenario, a finance intermediary is unnecessary. More scenarios, however, may require additional intermediaries; for example, for reputation screening of parties or for formally establishing electronic contracts between parties.

The multi-intermediary situation is shown in Figure 6.4, which illustrates an e-business organization structure at *level 2*. For reasons of simplicity and clarity, only two intermediaries are shown, labeled *Inter1* and *Inter2*. In practice, this can be an arbitrary number.

The second extension shown in Figure 6.4 is the identification of multiple communication channels between consumer and provider through which information or e-business objects can be passed. Multiple channels may each serve a different business function (as explained later in this chapter) or may serve the same business function in different ways (e.g., by means of different physical communication channels, such as telephone or internet). The latter is commonly referred to as *multi-channeling* (this is closely related to the *multi-channel business design* discussed in section 5.3.2). Figure 6.4 shows two channels for reasons of simplicity and clarity. In practice, the number can be arbitrary.

6.3 Intra-organization structures

In the previous section we have refined an organization model of a networked e-business market, but have kept the internal organization structure of the collaborating

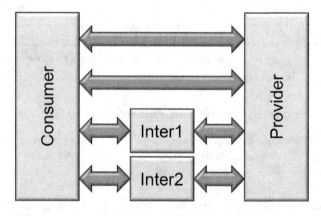

FIGURE 6.4 E-business organization structure (level 2).

parties opaque – they have stayed black boxes. In this section we further refine the organization structure by opening this internal structure and exploring intra-organization structures.

6.3.1 Front end versus back end

In Figure 6.4 the business functionality of both consumer and provider are shown as a black box; that is, without any internal detail. To completely design or analyze an e-business organization structure we need to open this black box.[4] We start with explaining what we need to find inside this black box.

The interaction between parties in a networked e-business context changes frequently, both as a consequence of changing business models (as discussed in chapter 5) and of changing technology (as discussed in chapter 8) – remember the joint forces of requirements pull and technology push as discussed in chapter 1. The core activities of organizations typically do not change that frequently, however. Take, for example, a telephone company selling its services over the internet. The interaction with its clients, for instance in the form of subscription packages offered, changes on a continuous basis. The core activities, providing infrastructure for phone calls and accounting its use, change only slowly over time.

The fact that internal business functionality and externally oriented business functionality change at different paces implies that we have to make a clear decoupling between these two types of functionality. Without a clear decoupling we cannot change the one without affecting the other. In other words, we need a separation of concerns implemented in the intra-organizational structure.

We see the result of the decoupling in Figure 6.5 (the organization structure at *level 3*). The core business functionality that has an intra-organizational goal (i.e., not exposed to the outside world) is commonly referred to as *back end functionality*. The business functionality that is in contact with external parties (hence, it has an inter-organizational goal) is commonly referred to as *front end functionality*. In administrative organizations, both types of functionality are often called *back office* and *front office*, respectively.

Decoupling the front end and back end means that in a concrete situation, it should be very clearly defined what is part of the back end, what is part of the front end and how the two ends interoperate.

6.3.2 Front end functionality and channels

The final refinement step we make here is the identification of individual functionalities in the overall front end functionality. A party (with a consumer or provider role) has a number of distinct business functionalities that it requires to collaborate with external parties, such as advertising for the objects that it offers on a market, negotiating about prices or delivery conditions, buying objects and paying for bought objects (and typically quite a few more). As flexibility in functionality is of the utmost importance to follow (or initiate) market developments, it is usually a good idea to allocate these distinct business functionalities to distinct organization

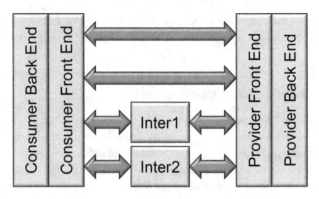

FIGURE 6.5   E-business organization structure (level 3).

building blocks. These building blocks are referred to as *organizational units* or *organizational modules*. This is shown in an abstract way in Figure 6.6 as an elaboration of Figure 6.5, resulting in an organization structure at *level 4*. The CF*x* modules represent consumer front end modules; the PF*x* modules represent provider front end modules. The number of front end modules depends on the e-business scenario at hand.

For illustration purposes, the abstract picture of Figure 6.6 is made more concrete in Figure 6.7 by filling in the front end modules and intermediaries with an example selection. We come by more examples when discussing our three running cases at the end of this chapter.

It is of course possible to also modularize the back end functionality (as shown in Figure 6.6 and Figure 6.7). We have not shown this here, because it is not specific for e-business in the O aspect of BOAT: traditional business requires a modular back end organization as well. When we move to the BOAT architecture (A) aspect in the next chapter, however, this issue becomes more interesting.

In the case of B2C e-business, the C side usually has very limited business functionality. If so, the distinction between front end and back end functionality is not very helpful. A limited set of functional modules (e.g., only buying and paying, as shown in Figure 6.8 with the C side on the left) may be sufficient – or even a single module to represent all of the activities of the consumer.

If an organization employs multiple channels for the same business function (multi-channeling, as discussed before), it may be wise to have one organizational module for each channel. This further increases the level of flexibility of an organization (obviously at the expense of a larger number of modules and, hence, possibly more complexity). If the provider organization of Figure 6.8 takes orders via the web (W) and via email (E), its organization structure may reflect this as shown in Figure 6.9. Note that this structure requires synchronization between the modules supporting the same business function to keep business processing consistent, which adds to complexity. This is a case where a trade-off between flexibility and complexity needs to be chosen explicitly.

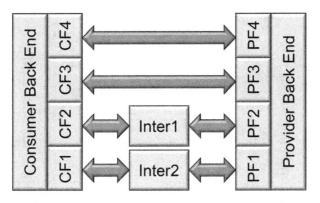

FIGURE 6.6 Abstract e-business organization structure (level 4).

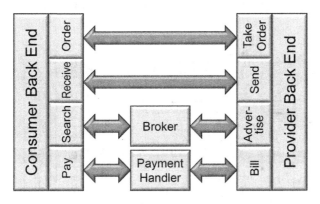

FIGURE 6.7 Concrete e-business organization structure (level 4).

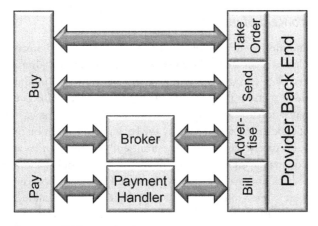

FIGURE 6.8 Concrete B2C organization structure.

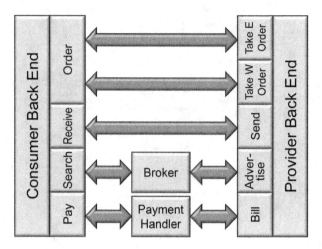

FIGURE 6.9 Concrete organization structure with multi-channeling.

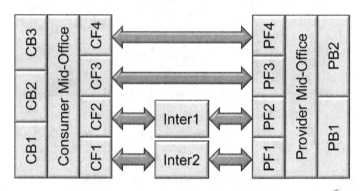

FIGURE 6.10 Organization structure with mid-office.

6.3.3 *The concept of mid-office*

In some organization design approaches, front end and back end organization modules are coupled by a *mid-office*. This mid-office functions as an 'advanced switching board' between back end organization modules and front end modules, thus linking the business functions they perform. The purpose of a mid-office is to further enhance organizational flexibility. Its functionality includes, for example, flexible integration of basic products provided by the back end organization into composed products towards diverse channels in the front end organization. As an example in the financial domain, basic banking products (such as accounts and loans) administrated in the back end may be flexibly combined in the mid-office into financial packages that are offered to customers via the front end. The resulting organization structure is shown in Figure 6.10 (based on the one in Figure 6.6). In this figure we have detailed the back ends of the consumer (CB*x* modules) and provider (PB*x* modules) organizations to better show the integrative function of the mid-office.

For reasons of clarity and brevity, we don't use the mid-office concept in the remainder of this book. If required, the discussions that follow can be easily extended to include this concept, however.

6.4 Business functions

In the previous section we have discussed how organizational modules (units) implement business functions in networked e-business organizations. We have not discussed, however, how to identify these business functions in a systematic way. In other words, we have not discussed how to arrive at an orderly set of business functions that we can use in an organization structure. We do this in this section.

We first take a look at business function models as a basis and explore one specific model. Then, we analyze how the distinction between front end and back end functions can be placed in this model. Based on this, we extend the function taxonomy of this model towards a taxonomy that is fit for e-business scenarios. In doing so we arrive at a set of front end business functions and a set of back end business functions. These sets can be used as simple catalogs (reference lists) for the identification of business functions in a concrete e-business scenario.

6.4.1 Business function model

Business function models provide a conceptual structure for the identification of general business functions. These models help in constructing complete and non-redundant sets of functions in practical organization design.

Following, we start with discussing a well-known example of these models: Porter's value chain model. This model was originally designed for production companies, but it can be used in a broader context. Then, we 'overlay' this model with the distinction between front end and back end functions, as we have seen earlier in this chapter. Finally, we discuss how to adapt Porter's model to networked e-business. This discussion is the basis for the set of business functions identified in the following section.

Porter's value chain model

Porter's value chain model [Port85] is a general model of a (production) business organization highlighting its main business functions. A slightly simplified version of the model is shown in Figure 6.11.

The model distinguishes between two classes of business functions: primary and secondary functions. Primary functions are directly geared towards the main

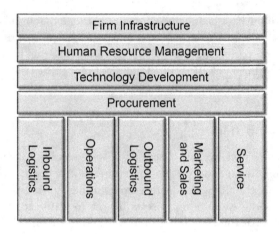

FIGURE 6.11 Functions in Porter's value chain model (adapted from [Port85]).

business goal of the organization: the production and delivery of goods. Secondary functions support the primary functions by providing a necessary context in which to execute the primary functions.

Primary functions are shown as vertical columns in the bottom half of Figure 6.11. The *inbound logistics* function enables the transport of materials used as input in production. The *operations* function performs the actual production of goods. The *outbound logistics* function enables the transport of produced goods to consumers of these goods. The *marketing and sales* function takes care of attracting these customers and arranging the actual sales. Finally, the *service* function is responsible for post-sale service to customers.

Secondary functions are shown as horizontal layers in the top half of Figure 6.11. The *procurement* function takes care of ordering the goods and services required in the other functions (most importantly the *operations* function). As its name suggests, the *technology development* function concentrates on the development of new technologies used in the *operations* function or in the produced goods. The *human resource management* function manages the personnel of the organization. Finally, the *firm infrastructure* function is responsible for providing the general infrastructure of the organization, such as the (financial) administration.

Front end and back end functions

In the previous section we have seen that in networked e-business it is important to distinguish between front end and back end functions in primary business functions. The front end functions implement the collaboration in an e-business scenario; hence, they mostly determine the e-business character of an organization.

Which business functions are important in the front end of an organization depends on the role that the organization plays in the scenario: provider with a sell-side perspective or consumer with a buy-side perspective.

When we map Porter's model to the provider front end perspective in this context, we obtain the selection highlighted in Figure 6.12: the most important functions are *outbound logistics, marketing and sales* and *service*. Obviously, most organizations require all the other functions, too, but they are not part of the provider front end perspective.

If we do the same for the consumer perspective, we get the function selection shown in Figure 6.13. Here, the focus is on *procurement* and *inbound logistics*. As with the provider perspective, the other functions are present in most organizations as well, but they are not part of the consumer front end perspective.

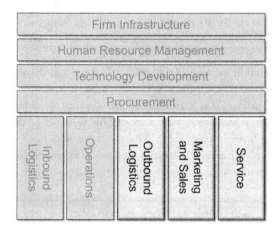

FIGURE 6.12   Provider (sell-side) front end business functions.

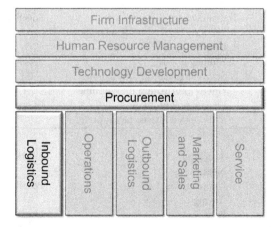

FIGURE 6.13   Consumer (buy-side) front end business functions.

Adapting Porter's model to networked e-business

Porter's model was designed for 'traditional' production organizations where physical production and transportation are of major importance. Therefore, we cannot effectively apply the model directly to a networked e-business context. Because it is a widely accepted model, though, we use it as a basis for the identification of e-business functions. Hence, we need to extend and detail Porter's model. We do this in the next two subsections for front end and back end e-business functions, respectively.

6.4.2 Front end business functions

We take the front end functions from Porter's model (as identified in the previous section) as the basis for the structured identification of front end functions for networked e-business. In doing so, we arrive at the basic set shown in Table 6.1. In the left column of the table, we find the business functions identified in Figures 6.12 and 6.13. In the middle column of Table 6.1 we have detailed and specialized these functions for networked e-business. While the table is certainly not the 'ultimate set' of business functions, it is a structured starting point for networked e-business design and analysis. It also shows how a set of functions can be derived in a structured way starting from a well-accepted business framework, such as Porter's model.

Note that the placement of logistics functions as identified in Table 6.1 is best applicable in e-business scenarios dealing with physical goods (see section 3.5) – not

TABLE 6.1 Simple catalog of front end e-business functions

Porter function	Networked e-business function	Comment
Provider Side		
Marketing and sales	Advertising	Usually via intermediary
	Negotiating	
	Contracting	Possibly via intermediary
	Selling	
	Billing	
Outbound logistics	Sending goods	Possibly via intermediary
	Status information provisioning	
Service	Goods information provisioning	
	Update provisioning	In case of digital goods
	Value added service provisioning	
Consumer Side		
Procurement	Searching	Usually via intermediary
	Negotiating	
	Contracting	Possibly via intermediary
	Buying	
	Paying	Usually via intermediary
Inbound logistics	Receiving goods	Possibly via intermediary

too strange, as the table is based on a supply chain model. Especially in scenarios dealing with services as main e-business objects, the situation can be different: there may be no logistics of any importance or the logistics may be reversed in the sense that the provider side has inbound logistics and the consumer side outbound logistics. The former can occur with digital services. The latter can occur with physical services where the consumer transfers physical objects to the provider for servicing.

6.4.3 Back end business functions

We can perform the exercise we did for front end functions in a similar way for back end functions. Because back end functions are not as specific for networked e-business as front end functions, we perform this exercise briefly. The result is shown in Table 6.2. We do not distinguish between consumer side and provider side in the table, because the characteristics of these sides are mainly relevant for front end functions.

Note that we have included *procurement* in Table 6.2 (it is also listed as a front end function in Table 6.1). As a back end function it is now seen without the perspective of networked e-business: an organization that sells products in an e-business scenario at its output side may have to buy products in a traditional business scenario at its input side. Because this is not very relevant from the e-business perspective, we don't detail this function here.

6.5 Business processes

Organization structures for networked e-business (as discussed in section 6.3) describe the organization of business functions (as discussed in the previous section) of participating organizations in an e-business scenario. They do not, however, describe how the various business functions are activated in time during the execution of an e-business collaboration. To capture this, we need to introduce the notion of business processes in networked e-business and their models.

TABLE 6.2 Simple catalog of back end e-business functions

Porter function	Networked e-business function	Comment
Operations	Production	May be digital objects
	Stock keeping	Not applicable if digital objects
Procurement	Procurement	
Technology development	Product configuration	
	Catalog management	
Human resource management	Personnel selection	
	Knowledge innovation	
Firm infrastructure	Financial administration	Linked with e-payments
	IS management	

In this section we first discuss the essence of the business process concept. Then we show how to specify business processes – we introduce a simple graphical notation for this purpose. Because networked e-business concerns the collaboration between multiple organizations, processes in this context span multiple organizations. We discuss this aspect in section 6.5.3. After that, we are ready to actually describe business processes in networked e-business. We end this section by discussing the differences between static and dynamic business processes. The latter concept allows processes to be woven between organizations that set up collaborations on the fly while doing business, as required by a number of the reference business models that we have seen in section 5.6.

6.5.1 The essence of business processes

A business process is a set of business activities that are performed in a specific order to achieve a specific business goal. A business process can be geared towards primary business goals, such as selling a product – this is a primary business process. It can also be geared towards secondary business goals, such as making a monthly financial overview of a company – this is a secondary business process.

The activities of a process implement the necessary business steps to reach the business goal. These steps are performed by *actors* (also called *agents*) in an organization, which are located in organizational units as discussed in section 6.3. In the description of a business process, actors are often abstracted into roles. A *role* describes the required capabilities of actors to perform an activity, such that a specific actor can be chosen when the process is executed. Selecting an actor for a role is called *role resolution*. The activities of a business process are part of the business functions as discussed in section 6.4. The actors that perform activities are often human beings, but they can also be machines. In an e-business context the latter are typically automated information systems (think, for example, of the *completely automated business* direction discussed in section 5.3.5).

A business process is specified in a *business process model*. Such a model specifies the order of the steps. In the next subsection we will see how to actually specify business process models. Steps in a business process model can be elementary business activities or *subprocesses*. Elementary business activities are considered atomic units of business activity in a process and are not further refined in a business process specification. Subprocesses are business processes at a lower level of aggregation and are used to break up the complexity of business process models or to reuse parts of business process models for different business goals.

The ordering of steps in a business process model can be simple – for example, a linear sequence – or they can be complex – containing alternative paths, parallel paths and iterations. The ordering of steps in time is referred to as the *control flow* of a business process model. When discussing business processes the focus is on this control flow, not so much on the internal details of the individual steps in the process.

A business process model specifies the structure of a *type* of business process; that is, all possible executions of that process. For example, a model of a sales process specifies how all sales are to be performed. A single execution of a business process according to a business process model is called an *instance* of that model or a *business process case*. Performing one specific sale is thus an instance of a sales process.

6.5.2 Specifying business process models

In the previous subsection we have discussed the essence of business processes, treating the most important concepts of business process models. In this subsection we turn to the specification of business process models; that is, the way to represent them in documentation. Business processes are often specified in graphical models because these provide an easy overview of the structure and control flow of the model.

Figure 6.14 shows an example B2C e-business process model. We use a simple, informal process specification notation[5] consisting of process activities and arrows that connect these activities. The arrows denote temporal sequence; that is, they denote the control flow. Thus, an arrow from activity A to activity B denotes that B is executed after A has been completed (or, in other words, A precedes B in execution). The meaning of the process element types we use is shown in the legend in Table 6.3.

The example in Figure 6.14 is a simplified e-retailing process (operationalizing part of the e-retailer reference business model that we have seen in section 5.6.1). The process starts with a web shop customer browsing a catalog and selecting

TABLE 6.3 Legend of process specification element types

start	Start of process. Can occur only once in a diagram.	1	Alternative split. The process continues with only one of the outgoing paths.
stop	End of a process. Can occur more than once in a diagram.	1	Alternative join. The process continues when one of the incoming paths is completed.
activity	Process activity. Denotes an elemental business function.	A	Parallel split. The process continues with all outgoing paths in parallel.
sub-process	Sub-process. Placeholder for a refinement in another diagram.	A	Parallel join. The process continues when all the incoming paths are completed.

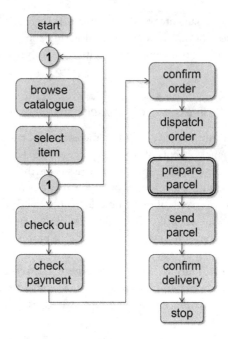

FIGURE 6.14 Example e-retail business process.

an item to buy (typically placing it in an electronic shopping cart). These two activities can be repeated multiple times, specified by the process loop between the alternative split and alternative join (forming an iteration). After finishing the selection of items to buy, the customer proceeds to check out. The payment is next checked. Then, the e-retailer confirms the order (typically by email) and dispatches the order to its delivery department. The parcel is prepared and sent to the customer (usually through a logistics partner – an intermediary). Finally, a delivery notice is sent to the customer (typically, by email). The *prepare parcel* step is a sub-process that contains more detailed activities. Its elaboration (refinement) is shown in Figure 6.15.

In Figure 6.15 we see that preparing a parcel starts with picking the goods to be delivered. Then, two paths are followed in parallel. This is specified by having two paths between the parallel split and parallel join. In one path, the parcel is composed and the bill and address sticker are added to it. In the other path, the stock administration is updated to reflect that items have been removed from stock.

The process specification in Figure 6.14 is simplified, because it does not show that the process can be aborted at various points. For instance, the customer can decide not to buy anything, may not proceed to check out, the payment may not be authorized and so on. This means that in the full process specification there are many more alternative paths leading to the end of the process. Also, the process specification is based on the fact that only goods are sold that are actually in stock.

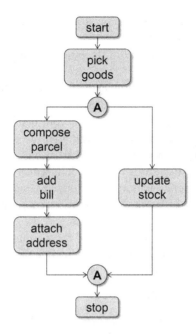

FIGURE 6.15 Refinement of sub-process of Figure 6.14.

Including activities to put a sales order in a waiting state and trigger an order for stock replenishment further complicates the process.

6.5.3 From intra- to inter-organizational business processes

Intra-organizational business processes are completely executed (also termed *enacted*) within the boundaries of a single organization. As such, focusing on intra-organizational processes is not very interesting in the scope of this book (as we are interested in inter-organizational e-business scenarios – see section 1.2). Therefore, we focus here on inter-organizational business processes. We first discuss the nature of these processes. Then, we pay attention to different process flow control types, which classify the distribution of the responsibility of process execution among the parties in an e-business scenario.

Inter-organizational business processes

Inter-organizational business processes[6] are executed by two or more collaborating parties, and hence are interesting from a networked e-business perspective. They are used to actually implement collaboration in business models as discussed in the previous chapter. We make a business process explicitly inter-organizational by allocating the steps in the process to specific parties in an e-business scenario – or, put very simply: we indicate who does what.

Figure 6.16 shows the business process of Figure 6.14 as an explicit inter-organizational business process. The inter-organizational character of the process is specified by indicating which part of the process is executed by which involved party.

In Figure 6.16 the situation is simple: the first two activities of the process are executed by the customer, the other by the e-retailer. The control flow distribution between the two parties is simple, too: the control of the process execution is passed from customer to retailer at one single point. To provide a good overview of the relationship between process parts and parties, a *swim lane* version [Wik14m] of a process model specification is often used, in which each participating party has its own vertical (or horizontal) segment of the diagram. The swim lane version of Figure 6.16 is shown in Figure 6.17, in this case a simple configuration with two lanes.

We show more examples when we get to the running case studies at the end of this chapter. Following, we discuss further the issue of control flow distribution.

Inter-organizational flow control types

Inter-organizational business processes exist in three flavors when it comes to the distribution of the flow control[7] of the business process; that is, the allocation of the responsibility to make the business process flow.

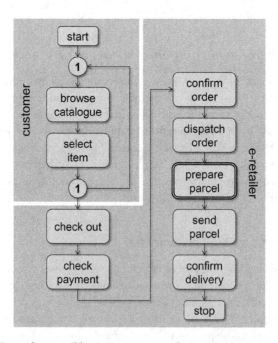

FIGURE 6.16   Example e-retail business process with organizations.

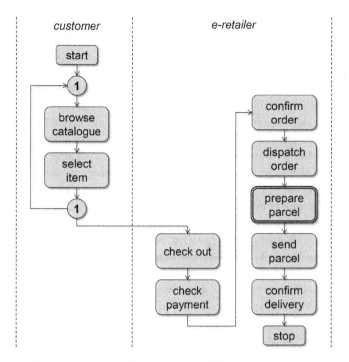

FIGURE 6.17   Swim lane version of example e-retail business process.

The simplest flavor is the one with *unilateral flow control*. In this type, one party completely controls the flow of the entire process. This means that this party makes all the routing and scheduling decisions in the process. The other collaborating party (or parties) participates in the process only by executing individual tasks upon request of the controlling party. These individual tasks can be executed, for example, using web-based interfaces to the systems of the controlling party – we discuss the technology for this in section 8.4.2.

More complicated is the case of *bilateral flow control*. In this type, two parties collaboratively control the flow of the business process. The business process is divided into two parts and each party is responsible for one part. This means that the two parties have to synchronize the states of their parts of the process and exchange process data to keep the entire thing running smoothly. This can be very simple, where one organization 'kicks off' the other (as, for example, in Figure 6.16), or more complicated, as in the case of multiple synchronization points.

The case of *multilateral flow control* is a generalization of the bilateral flow control case. Here the situation is similar, but there are more than two parties involved in process control to cater for flow control distribution among more than two parties. This flow control type can occur in virtual enterprise scenarios where multiple organizations collaboratively execute a complex business process [Gref09, Meha10].

An abstract example of a multilateral control flow is shown in Figure 6.18. Here, five organizations (indicated by the ovals) together execute an inter-organizational business process with activities (indicated by the small circles) executed by each organization. The process starts at organization A and ends at organization E. The process contains both intra-organizational control flow links (the solid arrows within the ovals) and inter-organizational control flow links (the dashed arrows between the ovals). The five organizations together are responsible for the flow control of the entire process; that is, the flow control is distributed among them.

Multilateral flow control makes synchronization more complex, certainly if the collaboration topology contains cycles (i.e., if organizations are 'connected' via more than one path). In this latter case, parties might even perform inconsistent activities if the processes are not well designed: decisions may be taken in parallel by two organizations that are inconsistent but join together further down the process. Swim lane diagrams can help to get overview of complex processes. A swim lane version of Figure 6.18 is shown in Figure 6.19. Here, we use the notation of Table 6.3 and assume that the local sub-process of organization C is a process with parallelism (as opposed to two alternative paths). Obviously, in any practical diagram the process steps are labeled with meaningful names – we have used abstract names here for reasons of simplicity.

In the bilateral and multilateral flow control classes, participating organizations need to expose the details of their business processes to the other organizations in order to synchronize their processes. They do not need to expose all of the details of their internal processes, however. The internal processes may contain details that are confidential (for reasons of competition) or simply irrelevant to other parties. Consequently, organizations expose abstractions of their *internal business processes* as *external business processes* at the inter-organizational level [Gre03b]. Such an abstraction is also referred to as *business process view* or *workflow view* [Chiu01].

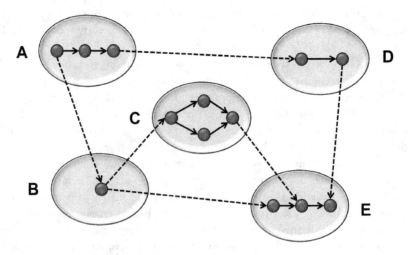

FIGURE 6.18 Multilateral control flow.

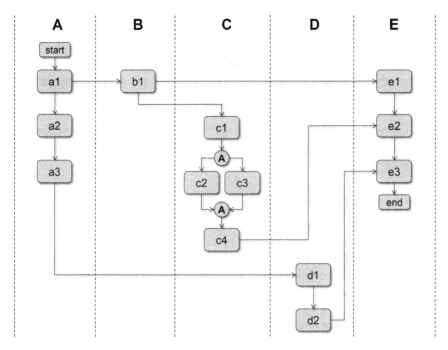

FIGURE 6.19   Swim lane diagram of Figure 6.18 (activity labels added).

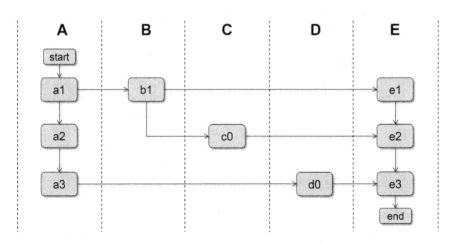

FIGURE 6.20   Version of Figure 6.19 with abstracted processes for C and D.

If in the situation of Figure 6.19 organizations C and D abstract their processes to black-box views, the process on the inter-organizational level is shown in Figure 6.20. In this figure the abstracted processes of C and D are labeled *c0* and *d0*, respectively.

6.5.4 Business processes in networked e-business

With the ingredients of the preceding subsections, we can turn to the discussion of business processes in networked e-business. Obviously, e-business processes are business processes, but they are business processes of a special kind. First, they are inter-organizational by nature. Therefore, it is important to map process steps to the right parties and within the parties to the right organizational modules. Second, they are typically complex, involving a number of e-business functions performed by two or more parties. Therefore, it is important to map process functions to an e-business function taxonomy. We discuss both aspects further on.

Process steps and organizational modules

An aspect that is more important in networked e-business settings than in tradi-tional business settings is the allocation of activities (steps) in a process model to the parties in an e-business scenario. This is so important because the process is per-formed by multiple parties that are usually autonomous with respect to each other. In other words, the allocation of activities to partners determines the feasibility of the implementation of a process model to a large extent.

We can go one step further and allocate the process steps to functional organization modules of involved parties (as discussed in section 6.3) and allocate inter-organizational connections between activities to channels between parties in a scenario. As an example, we can map a simple e-buying business process (as part of an e-retailer business model) to the organization structure of Figure 6.7. In doing so we get a hybrid organization/process diagram such as the one in Figure 6.21. Note that we have chosen a simplified process notation for reasons of simplicity here – circles denote process steps and splits and joins have been omitted. This diagram gives a high-level overview of how an e-business process progresses through the business functionalities of involved organizations.

If we require a more explicit process model than the one in Figure 6.21, we can use a proper process model specification as introduced earlier in this section. To show the sequence of activities of the involved business functions we use a swim lane layout with one lane per business function. The elaboration of Figure 6.21 in such a way is shown in Figure 6.22 (we have omitted the names of the process steps for reasons of simplicity). Obviously, this model is more concrete than the one in Figure 6.21. For example, it explicitly specifies the start and end of the process and explicitly specifies that the delivery and payment parts of the business process proceed in parallel (these aspects are implicit in Figure 6.21).

Note that the process shown in Figure 6.22 operationalizes only part of the e-retailer business model: the buying process. The advertising process, for example, is not included. Because advertising typically proceeds independently from selling, this is best modeled in a separate business process model.

Business process activities and e-business functions

In this section we have discussed business processes, the steps of which are e-business activities. As we have seen in Figure 6.21, these activities can be mapped to modules

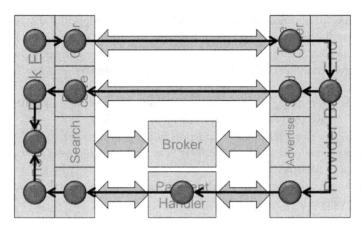

FIGURE 6.21 Networked e-business process mapped to organization structure.

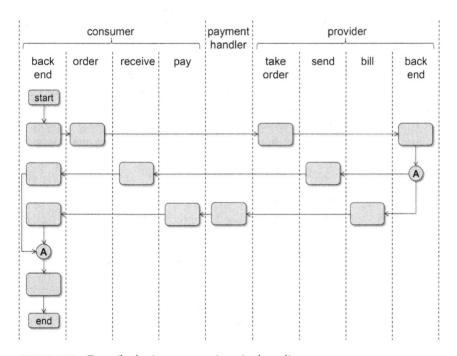

FIGURE 6.22 E-retailer business process in swim lane diagram.

in organization structures. Within these modules we find e-business functions, as discussed in section 6.4. The relationship between a business process and these functions is what we discuss here. We do this on the basis of the example we have seen earlier.

In Figure 6.16 we have shown a simple e-retailer business process. The activities in this process specification are of an ad-hoc nature; that is, they have been selected without using an underlying framework. To check completeness and consistency of the process specification, the steps in this figure can be mapped to the networked e-business function taxonomy that we have identified in section 6.4. As the process involves both supplier and consumer sides, we need functions from both perspectives. Thus, we can identify the following mappings (referring to Table 6.1):

- Steps *browse catalog* and *select item* belong to function *buying* (consumer side).
- Step *checkout* belongs to function *selling* (provider side).
- Step *check payment* belongs to function *billing* (provider side).
- Steps *confirm order* and *confirm delivery* belong to function *status information provisioning* (provider side).
- Steps *dispatch order*, *prepare parcel* and *send parcel* belong to function *sending goods* (provider side).

As can be seen, not all functions from Table 6.1 are included in the business process specification. Using a reference model such as Table 6.1, it is good practice to check why not all functions are included. The reason in this case is the fact that this business process does not operationalize all the functionality of the e-retailer business model, as noted before. Functions *advertising, searching, receiving goods* and all *service* functions are out of the scope of this process specification. As we have seen before the *advertising* function cannot even be part of the same process model as *buying*, because an advertisement has a different life cycle than a purchase order – the *advertising* function has its own business process. Functions *negotiating* and *contracting* are typically not applicable to standard e-retailing scenarios, so we do not find these in any business process specifications for this example scenario – but they do appear in business processes for other business models, as discussed in section 5.6.

6.5.5 Static versus dynamic processes

There is one aspect of business processes in networked e-business that remains to be discussed: the difference between *static processes* and *dynamic processes*.

We call an e-business process *static* if its specification is completely predefined without taking specific, individual e-business orders into account. The parties involved in the execution of a static process instance can be chosen during execution (e.g., a consumer may decide which provider to use in a buying process), but the activities and control flow of the process are not changed during the process. Selecting involved parties is role resolution within a scenario: specific organizations are assigned to roles, such as provider, consumer or intermediary, based on pre-specified roles.

We call an e-business process *dynamic* if its complete specification is determined right before the execution of a process instance on the basis of one individual e-business order – or, even during the execution of the process instance. The latter approach means that the execution of a process starts with an 'incomplete' specification, which is 'filled in' when all parties are selected. This implies that role resolution is coupled to on-the-fly process specification. The dynamic approach to e-business process management allows for high levels of flexibility in collaboration, but it also implies high levels of complexity (both in the organizational aspect and in the architecture and technology aspects).

An example of a dynamic e-business process is a process the specification of which contains 'blanks'; that is, placeholders for parts of the process that are not yet specified. Depending on the nature of a process instance, these 'blanks' can be filled in differently. If the instance handles a high-volume transaction, the blanks may be filled in with more details than in the case of a low-volume transaction.

In e-business research advanced approaches towards dynamic business process support have been used, for example, in scenarios using the *dynamic outsourcing* business structure (as discussed in section 5.5) for dynamic service outsourcing scenarios [Gref00] and the *dynamic partnering* structure for dynamic business network formation [Gref09]. In dynamic service outsourcing the 'blanks' approach, as discussed earlier, can be used to have these 'blanks' filled in by selecting specific business processes provided by external parties.

6.6 The service-oriented view

In section 5.8 we have introduced service-dominant business thinking for networked e-business. This thinking places value-in-use for customers at the forefront and realizes this through service delivery. This service-centric paradigm requires support in the organizational aspect of the BOAT framework to be executed in practice – comparable to the non-service-dominant paradigm that we have seen so far in this chapter. To get a good coupling to the service-dominant business paradigm we need to align organizational support. In this section we explain the main lines of this service-oriented view to the organization aspect.

We first show how services can indeed be related to business functions, as we have seen them in this chapter. Next, we explain how services relate to business processes. Finally, we address the organizational implications of dynamic business service networks.

6.6.1 Services as encapsulated business capabilities

In the service-oriented view of the organization aspect a *business service* is the central concept. A business service is a modular piece of business functionality that can be invoked by users (consumers) of that service, either within the boundaries of an organization or outside of these boundaries. A service 'wraps' (encapsulates) a business capability with a well-defined interface. A business capability is (a part of) a business function as discussed in section 6.4. The interface defines the operations through which the service can be used by service consumers. The anatomy of a business service is shown in Figure 6.23 [Gre13a] – we explain more details further on.

An example business service of an e-retailer is *manage shopping cart*. This service encapsulates the operational business capability to manage a shopping cart,

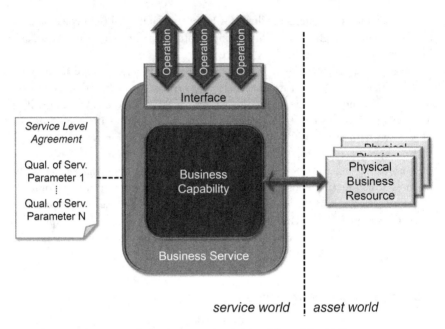

FIGURE 6.23   Anatomy of a business service (adapted from [Gre13a]).

consisting of part of the *take order* functionality (see Figure 6.7) and the internal business process implementing this capability. Operations of the service are *create new shopping cart, add item, empty shopping cart* and *process shopping cart*.

The fact that a business service encapsulates a business functionality implies that there is a strict separation between the external use of the service and the internal implementation. On the one hand, this means that the service consumer is not bothered with realization details that are non-relevant for the use of the service. On the other hand, this means that the service provider can change the internal realization of the business service freely, so long as it adheres to the specified interface. Consequently, the use of physical business resources can be determined internally by the service provider: there is a clear separation of the service world (which defines the functionality of services) and the asset world (which defines the management of physical resources, such as personnel and machinery).

To ensure that a business service delivers not only the right functionality but also does this in the right fashion, the concept of service level agreement (SLA) is of paramount importance in the service-oriented view (as shown in Figure 6.23). An SLA defines the non-functional characteristics of a business service in terms of a set of quality of service (QoS) parameters. Each QoS parameter specifies one or more metrics for service execution. Important examples of QoS parameters are response time (the time it takes to get a response from the service), availability (the fraction of the time the business service is actively available) and cost (the operational cost for invocation of the service). A QoS parameter can be specified for a

TABLE 6.4 Example (simplified) SLA specification

SLA business service: manage shopping cart		
Response time	Maximum	0.25 seconds
	Average	0.10 seconds
Availability	Minimum	99.99%
Cost	Average	€0.02

business service in general (and thus holds for all operations of that service) or for a specific operation of a service. A simplified SLA specification in tabular form for the example business service *manage shopping cart* is shown in Table 6.4. In this table we see three QoS parameters. The response-time parameter has two metrics, one for maximum response time and one for average response time.

6.6.2 Service compositions and orchestrations

To realize a value-in-use for a customer in a service-dominant scenario, we typically need the capabilities of more than one single business service. For example, to realize an e-shopping value-in-use we need more than the *manage shopping cart* service introduced before: we need a catalog browsing service, a payment service and so on. Consequently, we need to be able to compose a number of business services into a *complex business service* that delivers the value-in-use. To compose services we use them as elements in a *service orchestration*.

A service orchestration determines the sequence in which the individual business services are invoked. As such, a service orchestration is very similar to a business process, as we have seen in section 6.5 – where a business process specification describes the ordering of (parts of) business functions in time, a service orchestration specification describes the ordering of business services in time (using similar business process primitives as shown in Table 6.3).

6.6.3 Dynamic business service networks

In the service-oriented view of networked e-business organization, flexibility of collaborations is of great importance. Flexibility is, on the one hand, required to serve customers with diverse requirements, possibly even leading to mass customization, as we have seen in the discussion of the service-dominant view on the business aspects (see section 5.8). On the other hand, flexibility is required to deal with changing market circumstances that can be quite fluid in service markets.

Flexibility in service management can be achieved by the use of dynamic business service networks. In these networks complex services are created by dynamically composing services that are provided by various organizations in the network. Often, one party takes the role of the service orchestrator; that is, the party that performs the actual orchestration of a complex service. Typically, this is the party that will also deliver the integrated service to the customer (using the *e-integrator* business model that we have seen in section 5.6). We describe an example of this when we discuss the TraXP case study at the end of this chapter. Service orchestration implies a centralized responsibility for the synchronization of the component services. This responsibility can in principle also be distributed over a service network. In this case we speak of *service choreography*, and the synchronization is managed on a peer-to-peer fashion between collaborators in a network.

In dynamic service networks services are chosen on the fly, based on their functionality, and on the offered SLAs. To this aim, the markets in which these networks operate can be equipped with business service brokers: organizations that are matchmakers between service providers and service consumers.

6.7 Operations and change management

In operating a networked e-business organization (as in any other business organization), two main issues are of importance: keeping the existing situation operating smoothly and preparing for changing the existing situation. The former is called *operations management*. The latter, called *change management*, is extremely important in e-business – remember that change is the only constant in e-business. In this section we briefly discuss both types of management in the context of networked e-business.

6.7.1 Operations management

Clearly, operations management includes managing all the internals of organizations involved in networked e-business – but that is not the focus of this book. We focus here on two aspects that are specific to modern e-business: managing inter-organizational relationships and managing IT resources.

Managing inter-organizational relationships

Managing inter-organizational relationships at the operational level between organizations is obviously of paramount importance in networked e-business. In this context, operations management has three important elements:

- **Synchronizing business states** between partners involved in an e-business relationship. This may involve managing relationships defined in electronic contracts [Ang06a] by making sure that all rights and obligations specified in these contracts are handled in the appropriate way. Maintaining required levels of trust between business partners is a major issue here [Keen00]. Trust management between organizations in networked e-business typically has to be performed more explicitly than in traditional business, because business relationships are often not based on long-standing collaborations with personal contacts.
- **Synchronizing process states** of processes that are executed across multiple organizations in an e-business relationship (as illustrated in Figures 6.21

and 6.22). Synchronization is required to make sure that all collaborating parties have the same view on the progress of e-business processes (or service compositions, if we take the service-oriented point of view), both for monitoring and controlling purposes. Synchronizing process states includes the handling of exceptional situations, which may require advanced automated decision-making mechanisms or escalation to human decision makers. In scenarios where high levels of efficiency are required (as in the *completely automated business* direction, see section 5.3), manual handling of exceptions must be avoided as much as possible.

- **Synchronizing data states**; that is, making sure that the correct data is passed at the right moments during the execution of e-business processes (or complex services). Synchronization is required to ensure that all collaborating parties have the same view on the 'contents' of e-business processes, again both for monitoring and controlling purposes. Often, data synchronization relies on message passing between collaborating parties. In this case, strict communication protocols must be enforced (which may be supported by specific e-business technology, as discussed in chapter 8).

These elements of inter-organizational relationship management are summarized in Figure 6.24. Note that the three elements are in general not independent. A change in a business process state, for example, may imply a change in the corresponding data state. A change in a business state may imply a change in a business process state: a terminated business contract may trigger the abortion of running business processes.

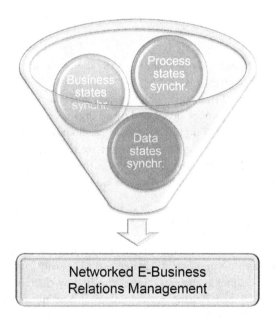

FIGURE 6.24   Ingredients of e-business relationship management.

Managing IT resources

Resource management is an important element in operations management for any organization – so, too, in a networked e-business organization. Information technology (IT) resources form one class of resources to be managed. IT resources include both software (such as e-business systems) and hardware (such as server machines and physical networks). In an e-business organization, IT resources are an even more key resource than in other organizations, because they are the main infrastructure for the execution of primary business processes. Failure of the IT infrastructure often means a direct loss for business. Therefore, IT resource management requires a good deal of attention in e-business organizations.

Important elements of IT resource management are:

- **Managing IT infrastructure capacity** and planning future capacity, taking into account variations in system load.
- **Keeping back-up infrastructure on standby** for immediate transfer of activities if the primary infrastructure fails.
- **Taking care of the security of e-business systems** to avoid unauthorized use of these systems. Security covers both the functionality of systems and the information they exchange. Note that e-business systems are by definition open to the outside world, so they can be vulnerable in this respect if not configured in the right way.
- **Making sure that system maintenance staff is available** to guarantee 24/7 operation of the organization (to provide the temporal reach, as we have discussed in section 5.2). Even relatively short down times of systems may imply a substantial loss of business, both in actual transactions and in customer confidence.

The first three elements may be coupled to the use of specific technology, some of which we discuss in chapter 8.

Note that the way IT resources are managed differs to a large extent between a situation where the resources are owned by an organization and a situation where they are used in a cloud computing scenario (as discussed in section 2.2.3). In the case of cloud computing, part of these issues are the responsibility of the cloud provider – hence, the operation management of the cloud-using party may be simpler (if, of course, a cloud provider with the right service levels has been selected).

6.7.2 *Change management*

Change management is essential in a networked e-business organization to ensure that the organization is prepared to change and to actually implement changes. As we have seen in chapter 1, changes can be triggered by changing market situations (requirements pull) or by changing technological possibilities (technology push).

Fast developments in the e-business arena make change management an even more pressing issue in e-business than in 'traditional' business. Change management is related to the topic of strategic alignment, as we discuss in chapter 10, because changes in various aspects of an organization need to be aligned.

Following, we briefly discuss the issues of enabling changes in organization structures, preparing staff in an organization for changes and of predicting the unpredictable in the networked e-business arena.

Enabling changes in organization structures

An important aspect of change management is preparing for new organization structures and realizing these; that is, reorganizing the business functionality of an organization. To be able to do so without rearranging everything from scratch over and over again, organization modularity is extremely important: by organizing business functionality in appropriate modules (organizational clusters), many changes can be realized by manipulating individual organization modules in isolation. We have seen earlier in this chapter how organization structures can be modularized to accommodate change.

Clearly, when organization structures are changed process and data structures defined in the context of these organization structures may need to be changed as well. But even without changing organizations structures, process and data structures may be subject to change.

Preparing an organization's staff for changes

In obtaining effective and efficient change management within an organization, the role of human resource management (HRM) is essential. In other words, the 'people side' of change management is crucial [Hiatt12]. The organization must make sure that well-qualified people are in pivotal places in the organization to enable changes. Apart from that, people must be in such positions that they can indeed keep track of changes in the context of the organization.

Preparing the people side of an organization for change is more than of average importance in a networked e-business organization, because the field of e-business changes frequently and often quite radically (see, for instance, the recent impact of the Big Five that we have discussed in chapter 2). This makes continuous knowledge acquisition or *lifelong learning* a sine qua non in an e-business organization.

Predicting the unpredictable

We just remarked again how changes in the e-business arena are frequent and often quite abrupt. Developments take place that may appear logical in hindsight but that were hard (if at all possible) to predict beforehand.[8] This is partly caused by the technology-push forces in e-business, partly by the open character of internet-based business and partly by the 'virtual character' of e-business – the combination of which allows drastic new ideas to be implemented quickly.

Consequently, it is hard to anticipate future changes when operating in networked e-business, certainly if these changes are further away than the near future. Only considering predictable, nearby changes, however, implies a great risk of lagging behind soon.

A way to explore the unpredictable is *extreme thinking*. In this approach future scenarios are sketched by taking one or two primary variables in a business model and assigning them extreme values – even if these values will never occur in reality. The scenarios are taken to be in the long-term future in e-business terms, say 5–10 years away. These extreme scenarios are next used to discuss the future (e.g., in BOAT terms) with an open mind. The technique of extreme thinking is in this respect closely related to that of *scenario planning* (see, for example, [Wade12]).

The extreme character of the scenarios forces people out of their comfort zone; that is, it forces them to think creatively. After the extreme future has been explored, the mid-term future is discussed by interpolating between the current situation and the developed extreme scenarios in the long-term future. The mid-term future scenarios combined with the current situation are a basis for change management. These steps are illustrated in Figure 6.25.

After this discussion of e-business operations management and change management, we turn our attention again to the BOAT framework to explore the relationship of the element in this chapter (the O aspect elements) to those in the previous chapter (the B aspect elements).

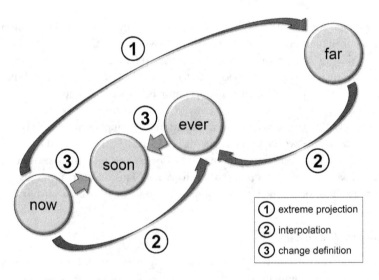

FIGURE 6.25 Extreme-thinking steps.

6.8 Mapping B elements to O elements

In chapter 5 we have discussed the business (B) aspect of networked
e-business, looking at classes of ingredients that contribute to business models. As we have seen in the current chapter, the organization
(O) aspect is an operationalization of the B aspect. As such, we should be able to
identify a clear mapping from B aspect elements to O aspect elements in a specific
e-business scenario.

In the subsections that follow, we discuss this mapping of B aspect elements to
O aspect elements. We do not have the intention to be complete, as a complete
mapping between the B and O aspect is highly complex and highly dependent on
the e-business scenario at hand. Rather, we provide a clear discussion of a small
number of important relationships such that the reader has a basis from which to
analyze other relationships.

We use the structure of the four classes of business elements that is used in
chapter 5 and illustrated in Figure 5.1: we discuss the operationalization of business drivers, business directions, business network operations and, finally, business
structures.

6.8.1 Operationalizing business drivers

In section 5.2 we have seen the concepts of *reach*, *richness* and *efficiency* as very basic
ingredients for e-business models: improvements related to these concepts are the
basic business drivers for networked e-business. In this subsection we focus on the
operationalization of the concepts of reach and richness.

The concept of *reach* clearly is related to communication between organizations in an e-business scenario. Hence, we can operationalize the concept in terms
of the communication channels between collaborating parties (as introduced in
Figure 6.6). Geographical reach, for example, can only be increased if channels
with the right characteristics[9] are placed between organizations; that is, channels
that help in bridging distance. Increased modal reach can be obtained by the use of
multi-channeling, as discussed before in this chapter.

The level of *richness* that can be offered by an organization is heavily related to
the functionality of the front office organization building blocks that we find in
the organization structure (see again Figure 6.6): the front office building blocks
'implement' the interaction with partners. To offer increased richness, the functionality of these building blocks has to be expanded, or new blocks have to be
introduced into the organizational structure. For example, in the O aspect a new
interactive advertising functional block may be added to obtain increased richness
in the B aspect.

We summarize these observations in Figure 6.26 by indicating where reach and
richness are located in the organization structure of Figure 6.6.

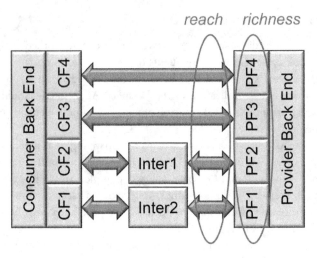

FIGURE 6.26 Reach and richness in organization structure.

6.8.2 Operationalizing business directions

One of the business directions that we have seen in section 5.3 is *multi-channel business*. As we have already shown earlier in this chapter, this business direction maps very directly to networked organization structures, as illustrated in Figure 6.9. A similar mapping can be observed for the *integrated bricks and clicks* direction: here we see how bricks-related and clicks-related functionality is clearly visible in an organization structure, both in the functional front-end modules and in the communication channels that are devoted to either the bricks or the clicks.

The other four business directions discussed in section 5.3 map less directly to organization structures. But still they can be operationalized in terms of O aspect elements. Take, for example, the *completely automated business* direction. To operationalize this direction, all business functions and business processes (as discussed in sections 6.4 and 6.5) must be completely specified in full detail to allow for their automation. Further, all regular roles in business processes must be linked to automated actors in role resolution.

6.8.3 Operationalizing business network operations

In section 5.4 we have seen how business networks can be modified by network operations related to the introduction of e-business concepts. The basic concepts here are *disintermediation, reintermediation* and *substitution*. These concepts can be easily operationalized in terms of the organization structures presented in this chapter.

When disintermediation or reintermediation pertains to an intermediary organization, it means removing and inserting, respectively, an intermediary between two collaborating e-business partners. This can easily be illustrated in a structure based on the notation as shown in Figure 6.6.

If disintermediation or reintermediation does not pertain to an intermediary organization but to a main e-business party, we get a different situation. In this case we remove or add a party that is between two other parties in the roles of consumer and provider, respectively, in an e-business scenario. Consequently, disintermediation means deleting this party from the chain and connecting the front ends of the other parties. Likewise, reintermediation means inserting this party in the chain by reconnecting the front ends to this new party.

An example of the operationalization of disintermediation of a main party is shown in Figure 6.27. The top of the figure shows a simple business chain from which a party is disintermediated. The bottom of the figure shows the result. Note that with disintermediation, some intermediary organizations can take the role of two intermediaries in the old scenario. Alternatively, there may be two intermediary organizations connected 'in sequence' between two main parties. The former situation is shown in Figure 6.27, where in the new situation *Inter2* takes the role of *Inter2* plus *Inter4* of the old situation. The latter situation is also shown in Figure 6.27 with *Inter1* and *Inter3*. A connected pair of intermediaries may occur, for example, if both main parties wish to keep using their preferred (and different) payment intermediaries; consequently, payments are handled by transactions between the two intermediaries.

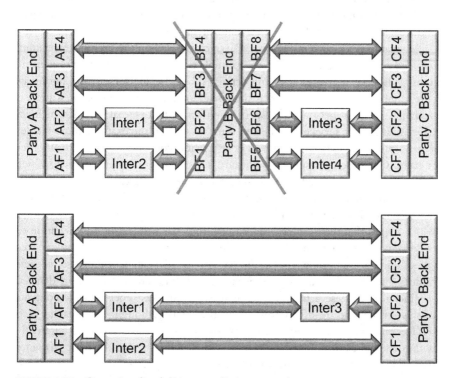

FIGURE 6.27 Operationalized disintermediation example.

In the case of the *substitution* business network operation, we replace a node in the network. To allow easy substitution (i.e., at low cost and with high speed) the communication channels of the old and the new node should be identical in structure. In this case substitution does not change the topology of the network – neither in the business aspect nor in the organization aspect.

6.8.4 Operationalizing business structures

In section 5.5 we have discussed a number of business structures that are structural patterns for networked e-business. Each of these patterns can be operationalized in terms of the O aspect elements discussed in this chapter. For reasons of brevity, we confine ourselves here to the operationalization of the *dynamic outsourcing* structure, specialized to dynamic service outsourcing.

As we have seen in section 5.5.2, dynamic service outsourcing is a networked e-business structure in which an organization has one or more of its non-core business activities performed by external parties for whom these activities are core competences. An external party is selected dynamically (possibly just in time), depending on market and client-order characteristics.

In this chapter we have seen how business processes are used for the operationalization of business models and their ingredients. Dynamic service outsourcing as a business structure can easily be mapped to the concept of business processes: outsourcing means 'transplanting' part of a business process to an external party that performs this process on behalf of the outsourcing organization.

An example is shown in Figure 6.28, which is based on the example e-retailing business process in Figure 6.16. In the example the e-retailer has chosen to dynamically outsource its parcel handling activities, because logistics is not among its core competences. This means that the corresponding part of its business process (activities *prepare parcel* and *send parcel*) is performed by external parties, which act as business process service providers to the e-retailer. In the example the e-retailer dynamically chooses between three service providers depending on the client order at hand. Outsourcing results in additional inter-organizational control flow (see section 6.5.3), as indicated by the dashed arrows in the figure.

Note that both outsourced process steps are regular activities in the process of the e-retailer. They appear as black boxes in the execution of the business process, which means that the e-retailer can observe the start and end of the execution of these activities but not the details of their intermediate state while they are executed. The corresponding steps at the service providers are sub-processes in their business processes. Because logistics is their core business they have a more detailed specification of these activities in their internal business processes. The contents of this refinement are of no concern to the retailer, though. This enables each service provider to implement their two externally visible activities differently within their organization while keeping the process interface to their customer the same for a specific logistics market. This is an application of *business process*

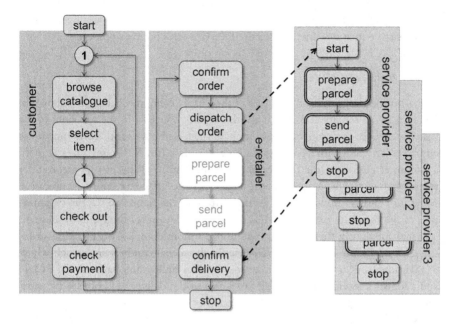

FIGURE 6.28 An example of operationalized dynamic service outsourcing.

abstraction from internal to external business process specification, as discussed in section 6.5.3.

6.9 Running cases

Here we turn our attention again to our running cases – POSH, TTU and TraXP – and apply the concepts from this chapter to them. For reasons of brevity, we do not apply all concepts to all three cases. We make a selection of interesting combinations of concepts and case characteristics.

6.9.1 POSH

As we have seen in chapter 5, POSH clearly follows the *e-retailer* reference business model. This means that in the O aspect we find structures that operationalize this business model.

POSH sells two kinds of products, which are handled in a different way. Small office equipment and supplies are delivered from their own stock by a logistics partner to clients. Large furniture is delivered from (and if necessary produced to order by) a furniture manufacturer with which POSH collaborates. This means that we can see the POSH scenario as a three-party scenario: supplier (POSH), customer and manufacturer.

We first elaborate the organization structure of the POSH e-business scenario. After that, we turn our attention to the POSH e-sales business process.

Organization structure

The e-business organization structure of the POSH e-business scenario is shown in Figure 6.29. As remarked earlier, it is a three-party scenario. In the top right of the figure we see the structure of POSH itself. In the left side we see the structure of the customer. The case with a business customer is shown (the B2B case). The case with a consumer customer (the B2C case) is a simplification of this case, as a consumer typically does not have separate organizational modules: the entire organization structure consists of one module. In the bottom of the figure we see the organization of the furniture manufacturer, as much as is relevant for the POSH e-business scenario (obviously, this party as a whole has a more complex organization structure). There are three intermediary parties in the scenario: a broker through which POSH advertises, a payment handler that handles billing and payment for POSH and a logistics service provider that takes care of the delivery of goods – the same service provider handles small and large goods.

Note that it is a design choice to model the furniture manufacturer as a third party. An alternative would be to consider it as an additional intermediary. The

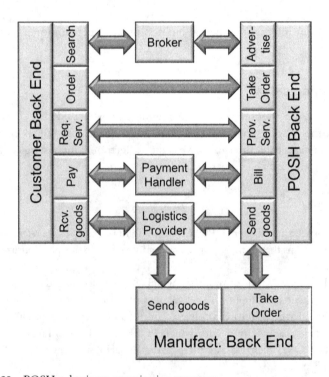

FIGURE 6.29 POSH e-business organization structure.

choice made is based on the observation that the manufacturer produces traded e-business objects (as discussed in section 3.5) and consequently takes a main role in the value chain of the e-business scenario. As such, it is not just an 'additional' service provider that has a minor role in the value chain.

Business functions and business process

In its e-sales business process, POSH makes a distinction between consumer (C) and business (B) customers. Business customers get a more advanced catalog for their order entry than consumer customers, a checkout procedure with more delivery options and they are billed offline for later payment whereas consumers pay directly (e.g., using their credit card).

POSH decides to have their e-sales business process cover the *marketing and sales* and *outbound logistics* function classes of Table 6.1. As each instance (case) of the e-sales process coincides with one sales transaction, the *advertising* function is not included in the e-sales process (advertising has its own process). The *negotiating* and *contracting* functions are not considered applicable to the business domain – although POSH considers including contracting at a later stage to cover large B2B orders, because these orders can incur large financial risks.

The high-level specification of the process is shown in Figure 6.30. Customers are required to make a choice when contacting POSH. Based on the choice, a split is made in the process between consumer and business customers.[10] Business customers have to log into to a pre-existing account to identify themselves. Both

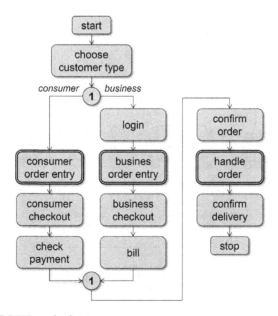

FIGURE 6.30   POSH e-sales business process.

order entry steps are sub-processes, which have elaborations comparable to the *customer* part in Figure 6.16. After payment and billing, respectively, the B2C and B2B cases follow the same steps. The *handle order* step is a sub-process with considerable complexity – within this step, the distinction is made between small goods delivered from POSH stock and large goods delivered from the furniture manufacturer.

6.9.2 TTU

TTU provides two very different kinds of services (as e-business objects, see section 3.5): document translation services and real-time interpretation services. In document translation they provide offline translation of physical documents and online translation of digital documents. In interpretation they offer interpreter services in telephone conferences and interpreter services in videoconferences. First we see how this impacts TTU's business functions and processes. After that, we discuss the way TTU handles change management.

Business functions and business process

To cater to the differences in services provided, TTU has a product-type-oriented e-sales process structure (as opposed to POSH, which has a client-type-oriented process structure).

The TTU e-sales process is shown in Figure 6.31. Because TTU only works for registered customers (typically business customers), they have to log in first. Then,

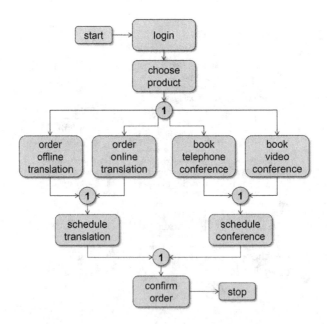

FIGURE 6.31   TTU e-sales process.

they choose the product they wish to order. Based on this choice the process proceeds further.

In contrast to the POSH e-sales process, e-business object delivery, billing and payment handling are not part of the TTU e-sales process. This is a process design choice. The reason TTU makes this choice is the fact that they prefer to bill after service delivery (as the amount depends on the delivered effort) and they don't consider delivery a part of sales.

Change management

TTU recognizes that innovation is of paramount importance to their existence. TTU does not employ translators or interpreters – they use freelancers who are hired in a just-in-time fashion. This means that TTU itself only offers digital services: on the one hand, they couple organizations requiring language services and individuals who can provide them; on the other hand, they make available electronic infrastructures supporting the delivery of these services. Hence, the TTU business model can easily be copied by competitors if it remains too static.

The facilitator for innovation within TTU is its R&D department. TTU is keen on keeping this department aligned with their business operations. For this reason, TTU has decided to have an innovation and change management (ICM) team consisting of key members from the organization – from management, R&D and operations departments. The ICM team has regular meetings to discuss possible new developments in an open atmosphere. Three points are always on the agenda:

1   New requirements to TTU services indicated by existing customers.
2   New technological developments in document translation, audio and videoconferencing.
3   New business opportunities; that is, possible new services and possible new customer groups.

Developments in automatic translation and telepresence technology [Wik14b] make point 2 a very important issue for TTU. For point 3, TTU uses the extreme-thinking approach (see Figure 6.25).

6.9.3 TraXP

Because TraXP follows the service-dominant business paradigm, the organization has designed its internal organization and its collaboration in its e-business network in a strictly service-oriented way (as we have discussed in section 6.6; [Gre13a]). This leads to strong modularity of business functionality and hence to a high level of agility: when requirements change in the business aspect, elements in the organization aspect can quickly follow with low redesign costs. This approach is based on the use of a business service catalog and the use of services from this catalog as activities in business processes. We discuss these two elements here.

Business service catalog

The TraXP business service catalog contains specifications of all business services that provide functionality that is relevant to TraXP customers (these are the customer-facing business services) – both internal services that TraXP provides itself and external services that are offered by other parties in the business network of TraXP.

Business services are organized in *business domains*, which are related to business functions in a traditional organization. Each domain has an *owner*; that is, a TraXP employee responsible for the domain.

A simplified overview of the TraXP business service (BS) catalog is shown in Figure 6.32. Here, we see a set of sixteen business services organized in five business domains. Dark-colored services are internal services; light-colored services are external services.

Each business service in TraXP's business service catalog has an SLA attached (as introduced in section 6.6.1). SLAs of internal services are mainly used to predict and monitor the behavior of internal business functionality. SLAs of external services are used to select external partners (e.g., in terms of costs or in terms of availability) and to monitor their performance during the execution of services.

To support a market offering to customers, a set of services is selected from the catalog to provide the business functionality required for this market offering. This set of services is the basis for a service composition (SC). In Figure 6.33 we see the selection of services for the service composition of TraXP's executive offering (denoted as /X).

Business processes

The services in a service composition are used as the activities for a business process (which acts as a service orchestration). The process is created from the composition by adding the control flow; that is, flow of the dependencies between the activities. Constructing a control flow on top of an existing set of activities is a relatively light-weight task that can be performed quickly by TraXP's business process designers. TraXP uses an advanced graphical business process design environment. This means that implementing a new business process does not require any programming effort.

A simplified version of the business process for TraXP's executive offering is shown in Figure 6.34. The activities in this process coincide with the services in the composition of Figure 6.33. This process manages one trip for a TraXP executive-level customer.

First, the customer's profile is updated if required. Next, the best location for the business goal of the customer is selected (e.g., the most convenient meeting location) and the best transport to this location is selected. Then, transport and accommodation are booked in parallel. After a travel guide (hard copy or digital, based on the profile of the customer) is generated, the trip can commence. During the trip the traveler gets personal notifications about the next steps in the trip so

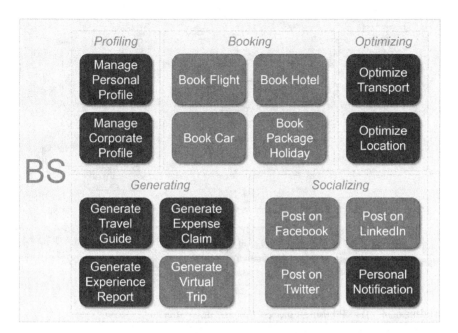

FIGURE 6.32 TraXP business service catalog.

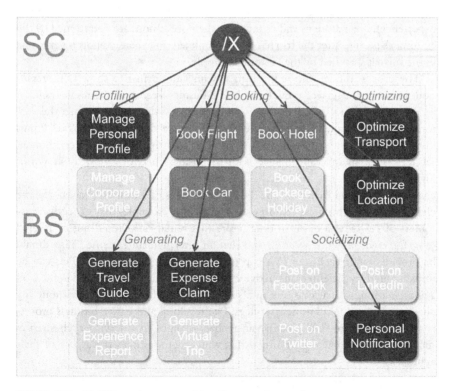

FIGURE 6.33 TraXP service composition from service catalog.

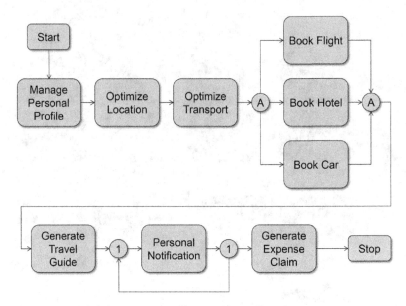

FIGURE 6.34 TraXP business process (for executive offering).

that he or she can travel completely worry-free (i.e., have the TraXP seamless travel experience). The nature of and channel for the notifications are determined by the customer's profile. After the trip has been completed, an expense report is generated in the format specified by the customer's profile.

The process model can be put into a swim-lane format to show the interactions between the service providers in the e-business scenario. The result is shown in Figure 6.35. TraXP formats the swim-lane process diagrams such that the customer is put in front, in line with the ideas of service-dominant logic. TraXP puts itself as the orchestrator between the customer and the providers of component services – this is in conformance with its business network view as shown in Figure 2.5.

Given the modularity of the business services, a business process can be changed easily if business requires so. Assume, for example, that executive customers of TraXP at a point in time desire that rental cars should not be offered (e.g., for environmental reasons) and that an intermediate expense claim should be provided after each step of a trip (to remain budget conscious). This can be implemented by deleting one activity from the business process in Figure 6.34 and repositioning a second one in a slightly modified control flow, without any change to underlying business services. The resulting alternative business process is shown in Figure 6.36. TraXP can realize changes to a service orchestration such as this one in a single business day, which demonstrates the agility of their approach.

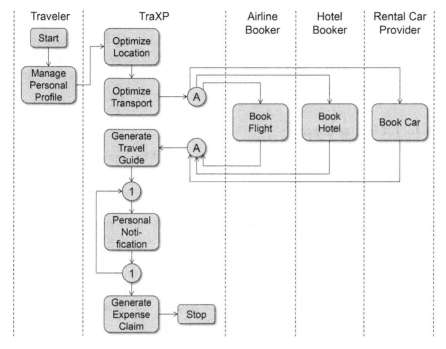

FIGURE 6.35 TraXP business process (for /X offering) in swim lane format.

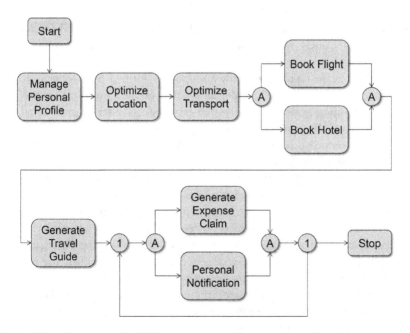

FIGURE 6.36 Alternative TraXP business process (for executive offering).

6.10 Chapter end

In this chapter we have treated the organization aspect of the BOAT framework. In this section we first summarize the main elements of this O aspect. Then, we provide a number of questions and exercises to allow the reader to apply the theory of this chapter.

6.10.1 Chapter summary

The first main ingredient of the O aspect is formed by organization structures for networked e-business. We distinguish *inter-organizational* and *intra-organizational* *structures*. The first class focuses on the interplay between parties in an e-business scenario. The second class focuses on the internal organization structure of individual parties in an e-business scenario. In the inter-organizational class we identify *main parties* (e.g., providers and consumers of e-business objects) on the one hand and *intermediary parties* (that support the collaboration of main parties) on the other hand. In the intra-organizational class we make a distinction between the *back end* and *front end* organization of an e-business party. The front end contains the organizational modules that implement the actual e-business collaboration. The back end contains core business functions with an internal orientation.

The second main ingredient of the O aspect is formed by *e-business functions*. Again we make a distinction between back end and front end to classify functions. Functions can be derived from standard business frameworks (such as Porter's value chain model) – extension and specialization towards e-business specifics of such models is necessary, though. In the service-oriented approach to networked e-business, we find business services that encapsulate (part of) business functions.

The third main ingredient of the O aspect is formed by *e-business processes*. E-business processes specify the order in which e-business functions are executed to achieve business goals. Main e-business processes are inter-organizational processes that cover the activities of multiple partners involved in an e-business scenario. In the service-oriented view, we find business *service orchestrations* that take the role of business processes.

Next to the core of the three main ingredients (structures, functions and processes), *operations management* and *change management* are important elements of the O aspect. Operations management is concerned with organizing e-business operations (i.e., the execution of e-business processes and functions) in an effective and efficient manner. Change management is concerned with keeping the organization prepared and agile for the adoption of new changes. The ever-changing world of e-business causes changes to be frequent, triggered by either the business context or the technological context. The O aspect ingredients are summarized in Figure 6.37. A clear mapping of B aspect elements to O aspect elements is required to enable well-structured change management.

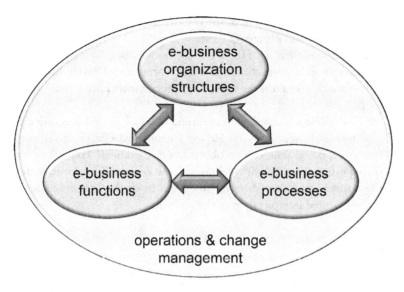

FIGURE 6.37   Main ingredient classes of the O aspect.

6.10.2   Questions and exercises

1. Try to find an existing networked e-business scenario with more than three parties. Specify the organization structure of this scenario in an e-business organization diagram. Explain why the scenario does indeed need this many parties by discussing that the parties are not intermediaries and that the scenario cannot be decomposed into two independent e-business scenarios.

2. Change the organization diagram of Figure 6.29 to the situation where the manufacturer is considered an intermediary (as discussed in the text). In other words, convert the three-party scenario to a two-party scenario.

3. At the end of section 6.4.2 e-business scenarios with reversed logistics are briefly discussed. Provide a practical example of such a scenario. Elaborate the business process including the logistics functions (see also Table 6.1).

4. The business process in Figure 6.22 contains a parallel split and a parallel join. Could this also be an alternative split and alternative join (see Table 6.3) in this specific process?

5. As discussed in this chapter, the process specification in Figure 6.14 is simplified. Extend this to the full specification. Note that this involves adding a number of alternative paths, using alternative splits and joins.

6. Design an elaboration of the *handle order* sub-process of the POSH sales process as shown in Figure 6.30. Allocate steps in the process to the involved parties. Note the different procedures for small goods (delivered from POSH stock)

and large goods (delivered from the manufacturer). Make further assumptions where necessary and document these.

7. Change the specification of the TTU sales process (see Figure 6.31) such that the *translation* and *interpretation* parts of the process are handled in sub-processes. In other words, transform the single-level process specification into a two-level specification.

8. One may ask how much down time (time in which no business activities can be performed) a year is acceptable for a networked e-business organization. How much down time can be planned and unplanned? Take a well-known existing e-business scenario (such as Amazon.com) and try to make an estimate. Analyze how this relates to parameters in service level agreements in a service-oriented interpretation of the scenario.

Notes

1 We revisit this issue when discussing change management in section 6.7.2.
2 This means that we take a step down the aggregation dimension of modeling.
3 Note that we use the term 'consumer' in two very different ways: it indicates a type of party (an individual person as opposed to a business or government party) and a role of a party (consumer as opposed to provider – as we use it here). Although this may be confusing, the term is generally used in both these ways and circumventing this would lead to unusual terminology.
4 This means that we take another step down the aggregation dimension of modeling.
5 The notation that we use for business processes can easily be mapped to standard notations with a more formal background, such as the Business Process Model and Notation (BPMN) [Freu12], UML Activity Diagrams [Fowl00] or Petri Nets [Aals02], or other informal notations such as Event-driven Process Chains (EPCs) [Wik14a].
6 Inter-organizational business processes are also referred to as *networked business processes* [Gre13b], *cross-organizational business processes* [Hoff00] or *collaborative business processes* [Liu07].
7 In our terminology, *process flow control* is executing the *control flow* of a process. In other words, *control flow* is a specification issue, *flow control* is an execution issue.
8 A book discussing the issue of predicting the 'unpredictable' in a broad context and a slightly polemic style is *The Black Swan* by Nassim Taleb [Tale07].
9 Note that we mean characteristics here in the O aspect; that is, characteristics that determine the way channels are used by organizations. Characteristics of a technical nature belong in the T aspect.
10 Note that the outgoing arcs at the split are labeled to provide more clarity to the process specification.

7

ARCHITECTURE ASPECT

Learning goals

- *Understand the concept of architectures for networked e-business and their organization in aggregation and abstraction dimensions.*
- *Understand the structure of hierarchically organized architectures for networked e-business.*
- *Understand the role of reference and standard architectures in a networked e-business context.*
- *Understand the role of service orientation for the architecture aspect of networked e-business.*
- *Understand the mapping of organization aspect elements (as discussed in chapter 6) to architecture elements.*

7.1 Introduction

Having discussed the business and organization aspects of networked e-business in the two preceding chapters, we now focus our attention on the architecture (A) aspect of the BOAT framework. Architectures in our context are blueprints for the design of information systems for networked e-business; that is, for the automated systems that support business functions and processes as discussed in the preceding chapter. In other words, architectures are designs of the structures of e-business systems – not so different from architectures in the building world where they are designs of the structures of houses or office buildings. In networked e-business, architectures form the interface between the non-IT elements (in the B and O aspects of the BOAT framework, as discussed in the previous two chapters) and the IT-related elements (in the T aspect of BOAT, which we discuss in the next chapter).

Given the scope of this book, we focus on architecture elements that are specific for networked e-business. This means that we do not discuss architecture in the broader context of general software engineering. Other good books are available that treat software system architecture in general (e.g., [Bass12, Tayl09]).

In the first section of this chapter we explain that architectures of systems for networked e-business are necessary to provide structure in a quickly changing context. After the need for architectures has been established, we move to the contents of architectures. We discuss the nature and main concepts of information system architectures, of which networked e-business architectures form a subclass. In the next three sections we discuss networked e-business architectures at three levels of aggregation (going from the structure of systems that span multiple organizations to the structure of systems that support part of a single organization): *market level*, *party level* and *system level*. As usual in this book, we end the chapter with our three running cases, a chapter summary and exercises.

7.2 The need for architecture

On the business side of networked e-business, we see a fast increase in required functionality of automated support for e-business operations. E-business systems become more and more complex as they cover an increasingly broad spectrum of business interactions. As we have observed with the *fully automated business* direction (see section 5.3.5), this may even lead to e-business systems covering (almost) all operational processes in an automated way. At the same time, an increasing level of quality is required of e-business systems as e-business operations are mission-critical for many modern organizations. E-business systems should not make errors, should have short response times, should be flexible, should always be available and so on. In the service-oriented view, quality requirements are made explicit in service level agreements (as discussed in section 6.6). Clearly, these two developments create a tension field between functional requirements and non-functional (quality) requirements: more and better are not always easy to combine.

On the technology side of networked e-business, we see something similar developing. A quickly increasing spectrum of diverse technologies is available, catering for all kinds of e-business functionalities. We discuss a selection of these technologies in the next chapter, and part of the functionalities is discussed in the introduction of the Big Five in chapter 2. The complexity that the deployment of a combination of all these technologies creates, however, requires an increasing level of e-business system structure to keep technology 'under control'. Without proper structure, e-business systems will end up becoming a heap of 'spaghetti' of interrelated technologies. Again, the abundance of technologies and the required structure create a tension field.

As we have seen in section 1.5, technology push and requirements pull (demand pull) forces reinforce each other. This increases the speed of developments in the networked e-business area in a cyclical way. This increasing speed of change further stresses the two mentioned tension fields. All these forces are illustrated in Figure 7.1.

To keep the relationship between the business and technology sides manageable, clear structures must be designed that describe the mapping of both sides to each other. These structures must be of an abstract nature, such that they are independent of specific, concrete choices made at either the business or the technology side. This independence of specific choices ensures that the structures remain stable over time.

In terms of the BOAT framework, these structures must form an interface between the B and O aspects on the one hand and the T aspect on the other hand. This is exactly what the *architecture* aspect of the BOAT framework is about: it has a pivotal function between the other aspects, as shown in Figure 7.2. This pivotal role is closely related to strategic business–IT alignment, as discussed in section 10.2.

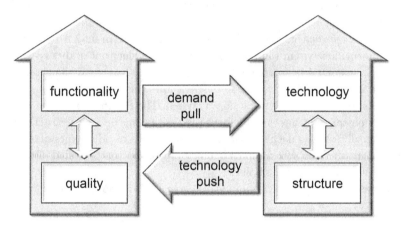

FIGURE 7.1   Tension fields in e-business development.

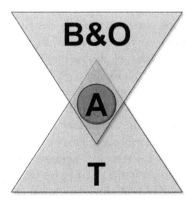

FIGURE 7.2   Architecture as a pivotal point in the BOAT framework.

7.3 A basis for networked e-business architecture

As discussed in the introduction of this chapter, architectures are blueprints for e-business information systems. We have seen how they form the pivot point between business-oriented aspects and technology-oriented aspects. Before we embark on the discussion of the structure of e-business architectures, we need a better understanding of what architectures exactly are. Providing this basic understanding is the goal of this section. We first discuss the concept of *networked e-business architecture*. Next, we discuss two dimensions along which we can position architecture descriptions. Then, we discuss several classes of architecture descriptions.

7.3.1 The concept of networked e-business architecture

Information systems have become more and more complex – we have discussed this as it pertains to networked e-business systems in the previous section, but this holds too for other types of information systems. To deal with this complexity, the concept of *architecture* has emerged in the information system field. An architecture of an information system can be seen as a high-level blueprint of that system that serves to understand its internal structure to aid in its design, redesign, configuration and maintenance. This is not so different from the (technical) architecture of a complex building, a bridge or a subway system. The fact that an architecture is a *high-level* blueprint means that the focus is on the main, conceptual structures and not on small technical details. Again, this is comparable to other types of architectures: the architecture of a complex building or bridge is not specified in terms of individual bricks or nuts and bolts.

We use the following basic definition of a general information system architecture:[1]

> *The architecture of an information system specifies the structure of that system in terms of functional software components that support specific functions, and interfaces that support the interactions among those components.*

The fact that an information system architecture describes software and interfaces means that hardware components (such as server machines) and physical connections (such as glass fiber links) between these are not part of the architecture. Hardware architectures exist too (see, for example, [PaOU05]), but they are not within the scope of this book.

As the previous definition states, an architecture describes a *structure* of a system. This means that we should use a clear method of representing that structure. Therefore, architectures are preferably described by means of diagrams (as opposed to a natural language textual description). There are specific diagram techniques for information system architectures (e.g., based on UML [Fowl00]), allowing for the specification of various kinds of characteristics of architectures. In this book, however, we use a simple, pragmatic notation. In the remainder of this chapter we will see examples of architectures.

The concept of *networked e-business information system architecture* is a specialization of the general concept of information system architecture discussed earlier. Obviously, the functions and interfaces supporting interactions between parties are of utmost importance in the networked e-business case, as e-business is about interactions between business parties enabled by automated systems (recall our definition of e-business from section 1.2). In the remainder of this book we will use the term *e-business architecture* as an abbreviation of *networked e-business information system architecture* – just to be brief.

7.3.2 Aggregation and abstraction levels

We can describe e-business architectures at various levels – from simple, high-level structures to more detailed, low-level structures. To be sure of what we describe we need to understand the nature of these levels. Following, we explain two important dimensions along which we can describe architectural levels: the aggregation and the abstraction dimensions.

The aggregation dimension

We can specify architectures of large information systems, but also of parts of these large information systems, of parts of these parts and so on. In other words, architectures can be specified at multiple levels of detail or, in the other direction, at multiple levels of *aggregation*. The aggregation levels are positioned along the aggregation dimension for architectures. When we move down this dimension (decreasing the aggregation level) we zoom in on architectures, analyzing smaller structures with a higher level of detail. When we move up this dimension (increasing the aggregation level), we zoom out, analyzing larger structures with a lower level of detail.

What holds for information system architectures in general also holds for e-business architectures: these can also be described at multiple aggregation levels. In this chapter we discuss e-business architectures at three aggregation levels:

Market-level architectures describe the structure of e-business systems at the level where multiple parties engage in business within a networked e-business market. Market-level architectures are inter-organizational architectures, because they focus on the relationships between systems of the parties in a market. This implies that they describe systems of multiple parties.

Party-level architectures describe the structure of e-business systems at the level of individual organizations; that is, individual e-business parties. As we describe e-business systems, the interfaces to the outside world (the e-business market in which the organization operates) are important, but the outside world itself is not covered. Hence, party-level architectures are intra-organizational architectures.

System-level architectures describe the structure of individual systems of an individual e-business party. An individual system can be a functional component in a party-level system that supports a specific business function (as identified in the O aspect of the BOAT framework – see section 6.4) or a general-purpose system that supports multiple business functions.

Market-level architectures can be refined[2] into party-level architectures, which can be refined into system-level architectures. The other way around, system-level architectures can be aggregated into party-level architectures, which can be aggregated into market-level architectures. We show both relationships in Figure 7.3. The number of party-level architectures related to one market-level architecture depends on the number of parties in a market (we show only two party-level architectures in the figure for reasons of simplicity). The number of system-level architectures related to one party-level architecture depends on the number of e-business systems used by the corresponding party (we again show two system-level architectures in the figure for reasons of simplicity). The number of systems depends on the complexity of the functionality supported by the party and the functionality offered by the systems: more complex functionality supported by a party typically implies more systems; systems with a greater functionality imply less systems.

Note that multiple similar parties in a market can share the same party-level architecture: this means that they have organized the structure of their e-business systems in similar ways. But they can also have different party-level architectures while conforming to the same market-level architecture.

The abstraction dimension

Information system architectures (end hence e-business architectures) can be described at various levels of *abstraction*: we can describe an architecture not only in

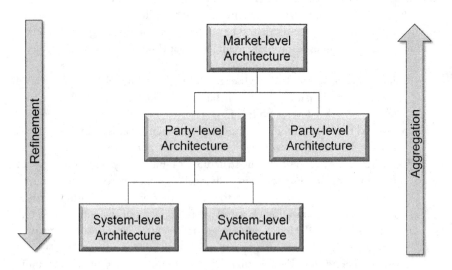

FIGURE 7.3 E-business architecture aggregation levels.

very abstract terms but also in very concrete terms – and in terms in between. The various abstraction levels are positioned along the abstraction dimension.

If an architecture is described in abstract terms the components in the architecture are specified very generally, typically by only labeling their functionality (or class of functionality). A label may be, for example, *e-payment system* or *enterprise resource planning system*. If an architecture is described in very concrete terms the components are described very precisely, typically by labeling the functionality plus the exact type of the component in terms of software vendor and software version. A concrete label is, for example, *XPay E-Payment Server Version 3.14a*. This is illustrated in Figure 7.4.

In the remainder of this chapter we explain that we use abstract architectures to show general structuring principles for e-business systems; that is, principles that are applicable to various scenarios. Here, we find, for example, principles regarding the structure of systems relating to the inter-organizational nature of e-business or the fact that e business systems must be flexible in their functionality. We use concrete architectures to show the structures of e-business systems in specific e-business scenarios. We discuss concrete architectures, for example, in the context of our running cases POSH, TTU and TraXP.

Aggregation versus abstraction

Where the aggregation level of an architecture is about the size or scope of the system (and hence about the number of bottom-level functionalities that are covered), the abstraction level is about the number of attributes of the components (the concreteness of description) in the architecture.

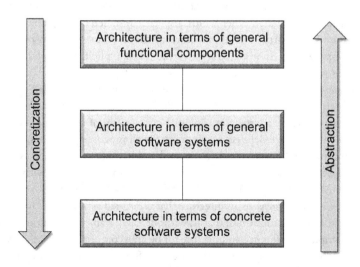

FIGURE 7.4 E-business architecture abstraction levels.

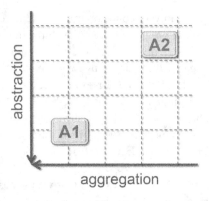

FIGURE 7.5 Aggregation and abstraction dimensions.

In principle, the abstraction level and aggregation level can be chosen independently for an architecture description: they are orthogonal, as shown in Figure 7.5. In this figure, architecture A1 is highly aggregated and abstract, and architecture A2 is detailed and concrete.

7.3.3 Reference, standard and instance architectures

When talking about information system architectures – and hence about e-business architectures – it is good to distinguish among various kinds of architecture, depending on their origin and goal. There are three kinds of information system architectures in this respect that one can distinguish:

- An *instance architecture* is the architecture of one specific information system in one specific context; in other words, a specific instance of a type of system. An example is the party-level architecture of the e-business system of one specific organization. An instance architecture is not explicitly designed to contain structures that can be reused in multiple contexts.
- A *standard architecture* is an architecture that is defined as a standard for a class of information systems within a specific organization context. This specific context is typically a large company or a consortium of companies. A standard architecture may be defined, for instance, for all procurement systems within a holding of companies. As such, a standard architecture can be used as the basis for the definition of an instance architecture of a specific system within its class and within the organization context of the standard architecture.
- A *reference architecture* is an architecture that is defined as a standard for a class of systems across organizations; that is, without having an organizational context. An example is a reference architecture for business process management systems in general (we discuss an example in section 8.4.2). A reference architecture is

often defined by an independent party, such as a standardization body or a government organization. A reference architecture can be used as a basis on which to define a standard architecture, or to directly define an instance architecture. A reference architecture can also be the basis for other reference architectures (where the other reference architectures are typically more elaborated).

The three kinds of architectures and their relationships are shown in Figure 7.6. The arrows between the classes indicate the 'can be based on' relationship between architectures.

A reference architecture is typically more abstract than a standard architecture, because a standard architecture contains organization-specific choices. A standard architecture is more abstract than an instance architecture, because an instance architecture contains specific choices for the one concrete situation for which it is designed. Hence, the three architecture kinds can be positioned along the abstraction dimension that we have discussed earlier in this section (see Figure 7.6).

Because interoperability between systems plays a very important role in networked e-business, reference and standard architectures are of great importance in this domain. The use of standardized architecture structures is a basis for ensuring that systems based on these architectures will 'fit together'; that is, they will be able to communicate and collaborate in automated processes, within the boundaries of an organization but very importantly also across the boundaries of organizations.

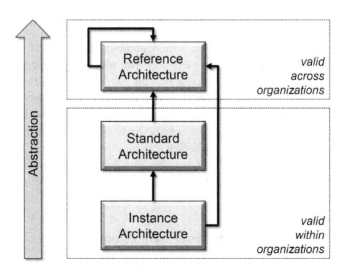

FIGURE 7.6   Reference, standard and instance architecture.

Now that we have completed our discussion of the basics of architecture, it is time to move on to actual networked e-business architectures.

7.4 Market-level architectures

In this section we discuss the highest aggregation level of networked e-business architectures: market-level architectures. We first discuss the concept of market-level architecture. Next, we explain the structure of such an architecture. Then, we pay attention to the role of reference and standard architectures at the market level.

7.4.1 The concept of market-level architecture

A market-level architecture describes how the main software systems interact that belong to the main organizations participating in an e-business scenario. These systems together form the networked e-business system for the e-business scenario. We use the following definition (a specialization of the general definition of information system architecture discussed in the previous section):

> The market-level architecture of an e-business system for a scenario defines the structure of that system at the inter-organizational level in terms of functional software components that support specific functions of the main business parties involved in the scenario, and high-level interfaces that support the interactions among those components.

There are several words in this definition that deserve some further explanation. A market-level architecture has an *inter-organizational* character. This means that a market-level architecture describes the information systems of all partners participating in an e-business scenario, not of a single partner. As we have seen in the previous chapter about the O aspect of BOAT, in a simple case this means two main parties are complemented with a number of intermediary parties. In a more networked scenario, multi-party scenarios also are possible, which leads to market-level architectures covering systems of more involved parties. In a market-level architecture, the emphasis is on support for collaboration between the parties. A market-level architecture contains *functional software components*; that is, software systems that support specific business functions. It also contains *high-level interfaces*; that is, the links between these software modules. The emphasis is on interfaces between software components belonging to different parties, as these implement the collaboration between the parties (i.e., the market-level interactions).

7.4.2 The structure of market-level architectures

After having discussed the concept of a market-level architecture, it is time to turn to its structure. Because a market-level architecture describes the interactions between the systems of the main parties involved in an e-business scenario, its overall structure is determined by the topology of these parties (the business network) collaborating in the e-business scenario. Typically, there is a strong congruence (structural similarity) between high-level models in the O aspect of BOAT and market-level architectures in the A aspect, as both contain interactions within the same business networks of organizations – the O aspect models interactions between organizations; the A aspect models interactions between systems of those organizations.

Figure 7.7 shows a simple, abstract market-level architecture. Here, the architecture has been elaborated for an e-business scenario consisting of two collaborating parties (party A to the left and party B to the right) and one intermediary party (party I in the bottom of the figure). The shaded areas in the figure indicate the party boundaries. Modules labeled with *BES* indicate back end component systems; that is, systems that support back end business functions as discussed in section 6.4. Likewise, modules label with *FES* indicate front end component systems. We show more concrete architectures at the end of this chapter when we discuss our case studies.

A market-level architecture focuses on the relationships *between* the involved parties, showing the systems and interfaces between the parties implementing these relationships. In the figure the systems are the boxes, and the interfaces are the arrows between the parties.

The interfaces are labeled with the types of messages they are meant to exchange (labeled from *m1* to *m6* in the figure); for example, *advertisement, purchase order* or *payment*. We will see more elaborated examples when we get to our running cases at the end of this chapter. Note that an interface often exchanges more than one message type (for a bidirectional interface usually at least two). Therefore, each message label represents a set of message types.

With respect to the systems in the example architecture, we clearly see the separation between front end systems and back end systems at all three parties. This separation is analogous to the separation between front end and back end functions in the O aspect (as discussed in section 6.3.1). The interfaces between front end systems and back end systems of one organization are elaborated in the party-level architectures, as discussed in the next section.

The front end systems support front end business functions, such as advertising, purchasing or paying (see the reference model in Table 6.1). As the interaction between systems of collaborating parties is modeled in a market-level architecture, the front end systems are individually identified. Note that there is not necessarily a one-to-one mapping between front end business functions in the O aspect and front end systems in the A aspect: one system may support multiple functions, or one function may require multiple systems. Note also that multi-channeling between two parties may have an impact on the architecture: each channel may result in a pair of front end systems with an interface.

All back end systems of a party are shown as a single 'black box' (i.e., an architecture module without internal detail), as their internal structure is not relevant for system interfaces at the market level: a party only 'sees' the front end systems of its collaborators. The back end systems are elaborated in party-level architectures (as we will see in the next section).

Note that it is possible to abstract a market-level architecture by aggregating all systems of a party into one composed system. If we do this for the example in Figure 7.7, we get the architecture shown in Figure 7.8. This aggregated architecture corresponds in level of aggregation with the level 2 organization architecture as shown in Figure 6.4. The architecture showing the individual front end systems of the parties is, however, much more informative about the interfaces between systems – which is the basis for support for e-business interaction. Hence, we skip the aggregated market-level architecture in our approach.

So far, we have seen a simple market-level architecture. Obviously, the architecture topology depends on the business scenario: there may be more than two collaborating parties, no intermediary at all or multiple intermediaries. A market-level architecture with many parties can get quite complex. We show a more complex example in Figure 7.9: this is a market-level architecture corresponding with the organization structure shown in Figure 6.3. Here, party A corresponds with the consumer, party B with the provider and party C with the set of provider's providers. Parties I and J are the intermediaries in the e-business scenario.

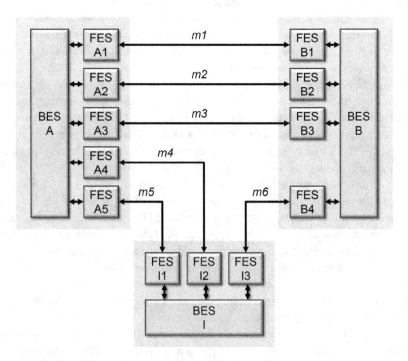

FIGURE 7.7 An example abstract market-level architecture.

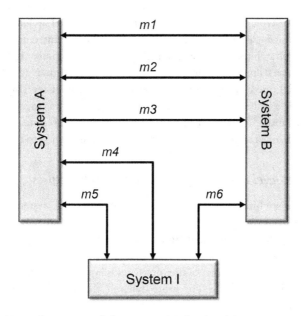

FIGURE 7.8 Example aggregated abstract market-level architecture.

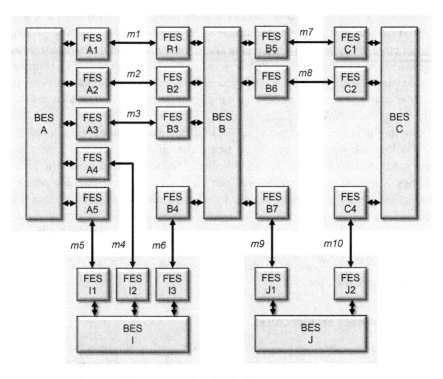

FIGURE 7.9 Abstract multi-party market-level architecture.

Note that we typically model *party types* in a market-level architecture: if there are multiple similar parties in a scenario, we show their architectures as one type in a market-level architecture. In a retailing scenario, for example, there typically is one provider (the selling party) and a large number of consumers (the buying parties) – we model one class of consumer systems in the market-level architecture. In Figure 7.9, there is only one party A system and one party C system, even though the scenario covers more concrete organizations. The party type is instantiated multiple times when realizing a market-level e-business system conforming to the architecture.

7.4.3 Market-level reference and standard architectures

In market-level architectures, interoperability of e-business systems of multiple autonomous parties is a major issue – if not *the* major issue. Hence, standardization of the functionality of components in an architecture is very important: this way, other parties know what to expect when contacting an e-business system of another party. Obviously, standardization of the interfaces is equally important, as they actually implement this contacting. The more dynamic the time scope of a scenario is (as discussed in section 3.6), the more urgent this issue becomes: in static scenarios, there may be time to 'repair' lacking interoperability, but in dynamic scenarios, things 'should fit' on the fly. Reference architectures (and standard architectures in smaller organizational scopes) can be used to obtain standardization across parties.

Because e-business scenarios can be classified, it can be expected that there will be similarity in architectures for scenarios within the same class. Classification can, for instance, be performed on the basis of the business model of the scenario (as defined in the B aspect of the BOAT framework – see chapter 5). For example, market-level architectures for e-retailing scenarios will all have similarities because they require support for a number of standard business functions (as identified in the O aspect of BOAT – see chapter 6).

In the architecture (A) aspect of BOAT, reference architectures should be technology-independent: one should first focus on *what* functionality must be included, and later on how this functionality is actually realized in specific technology. Many 'reference architectures' that currently exist for e-business interaction, however, are technology-specific. In other words, they do not focus on the general, conceptual interaction of e-business systems in terms of abstract functionality but focus, rather, on describing the structure of a specific technological solution for e-business interaction. Therefore, this kind of architecture belongs in the technology (T) aspect of the BOAT framework. In chapter 8 we discuss examples from this class.

7.5 Party-level architectures

In the previous section we have discussed market-level architectures for networked e-business systems. In this section we take one step down the aggregation hierarchy (as in Figure 7.3) and discuss party-level architectures. We first discuss the concept of party-level architecture. Next, we discuss the structure of party-level architectures.

Then, we pay attention to the role of reference architectures and standard architectures in the design of party-level architectures. We end this section with an explanation of the relationship between party-level architectures and enterprise architectures.

7.5.1 The concept of party-level architecture

A party-level architecture for networked e-business systems describes the system structure of one single party (possibly an intermediary) in an e-business scenario. We use the following definition (again, a specialization of the general definition of architecture discussed in section 7.3.1):

> *The party-level architecture of an e-business system for a party in an e-business scenario defines the structure of that system at the intra-organizational level for that party in terms of functional software components that support specific functions of that party, and high-level interfaces that support the interactions among those components as well as interactions with other parties in the scenario.*

Where a market-level architecture is inter-organizational, a party-level architecture is intra-organizational. As such, a party-level architecture is a refinement of a part of a market-level architecture – the part that coincides with one specific party. This implies that a complete elaboration of a market-level architecture leads to more than one party-level architecture; that is, one per party involved in the e-business scenario (as shown in Figure 7.3). The complete elaboration of the architecture in Figure 7.9 thus leads to five party-level architectures – if we include the intermediaries. All party-level architectures together form a partitioning of the refinement of a market-level architecture.

In a party-level architecture we provide more details than in a market-level architecture. The main refinements are the following:

- We detail the back end systems (which are black boxes in the market-level architecture).
- We show interfaces between back end systems.
- We detail the interfaces between front end systems and back end systems.
- We show main platform systems that are shared between business function systems, such as database management systems (including the main shared databases) and business process management systems. Platform systems do not provide functionality related to specific business functions, but support the business function systems that do provide business functionality.

7.5.2 The structure of party-level architectures

Networked e-business systems have party-level architectures with a general structure consisting of front end systems, back end systems and platform systems. We discuss this general structure in this section.

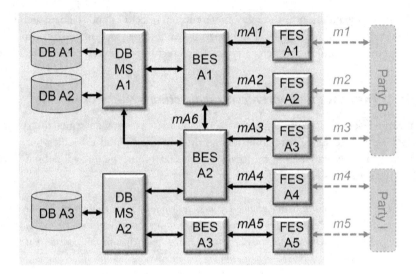

FIGURE 7.10 An example party-level architecture.

In Figure 7.10 we see an example of an abstract party-level architecture of a networked e-business system (we will see a concrete example when we get to our running cases at the end of this chapter). This architecture is the refinement for party A of the market-level architecture shown in Figure 7.7. In the figure the boundary of party A is indicated by the shaded area.

In the party-level architecture, we show the same front end systems as in the corresponding market-level architecture for the party at hand (*FES A1* to *FES A5* in the example). We show the other parties of the market-level architecture as *external entities*, depicted by rounded rectangles and dashed external interfaces to them corresponding to the market-level architecture. Note that message labels for external interfaces are consistent with the market-level architecture. The rest of the party-level architecture is an elaboration of the black-box back end system in the market-level architecture of the party at hand.

In the example we show three back end systems (*BES A1* to *BES A3*) and two platform systems: the database management systems *DBMS A1* and *DBMS A2*. The back end systems support the back end business processes of the party, such as financial administration, product management and inventory management. The database management systems manage the data for the back end systems. The data reside in databases *DB A1* to *DB A3*.

The interfaces between front end systems and back end systems, on the one hand, and between back end systems, on the other hand, are labeled with the message types (which can be sets of messages types, as in the market-level architecture). Note that we choose to include the party name (or an abbreviation of that in a practical situation) in the labels to avoid confusion with labels at the market level (e.g., when the number of market level interfaces would be increased).

7.5.3 Party-level reference and standard architectures

As for market-level architectures, reference (and standard) architectures are also important for party-level architectures. At the party level, reference architectures provide standard solutions for the high-level organization of complex e-business systems within one party.[3]

The use of standard solutions implies reusing existing knowledge to prevent 'reinventing the wheel' over and over again. As such, the use of reference and standard architectures can decrease both the realization time of e-business systems and the costs of this realization. Also, the number of flaws in an architecture design can be reduced, as reference architectures present 'proven solutions'. The use of standard solutions also improves the understandability of designs between different designers.

Another important advantage of the use of reference architectures is the easy adaptation of available standard software components. Obviously, when following standards the likelihood of a 'match' is greater than when using complete greenfield designs.

7.5.4 Party-level architectures and enterprise architectures

An *enterprise architecture* (also called *corporate architecture*) is an overall blueprint of the structure of all main information systems in an organization. In other words, an enterprise architecture specifies the structure of the complete information processing infrastructure of an organization. E-business architectures specify the information processing infrastructure related to a specific e-business scenario in which an organization participates. Consequently, there is a relationship between the corporate architecture and the e-business architecture(s) of a networked e-business organization.

Each party-level e-business architecture represents one e-business scenario. An organization may, however, be involved in multiple e-business scenarios (and in multiple traditional business scenarios as well). Therefore, a party-level architecture is a subset of an enterprise architecture tailored to a specific e-business scenario. In other words, a party-level architecture is an enterprise architecture projected onto one specific e-business scenario.

Typically, if a business organization engages in multiple e-business scenarios, it reuses part of its systems across the scenarios. Consequently, the party-level architectures for the different scenarios overlap within the enterprise architecture; that is, they share common functionality in terms of systems and interfaces identified in the architectures. This is illustrated in Figure 7.11 for an organization that engages in three e-business scenarios (we show a concrete example when we get to the case studies at the end of this chapter).

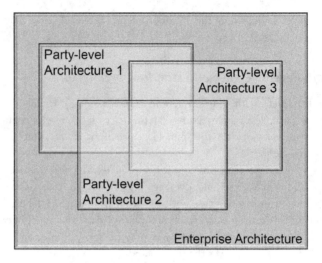

FIGURE 7.11   Party-level architectures in the context of an enterprise architecture.

7.6 System-level architectures

After the discussion of party-level architectures in the previous section, we now move one level further down the architecture aggregation dimension (see Figure 7.3) and arrive at system-level architectures for networked e-business systems. A *system-level architecture* is a refinement of one component in a party-level architecture, as discussed in the previous section. Here, we discuss the concept and structure of system-level architectures. We end the section by discussing the role of reference architectures and standard architectures at this architecture aggregation level, as we have done for the other levels in the preceding sections.

7.6.1 The concept of system-level architecture

A system-level architecture of a networked e-business system describes the system structure of one specific e-business information system of one party (possibly an intermediary) in an e-business scenario. We use the following definition (similar to the previous definitions of a specialization of the general definition of information system architecture discussed in section 7.3.1):

> *The system-level architecture of an e-business system defines the structure of one specific information system of one specific party in an e-business scenario in terms of functional software components that support specific sub-functions of a business function of that party, and interfaces that support the interactions among those components and between the components and their environment.*

Obviously, a system-level architecture is intra-organizational, because it is a refinement of part of an intra-organizational party-level architecture. A system-level architecture is the specification of the structure of either a front end system or a back end system identified in a party-level architecture. Platform systems are mostly standard systems that are bought 'off-the-shelf' – their internal architecture is usually not very interesting from the viewpoint of networked e-business.

7.6.2 The structure of system-level architectures

The structure of a system-level architecture heavily depends on the nature of the system that is described. Architectures of simple systems consist of a few components; those of complex systems may consist of many components.

Figure 7.12 shows an example of an abstract system-level architecture (we will see a concrete example when we get to the running cases at the end of the chapter). The architecture is the elaboration of system *BES A1* of the party-level architecture shown in Figure 7.10 (the boundaries of this system are shown by the shaded area in the figure). The system-level architecture shows that *BES A1* internally consists of four modules, labeled *BES A1.1* to *BES A1.4.*

As the figure shows, systems with which the system at hand communicates are shown as external entities, indicated by rounded rectangles. The interfaces to these systems must be consistent with those specified in the corresponding party-level architecture (both the interface topology and the message sets). Interfaces between the internal components of the system at hand are specified and labeled with message sets. These are *mA.BES_A1.1* to *mA.BES_A1.3* in the example – with the module label included in the message set label to avoid confusion at the party level.

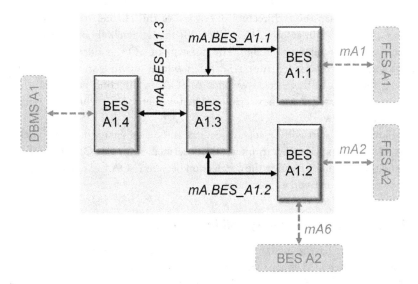

FIGURE 7.12 An example of system–level architecture.

7.6.3 System-level reference and standard architectures

At the system level of networked e-business architectures, reference and standard architectures play an important role as well, like they do at the party and market levels. At the system level, they define blueprints of structures of individual e-business systems.

Reference architectures define system structures that are generally applicable; that is, the application of which is not confined to a single organization. Reference architectures define standardized interfaces to standardized functional modules. Having standardized structures is of great importance to enable interoperability between systems (especially in case of front end systems) and reusability of (designs of) systems across different, autonomous organizations. Reference architectures exist for specific classes of business function systems, such as electronic contracting systems [Ange08]. Reference architectures also exist for classes of platform systems, such as business process management systems [WfM94].

Standard architectures have a similar function within the scope of a single organization. Consequently, they are less important for enabling interoperability and reuse across organizations. They are important, however, for standardizing structures in large organizations, which may have many instantiations of the same system type across departments of those organizations.

7.7 The service-oriented view

In sections 5.8 and 6.6 we have introduced the service-dominant view of the business aspect and the related service-oriented view of the organization aspect of networked e-business. In this section we continue the discussion of service orientation for the architecture aspect of the BOAT framework. In essence, this means that we map the architecture discussion of this chapter to the concept of service-oriented architecture (SOA) [Rose08] that is generally applied to information system architecture design. The concept of SOA is often linked to the technology of web services [Alon04, Papa07], which provides an implementation context for SOA. In this section we stick to SOA on the conceptual level – web services are discussed in the next chapter when we get to the technology aspect of the BOAT framework.

Following, we start with discussing services as the elementary building blocks in SOA. Next, we explain how to interconnect services from an SOA point of view. We end this section by treating the connection between SOA and cloud computing in the context of networked e-business.

7.7.1 Services as elementary building blocks

In section 6.6 we have seen how business services are the elementary building blocks for the service-oriented design of the organization structures of networked e-business. In the design of service-oriented architectures for networked e-business we have a very similar situation: services are the elementary building blocks for architectures.

A service in the architecture aspect is the specification of an encapsulated module of functionality with a well-defined interface. Each service in an architecture maps to a software service in the technology (T) aspect of the BOAT framework.

When moving to a service-oriented architecture concept, the first issue is to map the modules in architecture descriptions (as we have seen before in this chapter) to service structures. In doing so, the granularity of services is an important issue in SOA design. With granularity, we mean the 'size of services'; that is, the amount of functionality each service holds. Services should not be too large, because this makes them hard to reuse and compose. Services should not be too small, because this renders their functionality unclear from the business point of view. For architectural purposes, services can be clustered into groups, or *service containers*. With this clustering we can take as a point of departure for design that service containers coincide with business functions as we have identified them in the organization aspects (see section 6.4), and that individual services within containers coincide with activities in business processes (see section 6.5).

After we have mapped the functional modules, we have to map the interfaces between these modules as well. In the SOA concept, services collaborate by invoking each other's methods through their interfaces.[4] Method invocations activate the functionality of a service (from the service invoker to the service provider), possibly parameterized with data that is relevant for the service execution. As a consequence of the invocation, the service provider can return results to the invoker. This means that the message sets that we have seen before in this chapter for non-service-oriented architectures are replaced by parameterized service invocations.

7.7.2 Enterprise service bus as a connector

One of the main principles of service-oriented architecture is that of loose coupling between services. Loose coupling means that services can be connected easily to create new (business) functionality and that connections can be dissolved easily as well. Loose coupling is achieved by the application of two mechanisms: a mechanism for finding services with a specific functionality and a mechanism for easy interconnection of services. The first mechanism is typically found as a service broker, and the second mechanism as an enterprise service bus (ESB). Because the interconnection of services has a strong architectural impact, we focus on the concept of ESB in this subsection.

An ESB is used as a general connector between all functional components (services or service containers) in a service-oriented architecture. Each component is linked to the bus such that it can connect to all other components. This hides the actual functional connection between pairs of components; that is, the invocations of services in execution practice. The emphasis is on connectivity regardless of specific invocations – this implements flexibility in service orchestration.

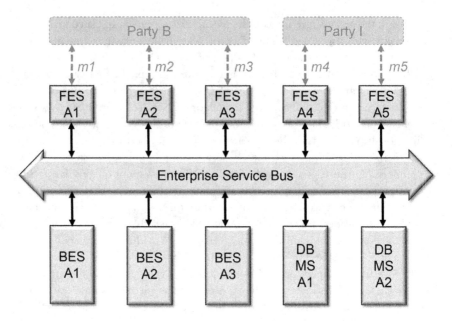

FIGURE 7.13 Enterprise service bus as connector in party-level architecture.

An example is shown in Figure 7.13. Here we see a service-oriented redesign of the party-level architecture of Figure 7.10. Each module in the architecture is a service container that contains a number of services. In this case *FES* is the acronym for front end services, *BES* for back end services and *DBMS* for database management services. Each container (and thus the services in it) is linked to the enterprise service bus. Because we have chosen the party level as the aggregation level for this architecture, the links to external parties are not channeled through the ESB. It is possible, however, to have inter-organizational connections in a market-level architecture also channeled through an ESB. In this case, either an inter-organizational ESB is required or multiple intra-organizational ESBs that are linked to each other. Note that Figure 7.13 does not show any databases: following service-oriented principles, data are encapsulated by services – in this case, the databases are encapsulated by the two *DBMS* containers.

7.7.3 Service-oriented architecture and cloud computing

Two developments that are often seen in connection are service-oriented architecture and cloud computing (see, for example, [Barr13]). As we have seen in this section, service-oriented architecture is a way to structure an information system architecture (in this book, a networked e-business system architecture). As we have seen in section 2.2, cloud computing is a way to make use of remote ('in the cloud') computing resources to achieve a number of advantages, such as flexibility in resources (elasticity).

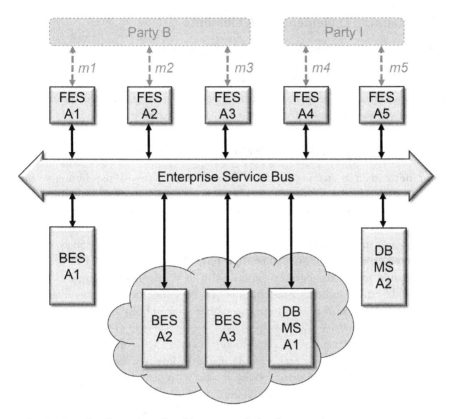

FIGURE 7.14   Service-oriented architecture and cloud computing.

In the modular setup of a service-oriented architecture with service containers and services, some containers or services may be provided by a third party in a *software as a service* (SaaS) cloud computing setting. This means that using cloud services does not change the functional service topology but the organizational allocation of some services. This is illustrated in Figure 7.14. Here, we see how the architecture of Figure 7.13 has been modified to allocate three service containers to the cloud. The fact that these containers are linked to the enterprise service bus implies that 'moving the containers to the cloud' has no impact on the other containers and the services in them.

Some networked e-business organizations may even consider moving their entire architecture to the cloud so that they no longer have to manage a computing infrastructure. This can be done using the SaaS paradigm such that an organization uses off-the-shelf service functionality offered by a cloud provider. This can also be done using a *platform as a service* (PaaS) or *infrastructure as a service* (IaaS) paradigm such that an organization uses its own functionality, but is remotely hosted. The SaaS approach may be easiest from a technology management point of view, but it may offer the least room for unique, distinguishing functionality in the service offering towards the customers of the organization.

7.8 Mapping O elements to A elements

As we have seen in this chapter, high-level architectures in the A aspect of the BOAT framework have structural similarities with organization structures in the O aspect. Obviously, this is not a coincidence: there is a mapping between O aspect elements and A aspect elements. In this section we discuss two principles that guide this mapping.

7.8.1 The form is function principle

For networked e-business, a close alignment of business requirements and information systems is essential to obtain good functional and non-functional behavior of e-business applications. This close alignment can be obtained by striving for isomorphism between organization structures (as defined in the O aspect) and information system structures (as defined in the A aspect). This is expressed by the *form is function principle* [Gre03a]: the structure of an architecture should follow the business functionality it is designed for. Important elements identified in the O aspect should also be visible in the A aspect, and the way they are organized with respect to each other in both aspects must have a clear mapping.

In the simplest case, there is a one-to-one mapping between high-level descriptions in O and A aspects: each module in the O level corresponds to a module in the A aspect. Often, however, reality is a bit more complex than this. Take, for example, the situation illustrated in Figure 7.15. At the left, we see the organization structure (at level 4) of an e-business party A (analogous to Figure 6.6; the other parties are omitted for reasons of clarity). At the right, we see part of a market-level

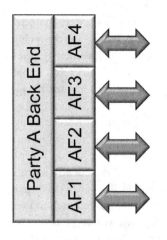
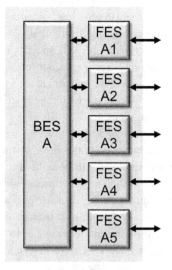

FIGURE 7.15   O aspect structure (left) versus A aspect structure (right).

TABLE 7.1 O to A aspect mapping matrix

		A aspect modules				
		FES A1	FES A2	FES A3	FES A4	FES A5
O aspect modules	AF1	X				
	AF2		X			X
	AF3			X		
	AF4				X	X

architecture of the same organization A (analogous to Figure 7.7; other parties are again omitted). The number of front end organization modules (four) is different from the number of front end architecture modules (five), so obviously there cannot be a one-to-one mapping.

Explicitly describing the mapping in a concrete situation is strongly advised, as this will make high-level dependencies explicit when changes occur. The description can have the format of a mapping matrix, an example of which is shown in Table 7.1 for the mapping of Figure 7.15. The matrix specifies which O aspect module relies on which A aspect module for its automated support. We see in the matrix that each organization module has its own architecture module, but that two organization modules rely on a second, shared architecture module as well.

7.8.2 Modular design of information systems

In complex architectures (such as those of most networked e-business systems), a strictly modular design greatly enhances the maintainability of the architecture. Modularity implies that an architecture is partitioned into functional modules, each of which plays a specific role in the architecture as a whole. This partitioning can be based on the partitioning of the organizational functions of an organization – following the *form is function principle* as discussed previously. Note that often functions in an organization are relatively stable, whereas their interconnection changes more quickly as business models evolve: modern business needs to be *agile*. Maintainability relates to a number of issues that are of high importance for networked e-business systems.

First, networked e-business systems (and thus their architectures) are subject to frequent change as a consequence of the volatile market in which they have to operate – remember that in networked e-business, change is the only constant factor. A modular architecture design means that it is possible to replace (or add or delete) specific modules in the architecture while leaving other modules as they are. This greatly enhances the level to which a system is 'future proof'.

Second, most networked e-business systems are of considerable complexity. This means that it is usually not feasible to build such a system from scratch. Where possible, one should rely on existing modules where they are available on the market (so-called *common-off-the-shelf* (COTS) components) and only build new modules where functionality is so specific (or new) that ready-made solutions are not available. Traditionally this is often referred to as the 'make-or-buy decision'. The 'buy' option may imply indeed buying software, or buying the use of software (e.g., using cloud computing, as discussed in section 2.2). Nowadays, this question is more and more answered with 'buy', where bought modules are parameterized (tuned) for the context in which they have to operate. Reference architectures can be of great help here. To be able to flexibly deal with the make-or-buy decision a modular architecture is required, where modules are identified based on the high-level (O aspect) business functions they perform.

7.9 Running cases

In this section we return again to our three running case studies and discuss their architecture aspect. For reasons of brevity, we do not elaborate the POSH, TTU and TraXP architectures in full detail (that would almost require a book on its own). Instead, we show a number of architecture models at the three aggregation levels to illustrate the concepts discussed earlier in this chapter. In the TraXP architecture discussion we use the service-oriented architecture concept introduced in section 7.7.

7.9.1 POSH

We first discuss the market-level architecture of the POSH scenario. Then, we elaborate the party-level architecture of POSH – we omit the party-level architectures of the other parties in the scenario for reasons of brevity. Of this party-level architecture, we further elaborate one module into a system-level architecture – we omit the elaboration of the other modules, again, for reasons of brevity.

Market-level architecture

The market-level architecture of the POSH scenario is shown in Figure 7.16. We see again the three parties in the scenario, plus the three intermediaries (organization boundaries are indicated by background boxes) as we have seen them in the organization aspect. We show the customer party on the left side of the figure and POSH on the right side of the figure to be consistent with the organization structure diagram in Figure 6.29. We show the architecture of one single B2B customer to represent the class of all customers. Obviously, not all customers have exactly the same information system configuration, but compatibility with the architecture is required to enable coupling of systems and hence enable participation in the e-business scenario.

Because the architecture shows the structure of the information systems that support the POSH business organization, there is a strong structural similarity with the structure of the organization (as discussed in the previous chapter and shown in Figure 6.29). This is a consequence of following the *form is function* design principle that we have seen earlier in this chapter. We can see, though, that the mapping is not one to one: there are systems in the architecture that support multiple organizational modules, both at the POSH and the customer side. For example, the *order management* system at POSH supports both the *take order* and *bill* functions identified in the organization aspect.

The architecture in Figure 7.16 shows the message sets (labeled *m1* through *m10*) that the parties use to communicate. They can be specified in a table similar to Table 7.2. Note again that a message set can contain more than one type of

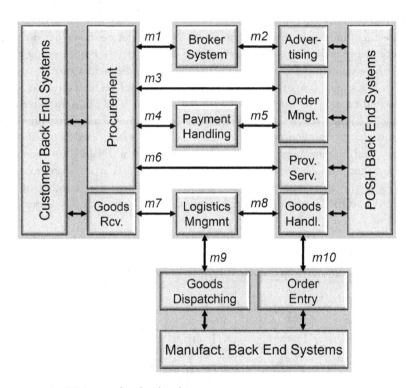

FIGURE 7.16 POSH market-level architecture.

TABLE 7.2 Message sets of POSH market architecture

Message set	Contents exchanged
m1	Provider search request; provider search result
m2	Provider profile; provider offer
m3	Order; order confirmation
m4	Payment order
m5	Payment notification
m6	Service request; service information
m7	Delivery notification; delivery confirmation
m8	Shipment request; shipment confirmation
m9	Shipment request; shipment confirmation
m10	Production order; production confirmation

message (as shown in the table). Each message type can be annotated with originator and recipient for additional clarity (this explains in which direction a message type flows along an arrow in the architecture diagram) – we have omitted this here for reasons of simplicity.

Party-level architecture

The party-level architecture of POSH is shown in Figure 7.17. We see the same front end modules and the same interfaces to external parties as in the market-level architecture (this should always be consistent). The modules are shown in a different layout order to make the resulting architecture diagram clearer. For reasons of brevity, we have omitted the specification of message sets in the architecture.

The back end systems module of the market-level architecture has been elaborated to show its internal structure. We see that POSH uses an enterprise resource planning (ERP) system as the core of its back end administration. The administration of providing furniture-related services is supported by a dedicated system. Both systems use a database management system (DBMS) for their data management. The *advertising* front end module uses data it retrieves from the ERP system – apart from that it has a dedicated data set in a number of files (there is no DBMS employed here because the data set is relatively simple and small).

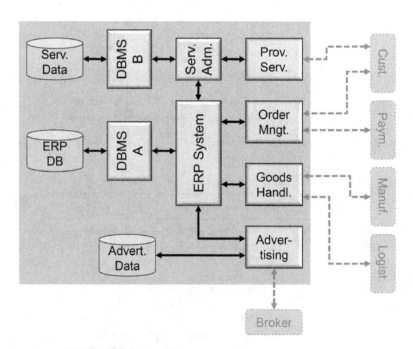

FIGURE 7.17 POSH party-level architecture.

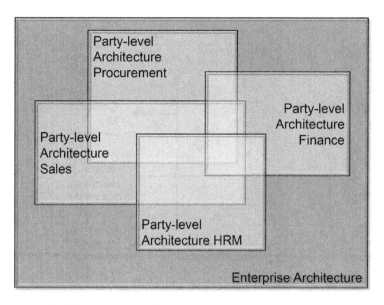

FIGURE 7.18   POSH enterprise architecture overview.

The presented party-level architecture is the architecture for the POSH sales e-business scenario. POSH is, however, also a party in e-business scenarios for procurement (to buy its products), human resource management (to have its personnel administered by an HRM service provider) and finance (to pay its bills). This results in an enterprise architecture overview as illustrated in Figure 7.18 (a concrete case of Figure 7.11).

POSH is currently considering moving its ERP functionality to the cloud using the *software as a service* (SaaS) paradigm. The reason for this is the fact that their current ERP system is getting outdated and that a solution based on cloud computing offers more flexibility in non-functional terms (such as performance). Given the nature of the business model of POSH, very specialized functionality in an ERP solution is not required, such that a relatively standard cloud solution will work well. This may lead to the party-level architecture shown in Figure 7.19 in the near future of POSH. Note that the use of a SaaS-based ERP solution removes the need for one of the DBMSs POSH uses in the current situation (as data management is encapsulated in the cloud).

System-level architecture

In Figure 7.20 we show the system-level architecture of the *order management* front end system of the POSH party-level architecture (see Figure 7.17). The shaded background denotes the system boundaries. Because the *order management* system is a front end system, there are interfaces to external parties and interfaces to other systems internal to POSH (in this case, to only one internal system). These interfaces

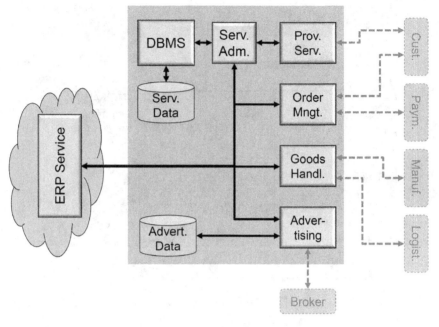

FIGURE 7.19 POSH party-level architecture with cloud-based ERP solution.

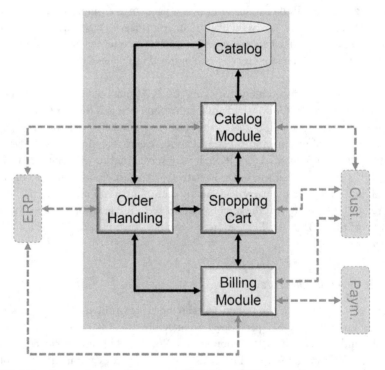

FIGURE 7.20 System-level architecture of POSH order management system.

are consistent with those in the party-level architecture. We have again omitted the specification of message sets.

As we see in the figure, the *order management* system consists of four modules: one that allows customers to use the electronic catalog of POSH and select items to buy, one that manages electronic shopping carts in which customers collect selected goods, one that performs the actual order handling and one that handles billing to customers. Three modules interact with the ERP system of POSH, in which stocks are registered and deliveries are planned.

7.9.2 TTU

Here we discuss the market-level architecture of TTU. We leave party-level and system-level architectures to the reader. After the discussion of the architecture, we provide a few words on reference architectures in the TTU context.

Market-level architecture

Figure 7.21 shows the market-level architecture of the TTU scenario. We see two elaborated main parties: TTU on the right side and a customer on the left side. The

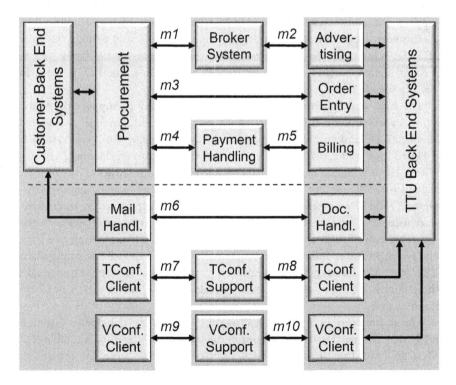

FIGURE 7.21   TTU market-level architecture.

TABLE 7.3 Message sets of TTU market architecture

Message set	Contents exchanged
m1	Provider search request; provider search result
m2	Provider profile; provider offer
m3	Order; order confirmation
m4	Payment order
m5	Payment notification
m6	Document to translate; translated document
m7	Teleconference details; teleconference contents
m8	Teleconference details; teleconference contents
m9	Videoconference details; videoconference contents
m10	Videoconference details; videoconference contents

architectures of the four intermediaries in the scenario have not been elaborated for reasons of brevity and simplicity.

We can see that the architecture consists of two 'functional parts' (as indicated by the horizontal dotted line). The part shown at the top of the figure supports the commercial processes of TTU: marketing, sales and billing. The part shown at the bottom of the figure supports the actual primary services of TTU: translation and interpretation. We concentrate on the latter part in the explanation herein – the former part is comparable to the POSH scenario described earlier.

The back end systems of TTU include functionality to support the translation of documents. Documents (both electronic and physical) are passed between TTU and customer through the *document handling* front end system at TTU and the *mail handling* front end system at the customer. The *mail handling* system has a connection to the back end systems at the customer to register the receipt of documents (similar to the receipt of other ordered goods). Telephone (*TConf.*) and video (*VConf.*) conferences are supported by intermediaries using the *software as a service* paradigm. Both parties have clients to the server systems of these intermediaries. The clients at TTU are coupled to back end systems to start and register conferences – because this is core business for TTU, they need a proper coupling to back end systems. At the customer side, these clients are stand-alone systems – dealing with conferences is not core business here.

The architecture in Figure 7.21 shows the message sets (labeled *m1* through *m10*) that the parties use to communicate. They are specified in Table 7.3. Message flow directions have been omitted from the table for reasons of brevity.

Reference architectures

TTU supports audio- and videoconferences across a spectrum of platforms, ranging from traditional telephone conferencing systems via broadly used communication platforms such as Skype (www.skype.com) to advanced telepresence platforms and dedicated meeting support systems. Currently, the interfaces to these platforms are not very well standardized. For TTU, it is important to couple these platforms to their back end systems such that conferences can be set up and joined automatically and activities in conferences can be registered automatically (for billing afterwards). Also, cross-platform interoperability is important to be able to link heterogeneous servers and clients into one conference, or even to couple multiple conferences. Development of reference architectures in this field is hence of prime interest to TTU to avoid an 'explosion' of different software structures and interfaces. For this reason, TTU actively participates in standardization committees that define these reference architectures.

7.9.3 TraXP

For the third case study of the architecture aspect we return to TraXP. In this section we first discuss the market-level architecture of TraXP – seeing that this is indeed a highly networked, service-oriented architecture. Next, we discuss TraXP's party-level architecture and the role of cloud computing.

Market-level architecture

Figure 7.22 shows the market-level architecture of TraXP. We see TraXP in the middle of the figure, the component service providers on the left and the travelers on the right. TraXP has chosen to have a service-oriented architecture so that it can stay as close as possible to its service-dominant business vision, which we have discussed in chapter 5.

TraXP has six main front end systems – three on the partner side and three on the traveler side. On the partner side we find systems for contract management (establishing a formal relationship with a partner), ordering (placing orders for travel elements, such as hotel reservations or airline tickets) and event handling (handling the travel-related events during travel execution, such as boarding a plane or checking into a hotel). TraXP expects mirrored front end systems with its partners (they may be sophisticated automated systems or simple email-based systems). On the traveler side of TraXP we find front end systems for registration and customer profile management, order entry (to enter requests for new trips) and communication to travelers (to send them travel plans or real-time travel instructions). A traveler is expected to only have a web browser and a communication system (that can accept electronic messages, such as a smartphone).

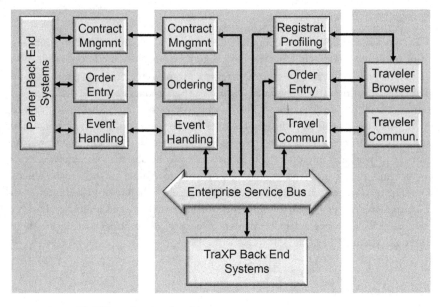

FIGURE 7.22 TraXP market-level architecture.

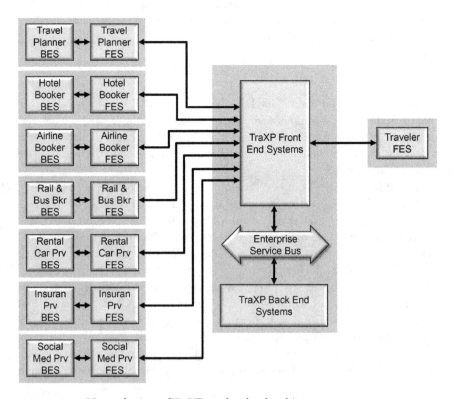

FIGURE 7.23 Network view of TraXP market-level architecture.

Note that on its partner side, TraXP deals with a wide variety of partner types, as reflected in its business network vision (illustrated in Figure 2.5). The front end systems have to interface to all these partner types. If we project this onto the market-level architecture (and aggregate the front end systems of each party into one module to keep the figure from becoming overly complex), we get the architecture of Figure 7.23. Note that in this figure each party represents a party class: TraXP may work with several parties of the same class (such as multiple airline bookers) and it certainly works with many customers.

This illustrates that a solid architecture design is essential for TraXP to deal with the complexity of its business model, and may be one of the leading advantages it has over existing competitors that cannot design an architecture from scratch; that is, have to deal with a legacy architecture.

Party-level architecture

The party-level architecture of TraXP is shown in Figure 7.24. We clearly see that the enterprise service bus (ESB) is the central interconnect in the architecture. Above the ESB we see the front end systems; below the ESB we see the back end systems.

TraXP has general-purpose systems for data management and business process management. Business process management is a key functionality to TraXP because

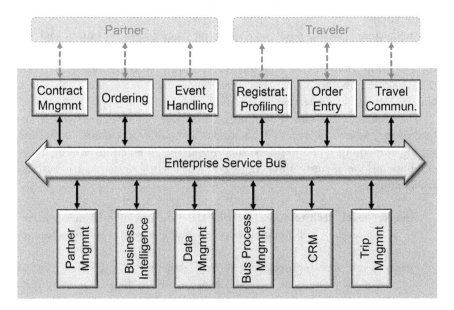

FIGURE 7.24   TraXP party-level architecture.

it functions as the spider in the web in the execution of travel plans in which many parties need to be synchronized. TraXP has a system for partner management and a customer relationship management (CRM) system. It has a trip management system to manage trips ordered by customers. Finally, it has a business intelligence system that it uses to make market analyses and forecasts – this is extremely important in the fast-changing travel market.

TraXP has decided to map its entire architecture to the cloud to minimize its upfront investments in hardware computing infrastructure and to be as flexible as possible with regard to capacity. Because it requires its systems to be completely state of the art, it does not use any functionality in the SaaS paradigm, but it deploys its own software using the IaaS paradigm.

7.10 Chapter end

We end the discussion of the architecture aspect of the BOAT framework with a summary of the most important concepts of this chapter and a set of questions and exercises.

7.10.1 Chapter summary

Architectures of networked e-business systems are required to manage the complexity and efficient developments of these systems. Architecture has a pivotal function between business and organization aspects, on the one hand, and technology aspects, on the other hand. Architecture is also the basis for interoperability between e-business systems, both within an organization and between organizations.

Architectures can be positioned along the aggregation dimension and the abstraction dimension. The position along the aggregation dimension determines the 'granularity' of the architecture (the size or scope of its components). The position along the abstraction dimension determines the concreteness with which components in the architecture are specified.

The architecture of an e-business information system defines the structure of that system in terms of functional software components, supporting specific functions, and interfaces, supporting the interactions among those components. We identify three aggregation levels for networked e-business architectures:

market-level architectures describe the structure of e-business systems at the level of collaboration between multiple parties in an e-business scenario;

party-level architectures describe the structure of e-business systems within the boundaries of a single party participating in an e-business scenario; and

system-level architectures describe the internal structure of individual e-business systems.

Party-level architectures are projections of enterprise architectures, because they describe the structure of the information systems supporting a single e-business scenario in which an organization (enterprise) participates.

Reference architectures describe proven system structures that can be reused across organizations. Standard architectures describe system structures that are reused within a single organization. Instance architectures describe structures of concrete systems. Instance architectures can be based on standard or reference architectures. Standard architectures can be based on reference architectures.

7.10.2 Questions and exercises

1. Specify the message sets for the party-level and system-level architectures of the POSH scenario (as shown in Figures 7.17 and 7.20). Use the format as shown in Table 7.2.
2. As discussed in the POSH case study, POSH considers moving its ERP functionality to the cloud using a SaaS solution. Would it also be possible to move its *order management* functionality (as illustrated in Figure 7.20) to a SaaS-based solution? Explain your answer.
3. The market-level architecture of the TTU e-business scenario is shown in Figure 7.21. Design a party-level architecture for TTU based on this market-level architecture. Discuss your major design choices.
4. Design a system-level architecture for the TTU *order entry* system. Use the TTU e-sales process shown in Figure 6.31 as input for your design, because this process is supported by the *order entry* system.
5. Select a real-world B2C e-business scenario and try to describe its market-level architecture. Make assumptions (educated guesses) where you cannot trace required details.
6. Select a real-world B2B e-business scenario and try to describe its market-level architecture. Make assumptions (educated guesses) where you cannot trace required details.
7. Does a system-level reference architecture for database management systems exist? Use the internet to try and find one.

Notes

1 Note that more elaborate definitions of the term 'architecture' also exist, which likewise pay attention to the way the structure of a software system is constructed (see, e.g., [Gref14]).

2 The term 'exploded' is also used in information systems modeling to indicate 'refined'.
3 In a sense, our distinction among front end systems, back end systems and platform systems can be considered a simple high-level reference architecture in itself.
4 These interfaces are (in a technical context) often referred to as *application programming interfaces*, or *APIs*. This term is, however, not specific to a service-oriented approach.

8

TECHNOLOGY ASPECT

Learning goals

- *Know the various classes of information technology used in networked e-business systems and understand their relationships.*
- *Understand basic internet and web technologies, as well as important advanced platform technologies for networked e-business.*
- *Understand the main classes of aspect-oriented technology for networked e-business.*
- *Understand the main classes of function-oriented technology for networked e-business.*
- *Understand how the main IT-based developments in the networked e-business domain (the Big Five) are related to the various technology classes.*
- *Be able to map architecture aspect elements as discussed in chapter 7 and business aspect elements as discussed in chapter 5 to technology aspect elements.*

8.1 Introduction

In this chapter we discuss the fourth aspect of the BOAT framework (see section 4.2): the technology (T) aspect. In the technology aspect we discuss how specific information technology classes are used to implement the information systems specified in the architecture (A) aspect (as discussed in the previous chapter).

In this chapter we start with the 'bare basics' of networked e-business technology: internet and web technology. After covering that we distinguish between three classes of advanced technology. First, we discuss *advanced infrastructure technology*; that is, information technology used to create a general, high-level basis (also called

TABLE 8.1 E-business technology classes.

		Functions	
		All	Specific
Aspects	All	*infrastructure technology*	*function-oriented technology*
	Specific	*aspect-oriented technology*	*not covered*

platform) for entire networked e-business information systems. Apart from infrastructure technology, there is more specific information technology. This technology can be subdivided into two classes. First, we have technology related to specific aspects of all (or most) business functions to be supported – we call this class *aspect-oriented technology*. Second, we have technology related to all (or most) aspects of specific business functions to be supported – we call this class *function-oriented technology*. The three technology classes are shown in relation to each other in Table 8.1. As indicated, we do not cover technology that is specific to one aspect of one business function – that would make things too specific for the scope of this book.

We discuss the three advanced technology classes in sections 8.3–8.5. The advanced infrastructure technology class contains a discussion of the service-oriented point of view – therefore, we do not devote a separate section to this view in this chapter (as we did in the preceding three chapters). After discussing the technology classes, we explain the relationship between the technology classes and the Big Five IT-inspired developments that we have introduced in section 2.2. In the two sections that follow, we pay attention to mapping issues between BOAT aspects: first to mapping from the A to the T aspect, then to mapping from the T to the B aspect.[1] Then we turn again to our three running case studies: POSH, TTU and TraXP. The chapter is – as usual in this book – concluded with a summary and exercise questions.

Note that this chapter focuses on technology that is of special relevance for networked e-business information systems. Clearly, most technology for information systems in general is also applicable to networked e-business systems. An example is general-purpose software engineering technology, such as object-oriented technology (e.g., CORBA [Bolt01], JavaBeans [Schi14], etc.). We do not cover this kind of technology in this chapter. Also, many technologies come (and sometimes go) – see, for example, Gartner's hype cycle report [Fenn05]. In this context, it is not the purpose of this chapter to be complete but, rather, to discuss the role of major technology classes in networked e-business. Other books are available that provide a more complete or more detailed description of e-business technologies (e.g., [Why01, Nels02,VanS03]) or information technology in a broader perspective (e.g., [Turb10]).

Note also that, although this chapter presents technology in various classes, one of the main challenges in the T aspect is the integration of multiple technology classes to arrive at 'seamless' networked e-business systems. A well-designed architecture (as discussed in the previous chapter) is an essential starting point to arrive at this integration.

8.2 The bare basics: internet and web technology

Obviously, the communication infrastructure on which most modern networked e-business systems are based is the internet and the web as a layer on top of the internet. As we have seen in chapter 1, the history of e-business is even heavily related to the history of the internet and the web. Therefore, the internet and the web form the technological 'bare basics' for modern e-business, or the basic infrastructure. Following, we briefly discuss the most important ingredients of internet and web technology to provide a basic understanding of this infrastructure.

8.2.1 The internet

The internet is the global network that forms the communication platform for most networked e-business scenarios. We have already discussed its history in section 1.3. The internet consists of a connected network of networks – which explains its name – to which internet hosts are connected. The operation of the internet relies on a stack of protocols that specify how computers communicate using the internet. A protocol specifies which messages are exchanged in which order between two or more computers.

The protocols in the stack are organized into four layers which make up the *internet protocol suite* (see Figure 8.1): the *link layer*, *internet layer*, *transport layer* and *application layer*. Following, we briefly discuss these four layers and the protocol suite. More details can be found in dedicated publications on internetworking (e.g., [Stev94, Come05]).

Link layer protocols

The basic network structure underlying the internet is defined using so-called *link layer protocols*. These protocols are defined for the operation of network links; that is,

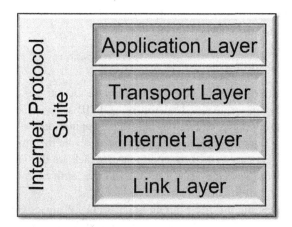

FIGURE 8.1 Internet protocol suite.

network connections at a low, technical level. These connections form the foundation for higher-level communication.

Link layer protocols support low-level communication functionalities. An important functionality is physically finding hosts on the internet. This can be performed by means of the *address resolution protocol* (ARP). Another important functionality is managing specific hardware networks. This is performed by means of protocols for specific network types, such as the well-known *ethernet* [Spur00].

Internet layer protocols

The basis for internet communication between internet hosts is formed by the *internet protocol* (IP). The internet protocol is defined on top of the link layer protocols. The IP sends data packets from one internet host to another without the requirement of first setting up a connection between these hosts. Therefore, IP is a connection-less protocol to operate a packet-switching (inter)network.

The internet protocol uses the *internet address* or *IP address* to identify a host. In IP version 4 (IPv4), the IP address is a 32-bit number, typically shown as four numbers in the range 0–255 (called *octets* because they each consist of eight bits) with dots in between, for example 121.122.123.124. As the range of IPv4 addresses is getting too small to accommodate the growth of the internet, the more recent IP version 6 (IPv6) uses a 128-bit address (consisting of sixteen octets).

Transport layer protocols

On top of the internet protocol, the *transmission control protocol* (TCP) is defined, forming the basis of the *transport layer* of the internet. TCP provides reliable, ordered delivery of a stream of bytes from a program on one internet host to another program on another internet host. TCP controls a number of traffic-related issues, such as message size, message exchange rate and network congestion resolution.

The combination of TCP and IP is often referred to as TCP/IP [Stev94, Come05] (pronounced as 'TCP over IP'). TCP/IP defines the basic communication mechanism for the internet.

Application layer protocols

TCP/IP is completely agnostic of any application on the internet. More functionally specific protocols are defined on top of TCP/IP as *application layer protocols*. These protocols support specific classes of internet applications.

Well-known examples of application layer protocols are the protocols for transmission of email messages, the most common of which are the *simple mail transfer protocol* (SMTP), the *post office protocol* (POP) and the *internet message access protocol* (IMAP).

Protocols for getting the web running (such as HTTP) are also application layer protocols based on TCP/IP, as we will see in the next subsection.

TABLE 8.2 Internet protocol suite structure

Protocol suite layer	Function	Example protocols
application layer	internet applications	POP, MIME, HTTP
transport layer	internet transport	TCP
internet layer	internet packet switching	IPv4, IPv6
link layer	network operation	ARP, ethernet

The internet protocol suite

Together, the *link layer* protocols, *internet layer* protocols, *transport layer* protocols and *application layer* protocols form the *internet protocol suite* (as illustrated in Figure 8.1 and summarized in Table 8.2). Given this protocol suite, the internet has a four-layer structure, which is also referred to as the *internet architecture*.

8.2.2 The (world wide) web

The *world wide web* (WWW), or *web* for short, is a communication infrastructure using the internet as its underlying platform and *hypertext documents* as its basic information structuring paradigm. A hypertext document is basically a document containing local content (such as text and figures) and *links* to other hypertext documents. The documents are commonly referred to as *web pages*. The web is navigated (or 'surfed') by following the links from web page to web page. Following, we first discuss *web protocols*, which define communication in the web. Next, we discuss the structure of *web addresses* (URLs) that are used by the protocols. Then, we pay attention to *web languages* that are used to specify the 'contents' of the web. We continue with a short discussion of the *semantic web*. We end this subsection with a few words on the *web 2.0* concept.

Web protocols

The *hypertext transmission protocol* (HTTP) is the basic protocol on which the web is built. HTTP supports the transmission of hypertext documents over the internet. HTTP is a request/response protocol in which a *client* (e.g., a web browser) requests the transmission of a web page from a *server* (a web server), which sends it as a response to the request. HTTP is defined as an application protocol on top of the internet TCP/IP protocol combination (see also Table 8.2).

The *hypertext transmission protocol secure* (HTTPS) is a combination of HTTP with the *secure sockets layer* (SSL) or *transport layer security* (TLS) protocol to provide message encryption and secure identification of web servers. HTTPS is commonly used for supporting transactions over the web that require the transfer of sensitive data, such as payment transactions.

Web addresses

Hypertext documents residing in the web are uniquely identified by a *uniform resource locator* (URL). A URL consists of an abstract domain address and an (optional) document address within a domain. The URL can be considered a pointer to a web page – each web page has a different pointer. The domain address points to an organization; the document address to a location within that organization. As such, a URL can also be seen as a web address.

The domain address of a URL has a hierarchical structure showing the hierarchy of web domains. Top-level domains are the last part of a domain address – they indicate countries (such as *.nl* for the Netherlands or *.mc* for Monaco) or global topical domains (such as *.com* for commercial organizations or *.org* for noncommercial organizations). Topical domains can also be organized per country, in which case one finds a combination in the URL (such as *.co.uk* for commercial organizations in the UK). Typically, organization names precede the top-level domain name in a URL. Before that, departments within organizations may be indicated, possibly with more than one level. A complete URL may thus look, for example, like one of the following:

> http://department.organization.country
> http://sub-department.department.organization.topicaldomain

A document address of a URL identifies a specific web page within the context of a web domain. It is specified after the domain address and can have a folder-like structure. As an example, the URL of the home page of the author of this book is:

> http://is.ieis.tue.nl/staff/pgrefen

The domain address of this URL follows the structure as explained earlier. The domain address indicates that this page is in the *is* sub-department of the *ieis* department of the *tue* organization in the Netherlands. The document address indicates that there is a web page with the name *pgrefen* within a folder structure named *staff*. When web pages are generated automatically to display temporary content, the document address may be a rather incomprehensible string to the casual observer. We see this, for example, with web pages displaying search results of search engines or product catalogs. A search on Google for e-business books can produce a URL such as this one:

> https://www.google.nl/?gfe_rd=cr&ei=MeddVKmJI4mD-waat4DoDQ&
> gws_rd=ssl#q=e-business+books

The *http://* prefix is often omitted when mentioning URLs. When a URL starts with *https://*, the HTTPS protocol is used to access the web page indicated by the address in a secure fashion. The structure of a URL is summarized in Figure 8.2.

FIGURE 8.2 URL structure.

Web languages

Hypertext documents are mainly specified using the *hypertext markup language* (HTML). HTML is a tagged language for specifying the structure of pages of human-readable information. A tagged language is a language that uses tags (specific labels) to identify characteristics in a text – in HTML, for example, the start and end of headings. HTML is mainly used to specify the structure of web pages of and links between web pages. Links between web pages are specified by embedded URLs. Using style sheets, the structure of a web page can be mapped to a specific layout such that a collection of web pages has a similar look.

Following the idea of a tagged language, the *extensible markup language* (XML) is a general-purpose tagged language that can be used to define specific tagged languages for specific purposes. As such, an XML-based language can be designed, for example, to specify financial transactions or to specify purchase orders between networked e-business parties. HTML can be defined using XML as well. XML allows the definition of the grammar of a specific tagged language using a *document schema definition* (DTD) or an *XML schema definition* (XSD) – the latter being the more modern standard.

Semantic web

The web protocols, addresses and languages as discussed earlier are mainly concerned with the structure of the web. Languages such as HTML describe the structure of web documents; that is, the *syntax* of these documents. A development in web technology is to try and describe the meaning of the contents of web elements such as documents and messages; that is, the semantics of web elements. This development is to result in a so-called *semantic web*. Having a semantic web, automated applications cannot only understand the structure of web pages but also reason about the meaning of their contents.

Semantics are usually based on the use of ontologies. An ontology is a conceptual structure in which the meaning of concepts and the relationships between concepts are specified, typically within a certain domain (e.g., a business domain such as banking or car manufacturing). Put very simply, an ontology is used as an 'extended dictionary' on the basis of which automated systems can interpret and reason about semantic messages. To achieve this, messages are 'annotated' with an identification of the ontology by means of which their contents can be interpreted.

As an example, we have taken the market-level architecture of Figure 7.7 and anno-tated the messages with ontologies, arriving at Figure 8.3. The figure shows that messages *M1*, *M2* and *M3* have to be interpreted with ontology *O1* and messages *M4*, *M5* and *M6* with ontology *O2*.

Languages have been developed for the specification of ontologies in the web context, the best-known of which is the *web ontology language* (OWL) [Wik14i].

Web 2.0

A term that appeared at the beginning of the twenty-first century is *web 2.0* [Wik14e]. The term refers to 'the second generation of the web'. Generally, this 'generation shift' is meant to indicate a change from the web as a set of static inter-linked web pages to the web as an integrated application platform for business and personal use, facilitated by a number of technological developments, such as:

- application logic that is built into websites (instead of into programs that reside on local computers);
- advanced levels of interactivity of websites and web-based applications, going beyond simple web surfing (see, e.g., web-based communication applications);

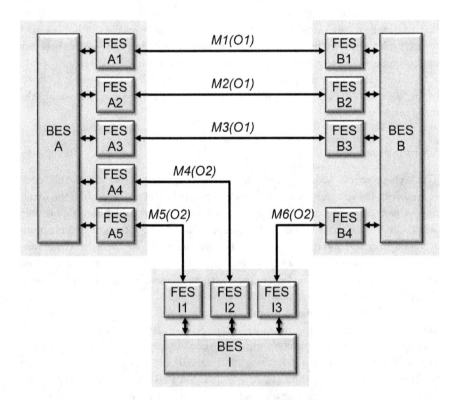

FIGURE 8.3 Market-level architecture with ontologically annotated messages.

- functional integration of websites and other information systems, making the web more than merely interlinked local sites (e.g., enabled by web services, which we discuss in section 8.3.3); and
- advanced use of multimedia characteristics, going beyond the text-and-simple-graphics approach that the web originally used to be based on; we find this, for example, in applications such as YouTube and Flickr (shown in Figure 8.4).

The application of web 2.0 technologies can contribute to increasing the richness of e-business communication (as discussed in section 5.2). Not everybody is convinced of the web 2.0 concept, though. This is not because the developments mentioned by web 2.0 enthusiasts are not considered important (there is little doubt about that), but because these developments can also be seen as a continuous evolution, such that there are no 'two versions' of the web but, rather, a continuum in time of new possibilities.

8.2.3 Some brief remarks

Two trivial but important remarks need to be made here to avoid the confusion that is often encountered 'in practice':

Figure reproduced with permission of Yahoo!. ©2014 Yahoo!. FLICKR and the Flickr logo are registered trademarks of Yahoo!.

FIGURE 8.4   An example web 2.0 application (with mobile client).

- First, the internet and the web are not the same thing (although many use the terms in an interchangeable fashion). The web is a hypertext based information structure using the internet as underlying communication technology. So, technically speaking, one cannot 'surf the internet' the same as one 'surfs the web'.
- Second, protocols and languages (for internet or web) are different things, although they are often intermixed. Protocols are used to specify *how* communication takes place, languages to specify *what* is communicated. In other words, put very simply: protocols are about transport, languages are about content.

Now that we have discussed the internet and web as the 'bare basic' technologies for networked e-business, we move on to more advanced technologies, starting with advanced infrastructure technology.

8.3 Advanced infrastructure technology

Advanced infrastructure technology provides a broad, general-purpose software platform for the implementation of networked e-business systems. This class of technology provides two main elements:

- a technological context in which functional modules (as identified in the architecture aspect) can be implemented; this context is a software engineering context that provides predefined primitives that cater to basic e-business operations (at some abstract level, depending on the kind of technology)
- a technological context facilitating the interoperability between functional modules; this context provides languages, protocols and mechanisms for exchanging information between software modules (where the abstraction level is again dependent on the specific kind of technology)

Because advanced infrastructure technology needs to provide quite a bit of functionality, its level of complexity is medium to high. To structure its functionality, a technology suite usually comes with a software architecture describing its structure. Note that an architecture of this kind may be easily mapped to an architecture in the A aspect of the BOAT framework if the infrastructure technology is structured at a high level of abstraction (i.e., close to business terms). The mapping may be harder in the case of lower-level infrastructure technology.

Following, we discuss four classes of well-known infrastructural technology: ebXML, RosettaNet, web services and multi-agent systems. For more detailed descriptions, the reader is referred to the material indicated in the reference list. ebXML is one of the older technology standards for networked e-business. We discuss it because of its well-structured nature – even if its application in current practice is limited. RosettaNet is a standard that has been applied mainly in the high-tech industry. Web service technology currently is considered 'the standard' for networked e-business. Finally, multi-agent systems form a class of technology that has been on the border of research and widespread practical application for quite a while.

After the discussion of these four classes, we take a short look at hybrid platforms, which employ more than one class of infrastructural technology. Note that many infrastructural technologies at this level assume an 'underlying layer' (actually an infrastructure or platform, too, as we have seen in the previous section) of internet or web technology.

8.3.1 ebXML

The ebXML standard is one of the older frameworks for the standardization of B2B networked e-business. It provides a framework for the implementation of software that supports e-business processes over the internet [OAS06]. As the name suggests, ebXML standards are based on XML (as discussed in the previous section). The ebXML development was initiated in 1999 by the standardization organization OASIS[2] and the United Nations/ECE agency, CEFACT.

Like most networked e-business frameworks, the ebXML framework supports dynamic collaborations between organizations. To accommodate this, parties that want to perform business transactions with each other can find each other through an ebXML registry (see Figure 8.5). This registry is an advanced form of an electronic yellow pages server. This registry can be considered an intermediary (in terms of the organization aspect of BOAT) that provides for dynamism in e-business relationships. This form of dynamism contributes to extending reach in e-business scenarios, as we have discussed in section 5.2.

As shown in the left side of Figure 8.5, conducting business following the ebXML framework requires performing a number of steps:

1   First, a process and information model is entered into an ebXML registry – this happens in the context of a specific industry group (related to a specific market). This step is typically performed by some form of business standardization body for the industry group.
2   Based on this, companies operating in the market can register their trading partner profiles (*collaboration protocol profile*, or CPP in ebXML terminology). Based on these profiles, companies can find interesting trading partners.
3   Based on their profiles, a trading partner agreement is specified (*collaboration protocol agreement*, or CPA in ebXML terminology), which defines the working business relationship between the companies.
4   The companies can next conduct actual business by exchanging business documents between their ebXML-compliant systems.

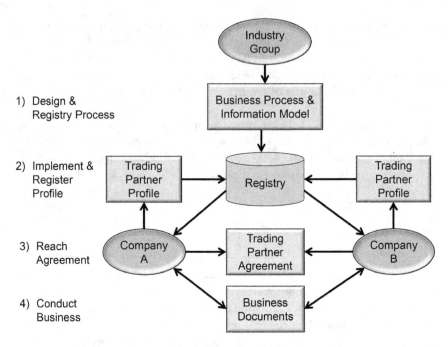

FIGURE 8.5 ebXML overview (adapted from [OAS06]).

ebXML defines a high-level technological framework, in which business documents and interactions are standardized. To fully adapt to ebXML, organizations have to adopt this complete set of standard documents and interactions. This makes the investment to start using ebXML substantial – hence the threshold is high for e-business situations where these investments may be less trivial.

8.3.2 RosettaNet

RosettaNet[3] is a non-profit consortium of major computer, consumer electronics, semiconductor, telecommunications and logistics companies that has created a set of standards with the same name for the support of open B2B e-business process interactions between organizations. In 2006 RosettaNet had more than 500 member companies [Boh07]. The RosettaNet standards allow companies in a supply chain in an industrial domain to more easily collaborate in an e-business context.

RosettaNet standards define message guidelines, business process interfaces and system implementation frameworks that support business interactions between organizations. RosettaNet standards are based on XML. As such, RosettaNet is comparable to the ebXML standard that we have discussed before.

In more detail, the aim of RosettaNet is to align the business processes of parties collaborating in supply chains [Rose09]. The alignment is implemented through the creation of so-called *partner interface processes* (PIPs). PIPs define how two business processes that each run in a different party are standardized and interfaced.

A PIP includes all business logic, message flow and message contents to enable the alignment of the two processes. The set in [Rose09] consists of about 100 PIPs.

8.3.3 Web services

Web service technology is currently considered the default platform of choice for new networked e-business applications. The web services framework specifies an internet-based set of technology standards for loosely coupled, distributed systems [Alon04, Papa07]. Following, we first introduce the web service concept. Next, we discuss the main standards making up the web services framework. Then, we place web services in the broader contexts of service-oriented computing and service-oriented architecture.

Web service concept

The basic concept of the web services framework is a *web service*, which is an encapsulated piece of software functionality that can be invoked through a well-defined web interface. It is encapsulated because only the interface is shown to the outside world – the implementation of the functionality shown in the interface remains invisible to the outside world. A service can itself invoke other services, such that complex services can be composed from simple services.

The main idea behind the web services approach is that of building complex functionality by composing modular functionalities in a loosely coupled way using a ubiquitous communication infrastructure. A composition of web services is loosely coupled because these services can be dynamically linked to each other at run time – this is in contrast to 'traditional software' in which connections between modules are defined statically at build time (hard-coded in software). The ubiquitous communication infrastructure is the web. This enables coupling services not only within the boundaries of organizations but also across these boundaries – obviously, the latter is of great importance for networked e-business.

In an e-business context, a web service typically implements a well-defined piece of business functionality. A web service may, for instance, implement an information service, an ordering business function or a payment service. By composing a number of these services, complex e-business systems can be constructed. In doing so, we are using a *service-oriented architecture* way of structuring a system, as we have discussed in section 7.7.

Web service standards

A number of standards exist that define the technical web services environment. We find standards for web service languages, web service protocols and web service software functionality.

The basic language for the web services environment is XML, as discussed before as part of the web basics (see section 8.2.2). All other web service languages are defined in XML. The basic communication protocol is the *simple object access protocol* (SOAP), a protocol defined on top of HTTP that allows basic object access via the web.[4] Following, we give an overview of the most important standards defined on top of XML and SOAP.

Two important languages exist in the web services environment. The central web service specification language is the *web service description language* (WSDL), which allows the specification of service interfaces. The *business process execution language* (BPEL or WS-BPEL) allows the specification of processes inside complex web services that use other web services (we revisit this language in section 8.4.2).

A number of protocols exist in the web services environment that provide specifications for the interaction between web services to obtain specific characteristics of their overall behavior. *The web services coordination* (WS-coordination) specification provides an extensible framework for defining protocols that coordinate the actions of distributed service applications. Such coordination protocols are used, for example, to reach consistent agreement on the outcome of activities that are distributed over multiple services. The web service transaction protocols are built on top of WS-coordination to provide transactional behavior to sets of web services. Two specific transaction protocols have been defined: *WS-atomictransaction* (WSAT) and *WS-businessactivity* (WSBA). WSAT provides a mechanism to implement atomic behavior over a set of services; that is, make sure that either all services in effect successfully complete or all services fail. WSAT is used to obtain all-or-nothing behavior of complex business transactions; for example, in the financial world. WSBA provides a mechanism to compensate (in effect undo) parts of a business process implemented in services. WSBA is used to undo parts of complex business transactions that have failed (and possibly try them again). *Web services agreement* (WS-agreement) [OGF07] is a web services protocol for establishing agreement between two parties that want to engage in business. *Web services security* (WS-security or WSS) is a protocol to apply security specifications in a web services environment.

A standard for brokering web services is defined as *universal description, discovery and integration* (UDDI) [OAS04], an XML-based standard for registries in which organizations can advertise their services or search services provided by other organizations. These registries provide advanced yellow pages functionality, comparable to the ebXML registries we have discussed earlier. A UDDI registry can be accessed through SOAP and contains WSDL specifications of services offered.

An overview of the discussed standards is given in Figure 8.6. In the figure we see the hierarchy of languages in the left column, the hierarchy of protocols in the middle column and UDDI as a software specification in the right column. The vertical dimension in this figure is an abstraction dimension. Standards at the bottom are lower-level, technology-oriented standards. Standards at the top are of a more abstract, application-oriented nature, using the standards below them in their column.

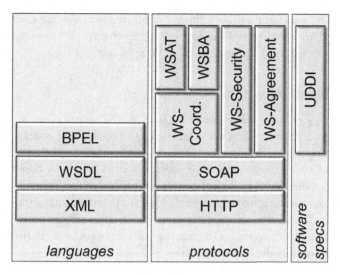

FIGURE 8.6 Overview of important web service standards.

Service-oriented computing and service-oriented architecture

The web service framework is the main basis for the *service-oriented computing* (SOC) paradigm, which (as the name suggests) has its roots more in computing and software engineering than in business frameworks. Although the SOC paradigm is not per se coupled to the web service technology (services can in principle be implemented in more traditional software technology), the combination is often made.

The fact that the web services stack is a rather open framework makes it easy to start using it for service-oriented computing: one does not need to adopt the entire framework for simple applications. In principle, the bottom two layers of Figure 8.6 suffice for very simple service-oriented applications. The implementation of full-blown, networked e-business systems may, however, require the application of quite a number of standards from the framework – hence causing considerable complexity.

When we use the SOC paradigm as a basis for the architectural design of information systems, we speak of *service-oriented architecture* (SOA) – as discussed before in section 7.7. Service-oriented architecture applied to enterprise e-business applications typically relies on two main technologies: *managed service platform* technology and *enterprise service bus* (ESB) technology. A managed service platform is a software platform that provides a set of basic mechanisms for the deployment and management of software services (such as data persistency and version control). An enterprise service bus implements the functionality to easily make interconnections between services – as we have seen in the architecture aspect of the BOAT framework in section 7.7.

The SOC paradigm has been further elaborated into the *grid computing* paradigm. This paradigm uses services to implement networks of computing resources called *grids* to support large-scale distributed applications.

8.3.4 Multi-agent systems

A technology class for networked e-business that is more or less in between a research and a practice status is the technology of multi-agent systems (MAS). In a multi-agent system, autonomous software modules (called *agents*) reason autonomously and communicate with their peers to achieve goals that have been given to them. In doing so, they do not merely react to commands given to them, but act on their own initiative to achieve their goals. As such, agents are autonomous, goal-oriented, proactive software components. Specific software frameworks have been developed for agents, of which the *belief-desire-intention* (BDI) framework [Rao95] is probably the best known.

The goal-oriented character of individual agents and the ability to communicate in agent communities makes them suitable for application in a networked e-business context (see, e.g., [Fas07a]); for example, to support automated negotiation between parties [Fas07b]. In such a context agents can represent parties that either collaborate or compete in specific markets to achieve the business goals of the parties they represent. Automated agents can engage in complex, repetitive negotiation protocols, which would be far too cumbersome for human negotiators.

A popular application field for agents is that of electronic auctions (see, e.g., [Vets08, Dobr09]). In these auctions agents place bids following specific bidding strategies depending on the kind of auction and the observed competition. Agents have also been used for other purposes where goal orientation and negotiation are important, such as the creation of dynamic virtual enterprises [Norm04, Meha10], related to the *dynamic partnering* business structure that is discussed in section 5.5.

8.3.5 Hybrid platforms

In complex settings the use of one advanced infrastructure technology class may be too limited to build a complete networked e-business system. The use of multiple classes may be necessary for several reasons. One reason is that multiple computing paradigms are required in different parts of a system because these parts have different basic functionality requirements. Another reason is that various pre-existing (standard) system modules are used as components in an e-business system and these modules require different platforms for their operations (i.e., they have been built using different computing paradigms). Following, we discuss an example hybrid platform that has been developed in a European research project.

The CrossWork hybrid platform

Figure 8.7 shows an example hybrid platform that has been used in the Cross-Work project [Gref09, Meha10] to support complex business processes in so-called *instant virtual enterprises* (IVEs). IVEs are highly dynamic virtual enterprises (see section 5.5) in which organizations cooperate in a peer-to-peer fashion. In CrossWork the IVE concept has been applied in the automotive industry to form business networks for the agile production of cars and trucks.

In the figure we see at the bottom a basic internet technology layer – as can be expected for a networked e-business system. On top of that we see both a multi-agent system (MAS) platform and a service-oriented computing (SOC) platform as advanced infrastructure layers. As shown in the figure, within the MAS and SOC platforms, respectively, more specialized technology is embedded. Business process management (BPM) technology is embedded in the MAS platform to handle the semi-automated construction of business process specifications. Workflow management (WFM) technology[5] is embedded in the SOC platform to execute constructed business processes. To enable communication to human decision makers, a user interface (UI) platform has been added on top of the other technologies.

In the CrossWork project the choice for a hybrid platform was made because one half of the system (the IVE construction part) requires goal-oriented reasoning technology, whereas the other half of the system (the IVE execution part) requires technology that facilitates interoperability to common-off-the-shelf (COTS) modules in a distributed topology.

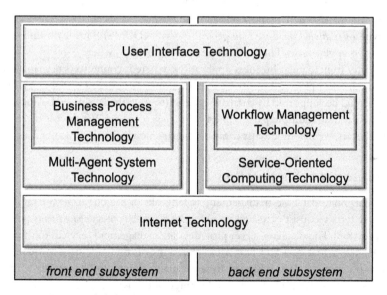

FIGURE 8.7   CrossWork hybrid platform.

8.4 Aspect-oriented technology

As discussed in the introduction of this chapter, aspect-oriented information technology supports specific aspects of a range of business functions. Mostly, these aspects belong in the non-functional category: they do not relate to *what* business functions do but, rather, *how* they do it. Typical aspects are, for example, security, transactionality [Wang08], performance and availability. As such, aspect-oriented technology can be related to a range of modules in the organization (O) and architecture (A) aspects – this in the sense that the technology supports specific characteristics defined for these modules.

In this section we discuss the following classes of aspect-oriented technology for networked e-business (noting that this is certainly not an exhaustive list):

*   data management technology
*   process management technology
*   human communication technology
*   security technology
*   performance technology
*   mobility technology

Each class of technology is discussed in the following subsections.

8.4.1 Data management technology

Clearly, data management is an important issue in networked e-business systems – as in every business information system. Data management is usually supported by a database management system (DBMS). In business applications we typically find the type of *relational database management system* (RDBMS). This is no different for e-business applications. There are some points, however, where e-business applications differ from 'regular business' applications where it comes to data management: multimedia data play an important role (e.g., in catalogs) and distributed transactions should be supported by database systems (to support data-based business transactions spanning multiple parties in an e-business scenario). We discuss these points here. To start, we briefly discuss database management systems, in general, as a basis.

Database management systems

Most corporate database management systems are of the client/server kind.[6] This means that they consist of a *database server* and a number of *database clients* (as shown in Figure 8.8). The database server provides data management services to the clients: it holds the actual data and performs operations on the data, such as queries and update transactions. It is designed to serve many clients simultaneously – in large organizations, this number can be in the range of thousands. Clients can be interactive interfaces for human users or information systems that require data management functionality.

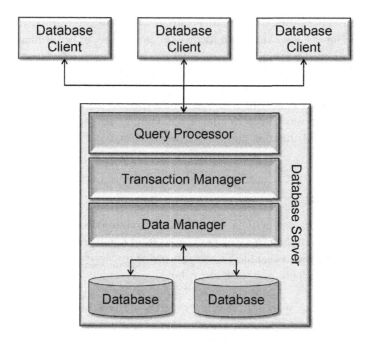

FIGURE 8.8 Simplified client/server DBMS architecture.

The database server consists of three main software modules (we have simplified things here a bit for reasons of clarity):

- The *query processor* takes commands (queries and updates) from the clients and transforms them into a format that can be easily processed by the other modules of the database server. Processing typically includes *query translation* and *query optimization*. Translation is required to transform a query from an external language to the language used internally in the database server − in this way, multiple external languages can be used. Query optimization is required to transform queries from a specification that is client-friendly to a specification than is execution-efficient − in this way, clients do not have to be aware of the efficiency of data management mechanisms in the server.
- The *transaction manager* is responsible for the enforcement of correct transaction semantics. Among other things, this means that *atomicity* and *isolation* of transactions must be managed. Atomicity means that a transaction consisting of multiple commands must be executed as a whole − we discuss this further on. Isolation means that each transaction should be executed without interference by other transactions. This is necessary because in a client/server environment, many concurrent transactions may be accessing and modifying the same data.
- The *data manager* performs the actual operations on the databases, such as the retrieval of query results, the insertion of new data and the modification or

deletion of existing data. The data manager can manage one or more databases – in Figure 8.8 we show two databases as an example. In performing database operations, the data manager uses auxiliary data structures called *indexes*, which enable efficient access to specific data in large databases.

As stated, networked e-business systems use database management systems to a large extent in a way similar to other types of information systems. Some aspects do require special attention in the e-business context, however – we discuss these further on.

Multimedia data

Because e-business applications often contain extensive electronic catalogs, there can be demand for the management of large sets of multimedia data (such as photographs, audio files, video files). This requires data management technology that is suited for this purpose. This technology should meet several requirements:

1   a large storage space for the data – in terms of the architecture in Figure 8.8, this means large databases;
2   the ability to find data quickly, based on a number of search criteria – this means that the data manager module requires indexes that can deal with multimedia data;
3   the ability to output large volumes of data quickly – this means that the data manager must not only be high performing but also that there must be a fast client/server connection.

The third requirement is important to handle peak loads, which may appear frequent in e-business scenarios. A typical example is an online music store that sells music in MP3 format. The release of a new song (or album) of a popular artist will create a very high peak load. For this purpose, internet data caching schemes exist, as well as organizations that exploit these on a commercial basis for third parties (we discuss an example when we get to performance technology in section 8.4.5).

Distributed transactions

In networked e-business, business transactions are conducted over the internet. These transactions are distributed, because they involve multiple autonomous parties. This means that one party performs one essential part of a transaction and another party performs another essential part. Although the transactions are distributed, they should be reliable in their effects. For example, when it comes to transferring money, it should be guaranteed that both a debit action for one party at one system and a credit action for the other party at another system are successfully completed – or none of them. In this case, *atomicity* of the transaction is required to make sure that no money evaporates (debit action succeeds but credit action fails) or appears out of the blue (debit action fails but credit action succeeds). To support this, we require distributed transaction processing (DTP) on top of data management. This means that the transaction manager of one database server must be able to synchronize with the transaction manager of another server to collaboratively execute one transaction.

We have already seen that the web services context provides transaction protocols (WSAT and WSBA, see section 8.3.2) that cater to distributed transactions. Database management systems used in web services should offer primitives supporting these transactions. An example standard for this purpose is the *X/Open XA protocol* [Wik14d] for distributed transaction processing.

8.4.2 Process management technology

In chapter 6 we have seen that business processes are a key element in the operationalization of networked e-business models. To obtain required levels of efficiency, the execution of these processes often must be supported by automated systems. Business process management systems or workflow management systems are specifically designed to support business processes [Leym99].

Business process management systems

In Figure 8.9 we see a high-level architecture of a business process (workflow) management system [WfM94]. This is the reference architecture designed by the Workflow Management Coalition (www.wfmc.org), a standardization body in the field of business process management. The core of the architecture is a *workflow enactment service*, consisting of a set of *workflow engines*. The workflow engines interpret workflow specifications (elaborated business process models as discussed in chapter 6) and activate agents according to these models. Agents can be human users or automated applications. The workflow enactment service communicates with its environment using a *workflow application programming interface* and a set of *interchange formats*.

Five interfaces are defined to the workflow enactment service (*IF1* to *IF5*):

Interface 1 (IF1) is the interface between WF enactment service and *process definition tools*. These tools are usually graphical editors used to specify a business process. After their definition, the process specifications are fed to the workflow enactment service to be enacted (executed).

Interface 2 (IF2) is used to invoke *workflow client applications*. Workflow client applications (also called *worklist handlers*) are used by human users in an organization to access the tasks that the workflow enactment service has assigned to them and to perform these tasks. These applications resemble email clients, but the user does not receive email messages to read but business tasks to perform.

Interface 3 (IF3) is used to invoke automated *applications* that perform tasks in a business process. These applications may run completely automatically, or they may be interactive and have interfaces to human users.

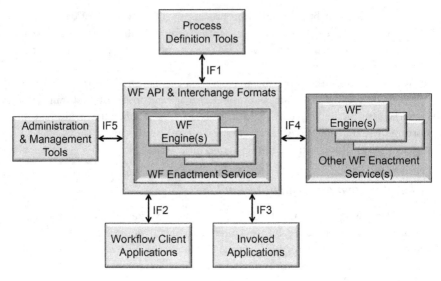

FIGURE 8.9 WfMC reference architecture [WfM94].

Interface 4 (IF4) is the interface to *other workflow enactment services*. These services may be employed by the same organization or by a different organization (in the case of inter-organizational business processes). Using IF4, a process enacted by one enactment service can invoke a process enacted by another service.

Interface 5 (IF5) is the interface to *administration and management tools*. These tools are used by a workflow administrator (WFA) to keep the workflow enactment services running smoothly and dependable.

Inter-organizational business process management

As we have seen in section 6.5, inter-organizational business processes are important in networked e-business. Here we first discuss the issue of process flow control in the context of the WfMC reference architecture. Then, we discuss concrete platforms for inter-organizational business process management.

In section 6.5.3 we have discussed the difference between unilateral, bilateral and multilateral process flow control. For unilateral flow control in inter-organizational business process management, the execution of a business process uses IF2 and IF3 of the WfMC reference architecture. In this case, business process flow control remains with one organization but the workflow clients or invoked applications may reside in another organization. A workflow client may be completely web-based, such that only basic web technology (see section 8.2.2) is required at a collaborating party: the workflow client is completely represented as dynamically generated web pages. This is certainly essential in highly dynamic e-business scenarios or B2C scenarios – in neither case it makes sense to install dedicated workflow clients for collaboration at a remote organization. For bilateral and multilateral flow control, IF4 is used to enable collaborative business process flow control. In this case, workflow enactment services of two or more organizations synchronize to enact an inter-organizational business process. In terms of the swim lane process diagrams we have seen in section 6.5, the workflow enactment service of each involved party manages the process part in its own swim lane and the IF4 interfaces are used to 'cross the lines' between the swim lanes in process execution.

Unilateral business process flow control is used practically nowadays, but multilateral flow control is not yet widely applied in practice. Advanced forms of inter-organizational business process management supporting various forms of flow control have been studied in research. Examples are the WISE, CrossFlow and CrossWork projects. The WISE project aimed at providing a software platform for process-based business-to-business electronic commerce in networks of small and medium enterprises [Alon99, Lazc01]. The CrossFlow project [Gref00, Hof01a] has developed prototype support for the business process management in dynamic service outsourcing business scenarios to form dynamic virtual enterprises (see section 5.5). The CrossWork project [Gref09, Meha10] has developed support for dynamic partnering scenarios (also see section 5.5) for dynamic virtual enterprises.

Business process management and web technology

We have mentioned how web technology can be used for the realization of workflow clients. Currently, we see that business process management technology is further converging with web technology. Web service technology plays an important role in this convergence. A major element in this development is the emergence of business process engines that enact business processes specified in BPEL (as discussed with web services in section 8.3.3). In process management these BPEL engines take the role of the workflow engine in Figure 8.9. Functionality of engines is sometimes still an issue here – in this development area, we currently find both proprietary (commercial) and open-source solutions [Harr13].

As an example, the CrossWork project mentioned earlier has used BPEL as the basis for the enactment of inter-organizational business processes. This is the main reason for having service-oriented computing technology as a platform in the CrossWork back-end subsystem (see Figure 8.7): this platform supports a BPEL engine that is used to execute inter-organizational business processes in a virtual enterprise. An inter-organizational business process in CrossWork consists of interlinked intra-organizational business processes that are supported by 'traditional' workflow management technology.

8.4.3 Human communication technology

Although many e-business scenarios rely on high levels of automation (with the completely automated business as an extreme – see section 5.3.5), human communication may be structurally required or as a means to handle exceptional situations. For this purpose, digital communication technology can be integrated into e-business systems to allow human communication over digital channels (usually, the internet).

We can distinguish the following main types of communication technology, based on the media supported:

Offline text communication technology provides the means to send text messages (often with file attachments containing other media) from one person to another in an offline fashion; that is, without the necessity of sender and recipient being online at the same moment in time. Email is the most prominent example in this class. Technology that interfaces to mobile phone texting also belongs in this class.

Online text communication technology allows two (or more) individuals to exchange text messages in an interactive, session-based way (often augmented with the possibility to exchange files containing other media in the same session). Chat technology such as that provided by various messenger services (e.g., WhatsApp; www.whatsapp.com) is the most prominent example in this class.

Audio communication technology provides the facilities to have a direct audio connection between two persons over the internet (using technology such as *voice over IP* or *VoIP*) – very much like a traditional phone call. A well-known provider of this technology is Skype (www.skype.com).

Video communication technology is similar to audio communication technology, but it also provides a bidirectional video link. Obviously, communication bandwidth is an important factor in the realization of video links. Simple forms of this technology are based on web cams and more advanced forms on video conferencing systems.

Telepresence technology is a technology that provides to communicating parties the experience of 'being present' at the same location [Wik14b]. This technology relies on high-end audio and video technology – typically using advanced set-ups of multiple video cameras, screens, microphones and speakers installed in dedicated telepresence locations. As such, telepresence is the 'next step' after video conferencing. The current costs of telepresence equipment are such that it is typically applicable to high-end B2B communication only.

Much of this technology is currently internet-based (in the past, communication infrastructures such as *integrated services digital network* [ISDN] were used for audio and video communication). We can observe a shift to web-based applications, thus removing the need for dedicated communication software at local sites (see also the discussion of web 2.0 in section 8.2.2).

8.4.4 Security technology

Security is a major issue in networked e-business for more than one reason. Obviously, an important reason is the fact that financial transactions are conducted in e-business. A second important reason is the fact that in networked e-business, information systems of an organization are opened to the outside world (via front-end systems, as we have discussed in chapter 7) and hence become potentially susceptible to misuse. A third important reason is the fact that sensitive information is exchanged in e-business, which may be information with privacy concerns or information with a competitive value.

We discuss two kinds of technology here. First, *user identification technology* is used to identify persons (or automated systems) in order to give them access to specific systems or specific functions of systems. Using such technology, registered customers can, for instance, be identified in e-retailing scenarios. Second, *cryptography* technology [Katz07] is used to provide certain security aspects in transmitting electronic information (documents) between collaborating business parties.

User identification technology

In all business information systems, user identification is an important aspect to make sure that only the right people get access to systems, and when having access the right people have the right access to specific functions or data. In networked e-business settings, access to systems is per definition important, because e-business systems are open to the outside world (remember our definition of networked e-business in chapter 1) and to a group of users that changes throughout time (both human users and external information systems).

The traditional method for user identification is having the user enter his or her *user identification* (UID) and password. This method relies on semi-static data only; that is, the access codes remain the same for relatively long periods of time (depending on the password renewal strategy of the user and the system). It is therefore only safe if the user manages to keep the password perfectly hidden and if the transferred UID and password cannot be intercepted by third parties. For the latter reason, they are typically transmitted in encrypted form (we will see how this works further on).

Keycards are a hardware means for user identification. A key card can have an embedded chip (with contacts or contact-less) or magnetic strip containing the user data. If a key card is used without further identification, the loss of a card poses great security risks. Therefore, the use of the card can be coupled to a *personal identification number* (PIN) that the user has to enter when using the card.

Hardware password generators are used, for example, in e-banking. These systems typically have a slot for a banking card containing a chip with user data, and they dynamically generate a password on the basis of a PIN and an input code supplied by the e-banking system. The fact that passwords are generated dynamically makes them usable once only – therefore, eavesdropping to obtain passwords is useless.

Biometric user identification is a relatively new technology where it comes to widespread practical application. It relies on detecting the specific body characteristics of a user, typically by means of a finger-print scan or an iris scan. It is not yet commonly used in e-business, however, because it requires dedicated equipment (scanners) with associated costs.

Finally, we currently see the emergence of *near field communication* (NFC) technology [Chan13] for identification purposes. In this case, a user caries an NFC-enabled device (usually a smartphone) to authenticate an e-business transaction. Application of this technology is typically for low-value transactions (as the loss of the NFC-enabled device would otherwise imply great risks).

Secure message exchange and cryptography

When exchanging messages in e-business, the messages should be exchanged in a secure way. Depending on the nature of a message, a number of security characteristic in exchanging electronic documents are important:

Confidentiality means that the message is only readable by the sender and the intended receiver.

Integrity means that the message cannot be changed during transport from sender to receiver by a third party without the intended receiver noticing this.

Authentication means that the identity of the sender of a message is assured to the receiver by the message.

Non-repudiation means that the sending of a received message is 'undeniable' by the sender in case of a dispute between sender and receiver.

To obtain these characteristics, *cryptography* is typically used. Cryptography relies on the use of *keys* and *encryption* and *decryption algorithms*. Keys are (large) numbers that are used in mathematical algorithms to transform a piece of information into another piece of information. Two basic forms of cryptography can be distinguished: *symmetric cryptography* and *asymmetric cryptography*.

Symmetric cryptography

Symmetric cryptography relies on a single secret key that must be available to two business partners that wish to exchange messages in a secure way, as illustrated in Figure 8.10. The sending party uses the key to encrypt a message into an encoded message. The original message is readable and referred to as *cleartext* message. The encoded message is unreadable and referred to as *ciphertext* message. The receiving party uses the same key to decrypt the encoded message into the original message. The encryption algorithm is such that it is virtually impossible to decrypt the message without knowing the key. In principle, one could of course try all possible keys,

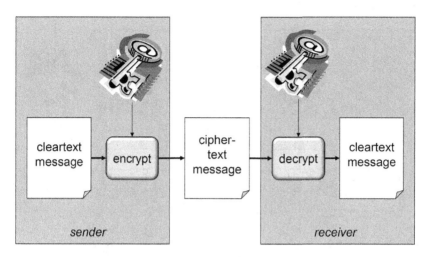

FIGURE 8.10 Symmetric cryptography.

but by choosing keys that are large enough, the number of possible keys becomes so large that this is practically infeasible.[7]

Symmetric cryptography ensures the confidentiality and integrity of a message. Authentication is supported to a limited extent, because a ciphertext message can only be produced by a party that has access to the secret key (but by any party with access in case of a multi-party scenario). Non-repudiation is not supported, as a receiver can construct a ciphertext message itself and claim that it was sent by a specific sender.

Although symmetric cryptography is safe, it has one great disadvantage: both parties need to have access to the same secret key. Obviously, it is not wise to exchange this key electronically in an unsecured message. It is usually not possible to exchange it in a secured message as there is no shared key available yet. Hence, keys are typically exchanged in a physical way for symmetric cryptography; for instance, on a person-to-person basis. This may be acceptable for long-standing business relationships, but not for dynamic e-business relationships (compare the *time scopes* dimension discussed in section 3.6). Asymmetric cryptography does not have this problem, at the expense of some additional complexity – we discuss this further on.

Asymmetric cryptography

Asymmetric cryptography uses a combination of a public key that can be exchanged freely between business parties and a private (secret) key that remains with one party. The cryptographic algorithms are such that a message that is encrypted with one key can only be decrypted with the corresponding 'sister' key.

Figure 8.11 shows the usage of asymmetric cryptography. The sender retrieves the public key of the receiver (which is publicly available), uses it to encrypt the

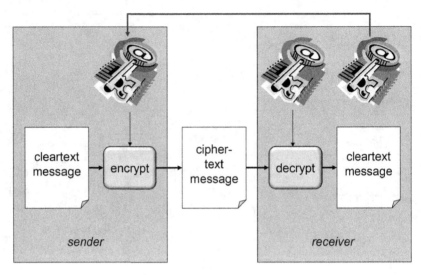

FIGURE 8.11   Asymmetric cryptography (protocol 1).

cleartext message and sends the obtained ciphertext message to the receiver. The receiver is the only party that has the private key that corresponds to its own public key, so it is the only party that can decrypt the ciphertext message.

The protocol of Figure 8.11 guarantees confidentiality and integrity of the sent message. Authentication and non-repudiation are not guaranteed, however, as anybody can retrieve the public key of the receiver and construct a ciphertext message. To guarantee these latter two characteristics, the keys are used in a 'reverse' protocol (as shown in Figure 8.12): the sender uses its private key to encrypt the message and the receiver retrieves the sender's public key to decrypt it. A message that can be decrypted with the sender's public key must have been encrypted with its private key, so it is guaranteed that the sender actually sent the message and the sender can never deny having sent it (as it is the only party who could have encrypted the message).

To ensure all four message security characteristics, a double encryption protocol is used that is the combination of those shown in Figures 8.11 and 8.12.

Asymmetric cryptography technology is the basis for *public key infrastructure* (PKI) technology [ITL97,Weis01,Vacc04], which underlies many security schemes in modern e-business systems. A PKI is a combination of software and policies to manage electronic keys and certificates in order to obtain trust in electronic business environments. PKI is in general a broad topic that has been evolving to meet the requirements of e-business [Weis01].

8.4.5 Performance technology

Obviously, proper performance of networked e-business systems is of utmost importance to keep an e-business organization running. Given the often volatile nature of e-business relationships (certainly in B2C scenarios), poorly performing

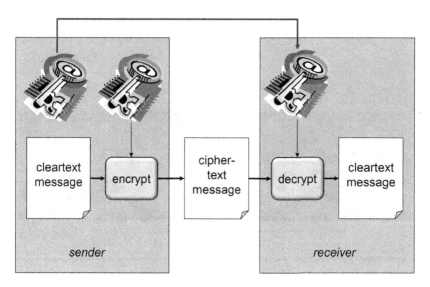

FIGURE 8.12 Asymmetric cryptography (protocol 2).

systems may cause collaboration parties (such as customers in e-retailing scenarios) to walk away quickly and look for a competitor that performs better. There are two aspects that we consider part of the performance aspect: response time management and availability management.

Response time management is concerned with guaranteeing that systems react quickly to user input. This is in general not an easy issue because users expect almost instantaneous reaction, and workload for e-business systems can fluctuate strongly. Various technologies are available for response time management, such as technologies that cater to advanced load balancing between e-business application servers and technologies that perform distributed caching of digital objects such that extended geographical reach does not degrade performance.

Availability management is concerned with making sure that e-business systems are indeed available when they should be. Given temporal reach considerations (see section 5.2.1), this often means 24/7 availability; that is, the systems should always be available. For availability management, we find replication technologies that enable the deployment of multiple copies of specific functional modules (or databases) of e-business systems, such that the failure of one copy will not cripple or even disable an entire e-business system.

Flexible management of response times and availability can often be obtained by good use of the cloud computing paradigm (as introduced in section 2.2.3). Apart from this, providing performance technology solutions is actually a business on its own in the internet world. Certainly when it comes to multimedia applications that are used by large numbers of users, explicit 'information logistics' is required to deliver a proper level of performance. There are companies that specialize in 'information logistics' in the internet. A well-known example is Akamai Technologies (www.akamai.com; see Figure 8.13).

FIGURE 8.13 Example internet 'information logistics' provider.

8.4.6 Mobility technology

E-business performed by users 'on-the-go' on mobile platforms is becoming increasingly important – we have identified this as *m-business* in section 1.4. From a technology push perspective, this development is fueled by two main developments:

- the availability of mobile internet access to computing devices (typically laptop computers, notebook computers and tablets), such that users can perform 'regular e-business activities at irregular places'
- the growth of the technical possibilities of portable communication devices (primarily smartphones), making them fit for use as computing devices in networked e-business[8]

The support for both types of e-business access can be considered *e-business mobility technology*. Although we treat it as aspect-oriented technology (for the mobility aspect) here, it can also be considered basic platform technology (for mobile platforms) as discussed in the previous section.

Mobility technology includes a wide range of basic technologies, such as:

- small-footprint (light-weight) versions of e-business software to be used on lightweight platforms such as smartphones (often in the form of *apps* running on mobile operating systems such as Android or IOS);
- context-awareness technology, such that the e-business options on a mobile device change per context; an important example is geo-location technology such as *global positioning system* (GPS) technology, which can be used

to adapt e-business functionality to the current geographical location of an e-business user;

- hardware and software technology that enables low power consumption of mobile devices (battery life being one of the major obstacles for high-performance, lightweight mobile devices) – and, of course, battery technology itself.

Detailed treatment of these technologies is not within the scope of this book. The reader is referred to specialized books, such as [Paav02, Nico13, Scha14].

8.5 Function-oriented technology

Function-oriented technology provides automated support for specific business functions. As such, it typically supports only a fragment of a complete networked e-business process. Function-oriented technology can often be related to specific modules, as identified in the organization (O) and architecture (A) aspects (as we have discussed in section 6.4 and section 7.5, respectively).

There are many types of technology in this category. Making an interesting selection from the wide variety, in this section we discuss the following types:

- catalog technology
- certificate technology
- payment technology
- contracting technology
- business intelligence technology

Because it is a selection, this list is certainly not complete. Other types of function-oriented technology for networked e-business are, for instance, electronic auction technology, collaborative authoring technology and reputation management technology.

8.5.1 Catalog technology

Electronic catalog systems are information systems that support the creation and the use of electronic catalogs. These are used, for example, in retail websites to support e-retailer business models (see section 5.6.1).

To some extent, electronic catalogs are similar to traditional paper catalogs, because they present objects offered by a seller in an organized way to a potential buyer. But there are some important differences.

- Both paper and electronic catalogs support *browsing*; that is, scanning a catalog following a predefined presentation order. In a paper catalog, this order is defined by the physical organization of the catalog. An electronic catalog can have multiple browsing orders; for example, browsing by object category, browsing by price or browsing by date of addition of objects.

- Both paper and electronic catalogs can support *searching*; that is, finding a set of objects using specific criteria. A paper catalog typically only has at most one index for searching (often alphabetically). An electronic catalog can allow searching on the basis of many criteria – even on combinations of criteria.
- The *presentation* of objects in a paper catalog is limited by the paper nature – it typically consists of text and one or a few pictures per object. Electronic catalogs can offer more elaborate texts, user reports, many pictures, audio and video presentations (see, e.g., Figure 5.2), virtual use presentations and even interactive configuration and display of objects (the latter is often used in the car industry, for example, to allow potential car buyers to configure exactly 'their car'). Obviously, this requires proper multimedia data management (as discussed in section 8.4.1).

8.5.2 Certificate technology

Electronic certificates are used to prove specific characteristics of a party to other parties in an e-business scenario. Certification is an important element in trust management. A certificate may prove, for example, that a party is member of a trade organization, conforms to specific quality norms (such as ISO standards[9]) or has a trustworthy banking representation. An electronic certificate is an electronic document that is secured by means of electronic signatures (which rely on security technology as discussed in section 8.4.4).

In electronic certification we typically find four roles (as shown in Figure 8.14). The *certification authority* (CA) is a trusted third party (TTP) organization that assesses other organizations with the aim of issuing electronic certificates to them. The method of assessment depends on the type of certificate. Issued certificates are registered by the *registration authority* (RA). This is a TTP that keeps record of issued certificates. In practice, the CA and RA roles can be performed by the same TTP. The *certificate owner* is the organization that requires an electronic certificate to prove specific qualities to parties it does business with. The *certificate requester* is the organization that wants to inspect a specific certificate before it enters into business with another party. It can receive the certificate from the certificate owner and check it with the RA.

In a highly dynamic supply chain scenario (see section 5.5.5), for example, the certificate requester might be a supplier of goods that is going to ship the goods to a buyer that it has not yet done business with. Before shipping the goods, the supplier wants proof of creditworthiness of the buyer by means of a banking certificate. In this case, the CA is the bank of the buyer. The RA may either be the same bank or another TTP, such as a chamber of commerce.

A problem arises in electronic certification if the certificate requester does not trust the CA. In this case, an issued certificate does obviously not have much value. To make a CA trustworthy to a certificate requester, the CA itself needs to be

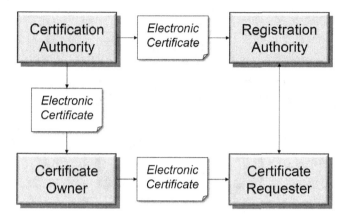

FIGURE 8.14 Parties in electronic certification.

certified; that is, it must have a certificate of another, higher-level CA that is trusted in a broader context. If even this higher-level CA is not trusted by the requester, this CA again needs an even higher-level certificate. For this reason, a CA hierarchy exists that has a so-called *root certification authority* at the top. Figure 8.15 shows an example CA hierarchy with three levels. The number of levels in a hierarchy depends on the type of certificate and the geographic scope of the scenario. Three levels may, for instance, correspond with a regional, a national and an international scope.

8.5.3 Payment technology

Electronic payment systems [OMah01, PáUT05, Kou10] provide the functionality to perform financial transactions in a distributed, electronic way in e-business scenarios. Typically, these transactions are based on information exchange and payment procedures, so they are not based on information technology only.

Electronic payment systems can be divided into three main classes:

- gateways to traditional payment systems
- facades to traditional payment systems
- systems that manage 'digital cash'

We discuss these three classes of systems.

Gateways to traditional payment systems

Gateways to traditional payment systems allow parties to make direct use in e-business scenarios of payment systems that are also used in traditional (non-e-business) situations.

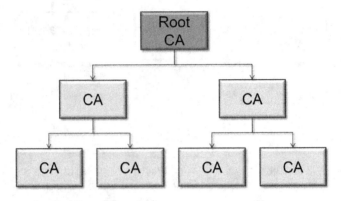

FIGURE 8.15 Certification authority hierarchy.

Widely used are e-business systems that include an interface to make credit card payments. When a customer buys one or more e-business objects, he or she enters his or her credit card details into the seller's system. Usually, the seller will verify these details and the client's credit status with the credit card company. Credit cards are, however, not generally used by the entire population in various countries.

A more recent development is the coupling of e-retailing to regular e-banking systems. In this case, a buyer makes a payment to a seller directly from his or her regular e-banking account. A good example of this class of e-payment systems is the Ideal system developed by the Dutch banking community, which we briefly describe further on.[10]

Using Ideal, a buyer is rerouted from an e-retailing system to the e-banking system of his or her own bank upon check-out. All banking account details are entered into the e-banking system of this own bank, comparable to regular e-banking transactions such as funds transfers. The payment is confirmed using the procedure of the bank (e.g., using a dynamically supplied transaction code). The retailer only knows which bank the customer uses, as the customer needs to be rerouted to this bank. Upon payment by the customer, the retailer is notified of this payment such that the sales process can be completed. The process from the customer perspective is shown in Figure 8.16. The fact that the customer does not need to disclose any account details to the retailer solves many trust issues: the customer only needs to trust his or her own bank (which he or she hopefully does).

Facades to traditional payment systems

Facades to traditional payment systems provide an e-business front end for payments that is linked to traditional payment systems, such as bank accounts or credit cards. It is a facade because it does not expose any banking details or credit card details of one party to another party. A well-known system in this category is PayPal (www.paypal.com).

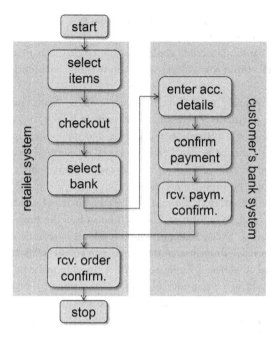

FIGURE 8.16 Ideal payment process from the customer's perspective.

PayPal provides a mechanism to perform payments and money transfers through the internet. It is an alternative to traditional, paper-based payment methods, such as checks and money orders. PayPal supports transferring money to practically anyone who has an email address.

Systems such as PayPal typically have two characteristics that distinguish them from gateways to traditional payment systems:

1 They are suited for making small payments (also called *micro-payments*) because they have small overhead and therefore can operate without substantial transaction fees.

2 They can often be used (partly) anonymously, which makes them fit for conducting transactions without revealing one's identity or one's financial details.

We currently see a development towards integration of this class of payment technology into communication technology classes to allow easy (C2C) payments. An example of the integration of payment technology and Twitter is Twitpay (although this initiative has not been very successful as of this writing).

Digital cash-management systems

Digital cash-management systems are systems that manage 'virtual accounts' in which *digital cash* (or *electronic money*) can reside. These accounts are mostly owned by individuals. Therefore, digital cash-management systems are mainly used in B2C and C2C e-commerce scenarios. Usually, funds are credited to these virtual accounts from traditional banking or credit cards accounts. Digital cash-management systems are typically well suited for making small, anonymous payments (as discussed for facade systems).

Digital cash typically resides in virtual accounts in the internet, where it can be used to make payments. There are also systems in which the digital cash resides in physical devices. An example is the Dutch *chipknip*, which is a smartcard that contains an offline virtual wallet.[11] Systems based on physical devices do, however, require dedicated interfaces (such as a smartcard reader), which makes them less usable for general e-business payments.

A special class of systems is formed by digital cash-management systems in virtual worlds or virtual communities. These systems often use their own 'virtual currency'. An example is Second Life, in which residents have accounts in the Linden Dollar (L$) currency, which has an exchange rate to the US$ currency (just like other non-virtual currencies). These accounts are used to make or receive payments in the virtual world or community. Although transactions are typically small, these worlds and communities can have substantial economic size.[12]

Finally, there is the relatively new development of *cryptocurrency*, a digital currency system that is built on cryptography technology. Bitcoin (https://bitcoin.org/en) is the best-known cryptocurrency, where the name indicates both the currency and the software to use it.

8.5.4 Contracting technology

Contracts are the basis for establishing formal business relationships between autonomous organizations. Traditionally, contracts are physical paper documents. In the development of electronic means for communication and collaboration between organizations, electronic contracts have emerged as a digital alternative for physical documents. In this subsection we first discuss two main forms of electronic contracting. Then, we focus on the structure of electronic contracts. Finally, we pay attention to electronic contracting systems.

Shallow and deep e-contracting

Electronic contracts are often used as a direct digital replacement for traditional paper contracts. Consequently, business processes in general and contracting processes in particular do not change much as a consequence of the use of electronic contracts – mainly efficiency of the contracting process is improved. Because this form of e-contracting does not change the way of doing business, we call this *shallow e-contracting*. As discussed in this book, new business settings have emerged in recent years. These new business settings require new contracting paradigms in which the use of electronic contracts becomes an essential element to obtaining a radical paradigm shift in contractual business relationships. We call this *deep e-contracting*.

Deep e-contracting allows for new contractual paradigms such as *micro-contracting* and *just-in-time contracting* [Gref02, Ang06a], which are better aligned with dynamic networked e-business models. We explain these two paradigms further on.

Micro-contracting is a form of contracting in which many small contracts are established instead of a few large contracts. Micro-contracts are typically small with respect to their time scope and the value of the exchanged goods they describe: they specify small business transactions that are executed in a short period of time. Micro-contracting allows organizations to create maximum variability in the contents of contracts: each micro-contract can be tuned to a specific situation. In this way, business relationships can be adapted very dynamically to current circumstances, following very dynamic e-business markets. An example domain where micro-contracting can be used is logistics [Gref00]: instead of bulk contracts, contracts can be established for the handling of individual shipments. In this way, contract-based dynamic service outsourcing can be realized (see also section 5.5.2). Obviously, micro-contracting processes need to be automated to a high degree to avoid enormous overheads of contracting in business processes.

Just-in-time contracting is a form of contracting in which contracts are established at the very latest possible moment, such that the conditions of that moment can be taken into account when specifying the exact contents of a contract. Conditions include specifics of customer orders, provider resources and market situations (such as current prices of e-business objects). To allow just-in-time contracting, electronic means are necessary to establish a contract in a very short time (in extreme cases in the order of a few seconds) – note that traditional 'pen and paper' contracting processes are not applicable here because they are simply too slow. Just-in-time electronic contracting can be used, for example, in dynamic advertising scenarios [Ang06b], where advertising campaigns are adapted, for example, depending on current weather conditions or the outcomes of sports events.

Electronic contract structures

Electronic contracts are typically complex documents. As they are often used in scenarios with dynamic partnerships, they must preferably be fully self-contained. In other words, because there is no pre-existing business relationship in dynamic, contract-governed e-business, all agreements between parties must be specified in a contract.

Because of this complexity, clear contract structures are needed. A high-level contract content structure is provided in the 4W framework [Ange03]. This framework distinguishes four classes of contract content or four contract clause types (indicated by the four W's):

- The *Who* clause type contains descriptions of the parties that engage in a contractual relationship. Usually, there are two parties, but multi-party contracts are possible, too [Xu04].

- The *What* clause type contains descriptions of the exchanged objects (as discussed in section 3.5). Often, one object is of a monetary type, but not necessarily so.
- The ho*W* clause type contains a description of the process for the exchange of the objects described in the *What* clause type. Possibly, it also contains a description of the process for the further use of the contract (such as complaint handling related to the contract).
- The *Where* clause type contains a specification of the context in which the contract is to be interpreted. Most important is the legal context, often specified by the country for which the contract law is applicable.

The contract clauses together form the contract content or the *core contract*. To make an electronic contract valid, electronic signatures of the participating parties need to be added. Together, we get the contract structure shown in Figure 8.17.

A structure such as the one in Figure 8.17 needs to be expressed in a specification language to obtain a transferrable document. For this purpose, electronic contracting languages are used that typically have an XML representation.

Electronic contracting systems

Electronic contracting systems [Ang06a] provide the functionality to establish and monitor contracts between business parties in an electronic way. A full-blown electronic contracting system supports all phases of a complete electronic contracting process:

- the *informational phase*, in which information is exchanged in a market between parties that explore possible collaboration;
- the *pre-contracting phase*, in which the details of a contractual relationship are negotiated and agreed upon in terms of a *contract offer*;
- the *contracting phase*, in which the contract is actually established by signing an agreed contract offer; here, electronic certificate technology is used (as discussed in section 8.5.2) for digitally signing;
- the *enactment phase*, in which the obligations specified in the contract are fulfilled by the respective parties in accordance with specified rights;
- the *evaluation phase*, in which the enactment is evaluated to confirm that all obligations have been fulfilled and all rights have been respected – if not, a settlement procedure is started to deal with contract violation.

Note that not all contracting necessarily includes all of these phases: in simple, clear markets, the informational phase may be superfluous; for simple, straightforward contracts, the evaluation phase may be superfluous.

An electronic contracting system enables the execution of all of these phases in an electronic way; that is, without the use of any physical documents. Obviously, this makes contracting processes a great deal more efficient than the traditional

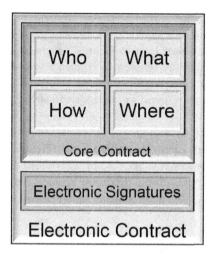

FIGURE 8.17   E-contract structure.

pen-and-paper approach. As a consequence of this improved efficiency, contracts can be used for a greater range of business collaborations (such as the micro-contracting paradigm that we have discussed earlier in this section), hence guarding the rights of parties in e-business scenarios.

8.5.5 Business intelligence technology

E-business can generate large volumes of business data, as activities are performed using automated systems, which can log all their activities.

Business-intelligence technology provides the basis for the functionality to analyze these large volumes of data, such as large sets of e-business browsing and transaction histories. Results from business-intelligence technology can be used as input to customer relationship management (CRM) systems and to tactic and strategic decision making systems. This type of technology is important in a networked e-business context for three reasons.

1   To understand the customer: because e-business is highly 'anonymous' as compared to traditional business (there are no personal contacts, there are no physical locations), meeting customer demands is one of the key distinguishing factors between competitors (see also section 5.3.2, where we discuss enriched customer relationship management as a business direction).

2   To understand market developments: e-business markets are often highly volatile, much more than many traditional markets; therefore, it is of major importance to closely and quickly follow market developments to be able to react or even pro-act (this issue is related to change management as discussed in section 6.7.2).

3   To manage risks: as networked e-business scenarios can get complex in terms of functions and processes and large in terms of the number of actors involved in a scenario, it is often hard to identify and manage risks (such as fraud). Business intelligence can be used to construct typical usage and transaction patterns, such that current business can be compared against these patterns to avoid risks before they appear or manage them after they appear.

Business intelligence technology is used to analyze business data. To store this data, often warehousing systems [Inmo01] are used. These dedicated systems enable business intelligence processes to proceed freely without disturbing primary business that runs against operational databases. Business intelligence technology is closely related to the *big data* development that we discuss in the next section.

8.6 Technology in the Big Five

In chapter 2 we have introduced the Big Five developments in e-business: social media, mobile computing, cloud computing, big data, and the internet of things. In this section we revisit the Big Five and discuss how these developments are related to the technologies that we have discussed in the previous sections of this chapter. We discuss each of the Big Five in the following subsections.

8.6.1 Social media

The current development of social media relies on most of the technology classes that we have seen in this section. Obviously, social media applications make use of the basic infrastructure technology found in the internet and the web. Less visible for the end users of these applications is the use of advanced infrastructure technologies by the social media operators. Given the size and complexity of modern social media, use of these technologies is a strict requirement.

Most aspect-oriented technologies that we have discussed are highly relevant for social media. Given the vast amounts of data managed in social media applications such as Facebook, advanced data management technology is a technology cornerstone of these applications. Human communication technology and mobility technology are important for obvious reasons. Security technology is of utmost importance to guarantee the privacy of the users of social media applications. Performance technology is important to guarantee smooth, fluent interaction between users and social media servers. Poor performance would have a negative effect on customer retention. Note that end-user social media applications are highly interactive, such that short response times must be guaranteed. The only discussed aspect-oriented technology that has a less clear link with social media is process management technology. The reason for this is that the use of social media mostly does not follow predefined business processes.

Most discussed function-oriented technologies are also relevant for social media. Catalog technology is important, but basically for another reason than in e-retailing: in social media, catalogs of social contacts are important to manage personal networks. Certificate technology is important to correctly identify parties involved in social media and enhance trust (even though the use of certificates is typically not very visible to the end user). Payment technology is gaining importance, as social media applications are moving into the e-retailing domain. Business intelligence technology is highly relevant to operators of social media to understand the overall behavior of subsets of their customers or to find closely linked clusters of customers. For the latter, techniques such as social network analysis [Wik14n, Golb13] can be used. Contracting technology does not (yet) play an important role in social media.

8.6.2 Mobile computing

As we have discussed in chapter 2, mobile computing has a profound impact on networked e-business. Mobile computing (obviously) relies on mobility technology, as discussed in section 8.4.6. Advances in both hardware (such as advanced screen technology and low power processor technology) and software (such as dedicated mobile operating systems like Android [www.android.com] and IOS [www.apple.com/ios]) have made mobile computing one of the fastest developing technology markets. But of course, mobile computing does not rely only on the mobility technology class.

Basic and advanced infrastructure technologies are important for mobile technology to enable the connection of mobile devices to server-side functionality. The advanced infrastructure class may not be visible at the 'mobile end' (i.e., the client side) of mobile computing, but it plays an important role in enabling the 'central end' (i.e., the server side). Connection of mobile devices to server-side functionality is more complicated than connection of stationary devices for two main reasons. First, mobile devices typically rely on less reliable wireless connections (such as cellular networks). Second, mobile devices can be *roaming*; that is, change their physical connection point to a network on a frequent basis.

For the aspect-oriented technology classes, mobile computing largely follows the same pattern as social media (which is not surprising, because social media applications are often used on mobile devices). As mobile computing is increasingly used to perform business transactions, security technology for mobile applications is of utmost importance [Dwiv10]. Note that data-management technology and performance-management technology are mostly relevant at the server side.

For function-oriented technology, the emphasis in mobile computing is on certificate and payment technology. Certificate technology is required to authenticate parties in mobile e-business scenarios. To enable adequate levels of trust, this technology relies strongly on security technology. Where payments are made from mobile devices, integration with payment technology as discussed in section 8.5.3 is essential.

8.6.3 Cloud computing

Cloud computing brings virtualized, flexible information processing facilities to parties in e-business scenarios, as we have seen in chapter 2. As its basis, cloud computing requires the application of basic and advanced infrastructure technologies, as discussed earlier in this chapter. To allow dynamism in the relationship between cloud users and cloud providers, an important aspect with respect to the advanced infrastructure class is support for the portability of e-business applications across cloud providers. Adequate support for portability allows cloud users to move their applications from one cloud provider to another, if market circumstances dictate so, and prevent lock-in with a specific service provider. Automated deployment frameworks such as the *topology and orchestration specification for cloud applications* (TOSCA) [OAS13, Binz13] play an important role here. These frameworks allow the specification of cloud computing configurations at an abstracted level that can be reused across providers.

In the aspect-oriented technology classes, as discussed in section 8.4, security and performance technology are of utmost importance for cloud computing. Security technology is important to make sure that cloud users can run their applications as secure in the cloud as on local systems (or perhaps even more secure). Security is important not only to shield unwanted parties that are external to the cloud provider but also to shield other parties that use the same cloud provider. Shielding other parties that use the same provider becomes more important when these parties share the same computing infrastructure. A number of small parties may, for instance, share the same database server in the cloud – with obvious risks for data privacy. This situation of sharing resources in the cloud is referred to as *multi-tenancy* [Mutc11]. The importance of performance technology is obvious: one of the reasons to use the cloud is to obtain flexible, high performance.

In the function-oriented technology classes, as discussed in section 8.5, we find few direct relations to cloud computing, because cloud computing is applicable to very diverse applications. Contracting technology may become important when relationships between cloud users and cloud providers become very dynamic and therefore have to be formally arranged in a quick and cheap way. In this case, cloud service contracts may be established effectively and efficiently using electronic contracting technology.

8.6.4 Big data

We have introduced the development of big data in section 2.2.4. The use of big data is becoming increasingly important for business intelligence in networked e-business. Big data technology relies on basic and advanced infrastructure technology as discussed before in this chapter. Internet and web technology are important for the transport of data from the data sources, where the data originates, to the big data repositories, where the data is stored for processing. Likewise, the internet and web are used for the transport of information distilled from big data to decision makers.

In the aspect-oriented technology classes, the emphasis is (of course) on data management technologies. Advanced data management schemes are required to effectively and efficiently deal with the huge amounts of data generated in e-business scenarios.[13] Take, for example, large e-retailers (see section 5.6.1) that may store not only transaction histories for millions of customers for accounting reasons but also their browsing history for marketing reasons. Security technology is important for guaranteeing the security of data transport and data storage in big data applications – certainly where privacy-related data or business-sensitive data are involved. Performance technology is important to guarantee high-performance data processing over very large databases: big data applications may run on large server parks, where effective load balancing technology is required.

In the function-oriented technology classes, business intelligence technology (as discussed in section 8.5.5) is strongly connected to big data developments. Business intelligence is not so important for the creation of large databases, but to extract relevant knowledge from them. Here, technologies such as data mining [Prov13], online analytical processing (OLAP) [Thom02] and process mining [Aals11] play important roles.

8.6.5 Internet of things

Like the other developments in the Big Five, the development of the internet of things (IoT) relies on basic and advanced infrastructure technology. Basic infrastructure technology is required to couple the 'things' to central information systems that process their state signals. For example, information from RFID scanners in logistics e-business scenarios is sent to central transport management systems [Yee12]. These central systems use advanced infrastructure technologies.

Nearly all discussed aspect-oriented technologies are relevant to the IoT, with human communication technology as the exception: communication in the IoT is centered at things, not at humans (although humans can be treated as 'things' to be automatically tracked – see the discussion of the TraXP case at the end of this chapter). Process management technology is relevant to the IoT to enable adaptive automation of business processes in which the 'things' are manipulated. Here, the IoT generates state change signals of things, which are fed to business process management systems used for controlling the enactment of processes [Zhao09]. An example application domain is logistics, where IoT technology is used to track the movements of goods and control business processes related to these movements.

In function-oriented technologies, the emphasis in the IoT is on certification technology to certify the identity of things (or of the systems that deliver identity information) to the central information systems and on business intelligence technology to distill decision management information from the real-time information generated by the things.

TABLE 8.3 Indication of relationships between Big Five and technology classes

		Social media	Mobile computing	Cloud computing	Big data	Internet of things
Infra	Basic	X	X	X	X	X
	Advanced	X	X	X	X	X
Aspect	Data management	X	X		X	X
	Process management					X
	Human communication	X	X			
	Security	X	X	X	X	X
	Performance	X	X	X	X	X
	Mobility	X	X			X
Function	Catalog	X				
	Certificate	X	X			X
	Payment	X	X			
	Contracting			X		
	Business intelligence	X			X	X

8.6.6 Overview

To provide a simple and indicative overview of the discussion in this section, the relationships between the Big Five and the discussed technology classes are shown in Table 8.3. Entries in the table indicate that a technology class is important for a development in the Big Five.

8.7 Mapping A elements to T elements

In the preceding sections of this chapter we have seen a broad spectrum of technologies in the T aspect of the BOAT framework. These technologies are chosen to realize (or, in another term, 'embody') the architecture specified in the A aspect. Therefore, A aspect elements should be mapped to T aspect elements.

The nature of the mapping from A aspect elements to T aspect elements depends on the class of T elements:

- The basic internet and web technologies underlie almost any modern networked e-business application. As such, they can often be assumed to be present 'by default' and hence do not explicitly appear in mappings between A and T aspects.

- Advanced infrastructural technologies typically underlie a complete architecture (or a major part of it). As such, they typically are not related to specific modules specified in the A aspect, but form a 'basis below' the modules. Hence, they do not show up in A aspect diagrams as separate modules, but can influence the choice of modules.

- Aspect-oriented technologies are typically used in various modules of a networked e-business system. Security technology, for example, is important in all front-end modules, because these have interfaces to the outside world. Aspect-oriented technology may in some cases be located in dedicated architecture modules showing up in detailed architecture diagrams (e.g., a database management system module, a business process management system module or a security management module) – this is mostly the case at the party level or the system level of architectures.

- Function-oriented technologies typically support specific business functions and can hence be related explicitly to individual modules identified in the architecture in the A aspect. In other words, modules in the A aspect may be dedicated to contain specific function-oriented technology (such as an electronic payment module or a contract management module). Typically, we find these modules in party-level architectures (see, e.g., Figure 7.10) or system-level architectures.

Realizing an e-business system typically requires the use of a number of technology types. Integration of these types is a major issue, both to 'get the system running' at present and to ensure flexibility of the system towards the future. Good architectural design (in the A aspect) is a main key to proper integration.

8.8 Mapping T elements to B elements

As we have seen in section 4.4, the BOAT model is preferably used in the 'wheel mode' in an e-business context. This means that we have to consider the mapping from T aspect elements to B aspect elements to 'make the wheel go round'. In other words, we have to think about the technology push aspects of e-business developments (as discussed in section 1.5).

It is not easy, however, to speak in general terms about the relationship from T aspect elements to B aspect elements, because they can have very different natures. We can give a few examples here to illustrate possible relationships.

- Obviously, the use of communication technology elements can have an impact on the reach element in the B aspect (see section 5.2): a more advanced communication platform can result in extended reach (typically modal reach, sometimes geographic reach). This holds both for system-to-system communication technology (such as web services) and human communication technology.

- The use of multimedia technology can have an impact on the richness element in the B aspect: the use of a full spectrum of media can increase the richness of the communication to business partners. The same goes for technology supporting interactivity in the internet context. As such, developments associated with the *web 2.0* concept (see section 8.2.2) can trigger new business opportunities.
- Specific technology classes can even directly foster the development of new business structures: the use of e-contracting technology opens new doors towards the formation of contract-based dynamic virtual enterprises (see section 5.5), for example.

A general 'recipe' does not exist for mapping T to B aspect elements. This is the reason for the fact that 'discovering' new business models based on emerging technology is still an 'art' in itself. The structured discussion of B aspect elements in chapter 5 may help to infuse some elements of business engineering into this art.

8.9 Running cases

In this section we turn our attention again to our three running cases. We use these to discuss the application of some of the technologies discussed in this chapter. For reasons of brevity, we do not discuss all technologies.

8.9.1 POSH

POSH uses standard internet and web technologies as basic infrastructure technologies for its e-business systems. For supporting its B2B activities, it is studying the use of more advanced platforms, such as RosettaNet.

The electronic catalog of POSH is essential to its business operation – it shows all the products they sell. For small goods, simple descriptions and photographs suffice. For large goods (such as office furniture), a detailed description with a set of photographs and a measurement diagram is included in the catalog. POSH considers using videos for the presentation of furniture lines it sells to give the customer a more lively impression than photographs can (here, the introduction of technology will affect *richness* in the B aspect of BOAT). This will imply, however, that POSH will have to upgrade the service-level agreement it has with the organization that hosts its website.

With respect to payment systems, POSH takes a traditional approach. For B2C orders, it requests either payments per credit card or pre-payments to its bank account. For B2B orders, POSH bills the customer offline after delivery of an order. The latter is possible, because POSH has pre-existing relationships with B2B customers (as reflected in its sales process – see Figure 6.30).

POSH considers using electronic contracting for large B2B orders. It sees two advantages here:

1   A contract provides a basis for guarantees between the customer and POSH with respect to mutual obligations. Large B2B orders represent substantial financial transactions, such that a contractual basis reduces risks.

2   A contract is a natural place to specify quality-of-service parameters, such as the delivery time of ordered goods, the mode of transportation and installation and the after-service provided by POSH. Using per-order contracts allows differentiating on a per-order basis, such that more flexibility is obtained.

8.9.2 TTU

Because TTU is a young company, it could choose freely what technologies to use for its networked e-business system platforms; that is, it does not have a technology legacy problem. TTU has chosen to use web service technology as its main platform (on top of basic internet and web technologies). It specifies all services it offers in WSDL.

Availability of its systems is essential to TTU, certainly when it comes to setting up online meetings for its clients: if important meetings need to be postponed because of unavailability of the systems of TTU, this will easily lead to loss of clients. Therefore, TTU has paid explicit attention to technology that allows functional back-up systems to seamlessly take over tasks of their primary systems. This can be considered a specific kind of performance technology as discussed in Section 8.4.5.

Given the market it operates in, human communication technology is obviously very important to TTU, most specifically audio and video communication technology. TTU is currently investigating the use of telepresence technology, such that its interpreters can join into teleconferences supported by telepresence. Mobility technology plays a role in more future scenarios, in which mobile teleconferencing may be required.

A point of interest to TTU is electronic certification. Because the organization works with freelance translators and interpreters and wants to guarantee high-quality service to its customers, some form of internal and external quality control is desirable. Having freelancers that are certified can help TTU's internal quality control system and provides opportunities to use explicit quality references in its marketing and sales processes. Electronic certification is, however, not yet available in the translation and interpretation market.

8.9.3 TraXP

Like TTU, TraXP is a new start-up company, so it can choose freely from technologies it wishes to apply, unburdened by any legacy choices. To show an alternative angle at the discussion of technologies in the context of a case study, we discuss the use of e-business technologies from the perspective of two of the developments of the Big Five.

A specific interest of TraXP goes to the internet of things. It interprets the abbreviation IoT as the *internet of travelers*: TraXP sees travelers as the objects that are tracked and monitored automatically in real-time across the internet. It is interested in this for two main reasons: first, this provides TraXP with necessary data to learn about travel patterns, which it uses to build user profiles; second, this allows TraXP to actually assist travelers in a real-time fashion, even without the need for the traveler to take initiative. Tagging and scanning passengers (similar to goods in supply chains) is not a good idea. Instead of this, mobility technology in the form of smartphones is coupled to IoT technology to serve as one of the prime data sources for this development: travelers are tracked and monitored via their smartphones.

Big data is an important development for TraXP for its business intelligence function. Consequently, data management technology is used extensively. Using data management algorithms, TraXP can actually construct the travel patterns mentioned earlier. Using OLAP technology, TraXP can analyze trends in the travel market and adapt its business offers to these in a tactic way.

8.10 Chapter end

As usual in this book, we end this chapter with a short summary and a set of questions and exercises.

8.10.1 Chapter summary

In this chapter we have provided an overview of networked e-business technology. We have distinguished among four classes of technology that are used as the basis for networked e-business applications (as illustrated in Figure 8.18):

- **Internet and web technology** are the bare basics for networked e-business systems, providing the basic communication and collaboration platform. This technology is based on a set of standard languages (such as HTML and XML) and protocols (such as HTTP).
- **Advanced platform technology** provides a layer on top of internet or web technology, offering more advanced collaboration primitives. The web services framework is currently a leading approach. It is based on the web services technology stack, consisting of a number of standard languages (such as WSDL and BPEL), protocols (such as WSAT and WSS) and software specifications (such as UDDI). ebXML, RosettaNet and multi-agent systems are other well-known platform types. In practice, hybrid platforms exist that combine multiple basic platforms.
- **Aspect-oriented technology** provides the support for specific aspects of networked e-business systems, such as security. Important aspects supported by this class of technology are data management, process management, human communication, security, performance and mobility.

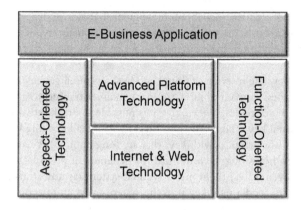

FIGURE 8.18 Technology classes as a basis for e-business applications.

Function-oriented technology provides the support for specific functions of networked e-business systems. Important functions supported by this class of technology are electronic catalog management, electronic certificate management, electronic payment support, electronic contracting support and business intelligence support.

The technology classes can be related to the Big Five developments. Integration of technology classes is a major point in realizing e-business systems. A well-designed architecture (as discussed in chapter 7) is the starting point to obtain this.

8.10.2 Questions and exercises

1 Study the electronic catalogs of a few well-known e-retailers in a specific shopping domain (such as music, books or house accessories). Compare the catalogs with respect to the support they offer for browsing and searching. Pay attention to the number of predefined browsing sequences, the number of search criteria (search dimensions) and the possibilities to combine these.

2 The X/Open XA protocol (discussed in section 8.4.1) uses a *two-phase commit protocol* to ensure that distributed transactions either completely succeed or completely fail (i.e., that no partially completed transactions can end). Find out how the two-phase commit protocol works.

3 In section 8.4.3 we have mentioned a double asymmetric encryption protocol. Elaborate this protocol and show that it indeed guarantees all four security characteristics discussed in that section.

4 Figure 8.16 shows the Ideal payment process from a customer's perspective; that is, the process steps a customer has to perform. Specify the Ideal payment process from a retailer perspective; that is, the process steps a retailer has to perform.

5 Try to find information about the practical usage of the RosettaNet and ebXML standards (in terms of market size, domain types, regional usage, etc.). Are there interesting differences between the usage patterns of the two standards?

6 Find out how the internet of things and business intelligence can be combined in the business domain of international container transport.

7 We have mentioned that *in principle* it is possible to break into a system secured with a digital key scheme (such as PKI) by trying all possible key values – but that this is not practical with keys that are long enough. Try and give a rough estimate of how long it would take to generate all possible key values for a 256-bit key and feed them into a secured system (assume, for instance, that it is possible to feed a new key into the system every millisecond – even if any practical system would, of course, refuse access very soon).

Notes

1 Note that with discussing this mapping after the previously discussed mappings, we complete analyzing the aspect-pair-wise dependencies in the cyclical BOAT view. We revisit the topic of dependencies in the complete BOAT cycle in section 9.4.

2 See http://www.oasis-open.org for more information.

3 See http://www.rosettanet.org for more information.

4 An alternative to the SOAP protocol standard is the *representational state transfer* (REST) architecture style to define so-called *RESTful* services [Rich08]. As REST is less standardized than SOAP, we do not further discuss this alternative.

5 In the CrossWork project, both the terms BPM and WFM are used and refer to the build time and execution time support, respectively, for business processes. Often, the terms are used as (near) synonyms (with BPM as the more modern alternative). We discuss BPM technology later in this chapter.

6 So-called *personal database systems* (such as many small database management systems designed to run on personal computers) do not have the client/server organization, as they serve one single user only.

7 As an example, modern implementations of the AES symmetric encryption scheme use 256-bit keys, which means that 2^{256} different keys are possible, which amounts to a decimal number of seventy-eight digits.

8 With modern smartphones, the distinction between smartphones and tablets is fading, giving rise to terms such as *phablets*, indicating a hybrid form between smartphone and tablet, such as a smartphone with a very large screen and ample computing power.

9 See http://www.iso.org/iso/iso_catalogue.htm.

10 See http://www.ideal.nl/?lang=eng-GB for more details.

11 Note that the current ubiquitous availability of connectivity reduces the necessity of offline payment technology. The Dutch *chipknip* technology was discontinued at the start of 2015.

12 For example, Linden Lab, the operator of Second Life, stated the following in August 2009 on their Second Life website: 'With nearly USD$35 million traded between residents each month, the Second Life economy has grown to become one of the world's largest user-generated virtual economies.'

13 Sizes of e-business databases are not easy to obtain, but estimates of large big data applications are available. These indicate existing databases in the order of magnitude of hundreds of terabytes and trillions of records (see, e.g., http://www.comparebusiness products.com/fyi/10-largest-databases-in-the-world, inspected 2014).

9

ANALYZING AND DESIGNING

Learning goals

- *Know and understand an approach to classify a networked e-business scenario.*
- *Know and understand an approach to analyze or design a networked e-business scenario.*
- *Be able to relate elements of the four BOAT aspects in a graphical way for an e-business scenario.*
- *Understand networked e-business developments in a temporal setting.*

9.1 Introduction

So far in this book we have explored the networked e-business space along a number of dimensions as outlined in chapters 3 and 4. This provides a conceptual 'tool' for analyzing and designing e-business scenarios, but does not yet explain how to precisely 'handle this tool' in practice. To use an analogy in terms of cooking: the ingredients are there, but the overall recipe is still missing. Therefore, we provide guidelines in this chapter of how to use the theory in this book for the following tasks:

- classify an existing e-business scenario (section 9.2)
- analyze an existing e-business scenario (section 9.3)

Designing an e-business scenario can in principle follow the same approach.

After describing the basic way to perform these tasks, we next pay special attention to two additional issues to obtain a complete analysis (or design) of an e-business scenario. First, we describe a technique to get an overview of the major dependencies between elements in the four BOAT aspects in an e-business scenario to understand the overall conceptual structure of that scenario (section 9.4). Second, we add the time aspect[1] to understand and describe development and evolution of an e-business scenario (section 9.5).

9.2 Classify a scenario

Classifying an e-business scenario is the starting point for the analysis of an existing scenario or the design of a new scenario. An e-business scenario can be classified in a well-structured way using the following steps.

1 Determine the scope of the scenario. This includes the following two tasks:

   a decide which organizations are included in the scenario (and also which organizations are excluded);
   b decide for each organization which activities are included in the scenario (and which activities are excluded).

   Note that this is not always a trivial task, certainly in complex supply chains or business networks. If this step is problematic, it may be an indication that one is actually trying to classify a combination of scenarios: an e-business network may consist of multiple, independent e-business scenarios (recall Figure 1.1). In this case, further dissection is required.

2 Classify the scenario in terms of the party types involved (see section 3.4). If this step is problematic, it may be an indication that step 1 has not been performed correctly. If there are parties that have an unclear role or that have 'superfluous' activities, a too broad scope may have been chosen. If a party with a 'logical' role is missing or a 'logical' function is not supported, a too narrow scope may have been chosen. In this case, redo step 1.

3 Classify the scenario in terms of the e-business objects that are manipulated (see section 3.5). Again, if this step is problematic, it may be an indication that step 1

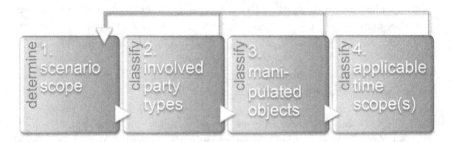

FIGURE 9.1   Steps to classify an e-business scenario.

has not been performed correctly. If many heterogeneous objects are identified, a too broad scope may have been chosen. In this case, restart from step 1.

4   Classify the scenario in terms of applicable time scope or time scopes (see section 3.6). If two very different time scopes are found, it may again be an indication that the scope of the scenario is too broad. In this case, restart from step 1. Note that an (ultra-)dynamic time scope is typically coupled to the life cycle (or rather 'trade cycle') of the objects identified in step 3.

These steps are summarized in Figure 9.1.

9.3 Analyze or design a scenario

An e-business scenario can be analyzed (or designed) after it has been classified as discussed previously. The following steps are used for a well-structured analysis (or design).

5   Describe the scenario with respect to the four BOAT aspects in global terms (see chapters 5–8). Make diagrams or graphical models where possible, as this will yield more structure and clarity than text only.
6   Analyze the mappings between the identified elements in the BOAT aspects in global terms. Make diagrams or graphical models where possible – we discuss a technique for this in section 9.4
7   Decide which BOAT aspect(s) are most relevant for the nature of the scenario; that is, choose which aspect(s) have a 'leading character'. Most relevant aspects are usually those that distinguish the scenario best from similar scenarios. Preferably, choose one aspect; two aspects if really necessary.
8   Analyze or design the results of steps 5 and 6 in more detail. Start with the aspect(s) identified as 'leading' in step 7. Usually, it is advisable to elaborate these aspect(s) most, as they most heavily determine the entire scenario.

These analysis (design) steps are summarized in Figure 9.2. This figure complements Figure 9.1: together, they summarize the complete classification and analysis (design) approach.

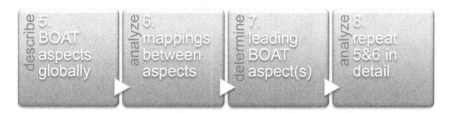

FIGURE 9.2   Steps to analyze an e-business scenario.

9.4 BOAT element dependency diagram

During the analysis or design of an e-business scenario, as out-lined in the previous section, the most important elements in the four BOAT aspects and their dependencies can be shown in a BOAT element dependency diagram (BEDD) to provide an overview of a scenario.

A BEDD is based on the wheel model of the BOAT framework (see Figure 4.4). In a BEDD, all four mappings between the BOAT aspects are summarized. These are the mappings that we have discussed at the ends of Chapters 6–8. As such, a BEDD represents the essentials of the complete wheel model of BOAT for a specific e-business scenario. The mappings are summarized by indicating the most essential elements in each aspect and using arrows between elements in different aspects to show important dependencies between them. A dependency between elements X and Y means that the characteristics of element X have a strong influence on the characteristics of element Y.

An abstract BEDD is shown in Figure 9.3 (it is abstract because it contains only abstract elements). For each of the four BOAT aspects, the most important

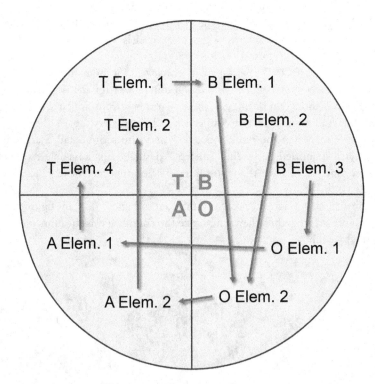

FIGURE 9.3 Abstract BOAT element dependency diagram.

elements are shown in the respective quarter of the diagram. The number of elements depends on the nature of the scenario, but should preferably not be too large – otherwise, the diagram looses its overview function. The arrows indicate the dependencies between elements of different BOAT aspects. The number of arrows crossing a boundary is an indication of the 'amount' of the coupling between two BOAT aspects. In the example, the coupling between B and O aspects is the largest. This may indicate that the B aspect is leading in this scenario. Note that this indication needs to be used with care, as the arrows do not indicate anything about the relative importance of the dependencies. It is possible to illustrate the relative importance by means of the weights of the arrows or their colors, but this makes the BEDD harder to interpret – often it is a better idea to include only the most important dependencies, as they represent the core of the relationships between the BOAT aspects.

We show a concrete BEDD (i.e., a BEDD of a concrete example e-business scenario) when revisiting the running case studies at the end of this chapter.

9.5 Analyzing networked business developments

As we have seen, the field of networked e-business is a field with rapid developments. Therefore, it is often interesting to analyze an e-business scenario over time; that is, to analyze its development (which we may also call its evolution). We can do this in a retrospective way; that is, look back at the past. We can also do this in a prospective way; that is, try to look forward into the future. We discuss both directions here.

9.5.1 Analyzing past developments

When analyzing past developments of an e-business scenario (which have been completed at the moment of analysis), typically two 'moments in time' are chosen:

1   *Past*: a carefully chosen moment in the past, typically one or a few years away from now, at which the scenario was in a clear state.
2   *Now*: a stable moment (without major changes going on) in the very recent past, preferably not more than a month ago.

For each of the two moments in time, a BOAT classification and analysis is performed as outlined in the previous sections of this chapter. Next, main differences are identified between the two outcomes. Very different outcomes from the two classifications may indicate that two different scenarios are compared, not two versions of the same scenario – this means that somewhere between the *past* and *now*, an old scenario was replaced by the current scenario.

It is of course possible to use more than two moments, but given the effort required to perform a good BOAT analysis, it should be clear why this is actually needed.

9.5.2 Analyzing future developments

When analyzing future developments (studying possibilities for scenarios to be realized), it is often a good idea to think in terms of three 'moments in time':

1   *now*: a stable moment in the short-term future or very recent past
2   *near future*: typically in the order of one year from now
3   *far future*: typically in the order of five to ten years from now

For the *now*, a BOAT analysis is performed as outlined in the previous sections of this chapter. For the *near future* and the *far future*, a BOAT design is performed. In this process, emphasis can (or even should) be placed on a leading BOAT aspect to better channel the design process. Obviously, this leading aspect should be chosen with care.

It is often worthwhile to think about the *far future* first to explore possibilities in an 'ideal world' in which extreme ideas are realizable. This avoids thinking in terms of too pragmatic 'current limitations' (e.g., in terms of technology or regulations). When a 'vision' has been established for the *far future*, the *near future* can be deduced by interpolating between *now* and *far future*. This can be compared to the approach of *extreme thinking*, as explained with change management (see section 6.7.2).

9.6 Running cases

In this section we continue the discussion of the three running case studies that we have seen throughout this book. For reasons of brevity, we choose one element from this chapter per case study. For POSH we elaborate a BOAT element dependency diagram as discussed in section 9.4. For TTU we perform a near-future development analysis as discussed in section 9.5. For TraXP we focus on the first analysis step of the approach outlined in section 9.2: the determination of the e-business scenario scope, given their service-dominant approach.

9.6.1 POSH

A BOAT element dependency diagram[2] for the POSH scenario is shown in Figure 9.4. It shows the main elements of the four BOAT aspects of the scenario and the cross-aspect dependencies between these elements.

In the B aspect, *extending reach*, *extending richness*, *disintermediation* and *enhanced customer relationship management* are the main elements (as discussed in section 5.9.1). In the O aspect, the front-end processes of POSH are key elements. POSH selects the *e-sales process* (discussed in section 6.9.1), the *service process* and the *logistics process* as the main processes. In the A aspect, the *front-end architecture* is key to POSH (see section 7.9.1). The structure of their *order management system* is considered an essential e-business element as well (also see section 7.9.1). In the T aspect, *e-catalog*

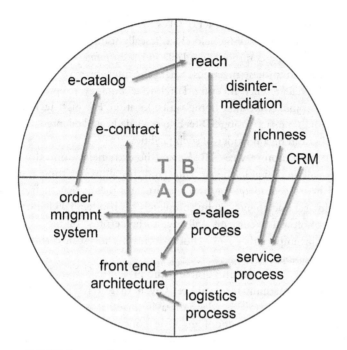

FIGURE 9.4 BOAT element dependency diagram for POSH scenario.

technology is of prime interest to POSH in the current situation; *e-contract technology* is added for future developments (see section 8.9.1).

The arrows show the main dependencies. For example, extending reach and disintermediation determine the existence and the nature of the e-sales process of POSH. Realization of reach and disintermediation depend on the implementation of these processes. In other words, the processes enable reach and disintermediation (as O aspect elements should be operationalizations of B aspect elements).

The diagram shows that most dependencies exist between the B and the O aspects and between the O and the A aspects. This suggests that the O aspect is the leading aspect for the POSH scenario. As there is only one dependency between the T and the B aspect, the POSH scenario is certainly not a technology push scenario.

9.6.2 TTU

For TTU we perform a future analysis (as discussed in section 9.5.2). In terms of this analysis, TTU projects the *far future* at about ten years from now. The T aspect will be the leading BOAT aspect for TTU, as communication modalities will rely heavily on technology developments. TTU analyzes the future with respect to the two kinds of services it offers: interpretation and translation.

For its interpretation services, TTU takes the extreme position that all international business meetings will be held electronically using multi-party telepresence systems, which will be commonly available in the *far future*. Interpretation services will still be needed in these meetings, where the interpreter will join a meeting as a party in the telepresence meeting. For low-technology telepresence meetings, interpreters can join from their home-office location. For high-technology telepresence meetings (possibly using 3D technology), dedicated telepresence set-ups are required. TTU can be a provider of such facilities.

For their translation services, TTU takes the extreme position that all business documents will be digital in the *far future* (and that all pre-existing, historic documents will have been adequately dealt with). This means that their activities for handling physical documents can be completely dismantled. TTU also expects that translations of official documents will have to be certified by means of electronic certificates. This implies that TTU choose to further invest in certification procedures and technology.

TTU uses the far future situation and the present situation to make an interpolation for the medium-term future. Given that it is and will remain in a technology-push market, it decides to heavily invest in knowledge of and experience with telepresence technology. One concrete step is the installation of TTU-owned, high-end telepresence facilities at two top-notch business locations, such as London and New York City. These facilities will be used for high-profile business meetings and for positioning TTU as the globally leading provider in this market.

9.6.3 TraXP

For the TraXP case study we concentrate on the first step of networked e-business analysis: determining the scope of an e-business scenario (see Figure 9.1). Finding the right scope for a new business model is very important to TraXP, as this determines which parties will be included and how the distribution of costs and benefits will be in a highly networked e-business scenario (and hence what the revenue model will be, as discussed in section 5.6). Following TraXP's service-dominant view on business, the answer to the question *"Which parties to include in an e-business scenario?"* is based on the choice of offered value-in-use and targeted customer segment.

To perform this analysis task, TraXP uses a multi-party business modeling technique that has been developed specially for service-dominant business: the service-dominant business model radar [Lüft13, Lüft14]. This multi-party business model diagramming technique is shown in Figure 9.5 and is further explained in the context of TraXP further on. The technique takes the business network of an e-business scenario as a starting point and is therefore complementary to the business model specifications that we have discussed in section 5.6 (which are party-centric; that is, take a single organization as the focal point).

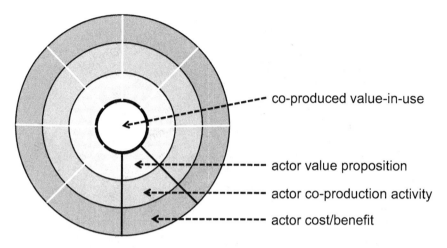

co-produced value-in-use

actor value proposition

actor co-production activity

actor cost/benefit

FIGURE 9.5   Service-dominant business radar technique.

The service-dominant business model radar for the most complex e-business scenario of TraXP is shown in Figure 9.6 (with Figure 9.5 acting as a legend). This is the scenario developed to offer the *seamless travel experience* value-in-use to the customer group of executive business travelers. This value-in-use is shown in the center of the diagram: the *seamless travel experience* /X – where the /X indicates the executive variant. Around it, we see pie slices of the diagram. Each pie slice represents one party in the e-business scenario, without any particular order. Having eight pie slices in the diagram means that this is an eight-party e-business scenario – so the scenario has considerable complexity.

The inner ring around the value-in-use contains the *actor value propositions* per actor; that is, per involved party. The actor value proposition is the part that the actor contributes to the overall value-in-use in the center of the radar. For example, TraXP contributes the overall execution of the travel experience, and a transport actor (such as an airline company) contributes the relocation (transport) part of the travel experience. Using the radar diagram, the completeness of the e-business scenario can be assessed by checking whether the complete value-in-use is covered by the combination of the actor value propositions.

The middle ring of the radar contains the *actor co-production activity* per actor. This is the business activity that an actor performs to produce its actor value proposition. To execute the travel experience, TraXP performs the overall business process orchestration and the customer profiling. The included activities are the (abstract) basis for the design of e-business processes, as we have seen in chapter 6.

The outer ring of the radar contains the *actor costs and benefits* per actor; that is, the costs an actor is incurred in to perform the actor co-production activity and

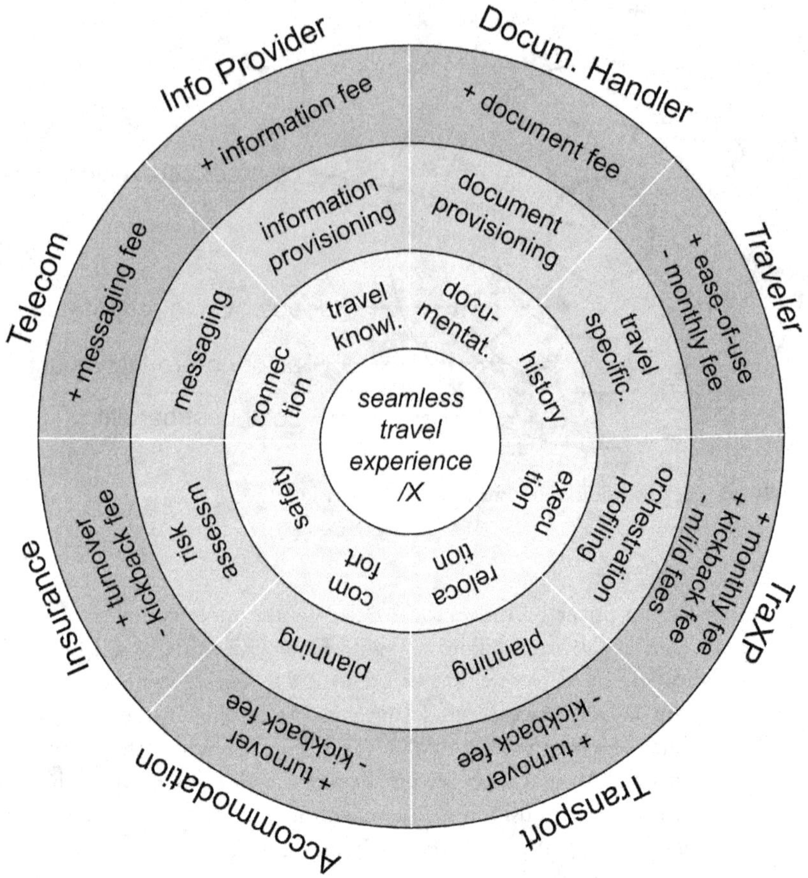

FIGURE 9.6 Service-dominant business model radar for TraXP.

the benefits it receives for this activity. Note that in this approach, actor costs and benefits can be both of a financial and a non-financial nature. The balance of costs and benefits per party and for the entire scenario can be analyzed in a qualitative way to assess the economic viability of the e-business scenario.

Given the business model radar for their /X business offering, TraXP finds a consistent scope of an e-business scenario, which is the basis for further analysis and design as outlined in this chapter.

9.7 Chapter end

This chapter on analyzing and designing e-business scenarios is ended with a short summary and a set of questions and exercises.

9.7.1 Chapter summary

Analyzing or designing an e-business scenario starts with determining the exact scope of the scenario in terms of parties and activities of these parties. Next, the scenario is classified in terms of party types, objects and time scope(s). After scoping and classification, a BOAT analysis or design is performed. First, a global analysis of BOAT aspects is made, after which the dependencies are analyzed. A BOAT element dependency diagram can be used as a summarization technique here. A leading BOAT aspect is chosen (two if really necessary). Then, a detailed analysis or design is performed, where the leading BOAT aspect is elaborated in most detail.

In analyzing past and future developments, points in time should be chosen with care. For future analysis, it can be a good idea to start with a far future scenario, which is analyzed by means of extreme thinking. A near future scenario can be obtained by interpolating between a far future scenario and a current scenario.

9.7.2 Questions and exercises

1   Explain all dependencies in the BOAT element dependency diagram of the POSH scenario, as shown in Figure 9.4.

2   Construct a BOAT element dependency diagram for the TTU scenario. Use the description of TTU in chapters 5–8 as input for the construction process.

3   Take a real-world e-business scenario. Perform a short, high-level BOAT analysis of it. Summarize the dependencies between the most important identified elements in a BOAT element dependency diagram.

4   Future developments are analyzed at various points in time, among which is the far future. How far away this far future actually is depends on characteristics of the scenario at hand. Find three characteristics that determine this in practice.

5   The BOAT dependency diagram of the POSH scenario (see Figure 9.4) indicates that the technology push forces of networked e-business are not too strong in this scenario. If the POSH organization would have more interest in these technology push forces, would this open ways to new business possibilities? Motivate your answer.

6   TTU projects the extreme future of business meetings as all-virtual, using telepresence technology (see section 9.6.2). Analyze the extreme other end of the future, where telepresence technology has lost all appeal in the business field and meetings are all face-to-face. Try and design a business future for TTU in this case.

7   Explain all costs and benefits shown in the business model radar of Figure 9.6. Determine which costs and benefits are directly coupled (note that each benefit received by one party should be contributed as a cost by another party).

Notes

1 Note that this is essentially different from the *time scopes* dimension introduced in section 3.6. The *time scopes* dimension is used to classify the time aspect of e-business transactions; that is, of the *operations* of an e-business scenario. The time aspect in this chapter relates to the *development* of an e-business scenario.
2 Note that we say *a* BOAT element dependency diagram, not *the* diagram. Constructing a BEDD is matter of making choices – different choices lead to a different BEDD.

10

BUSINESS STRATEGY

Learning goals

- Know and understand the concept of business strategy in the context of net-worked e-business.
- Know and understand the relationships among the concepts of business strategy, business model and e-business scenario.
- Understand the concept of strategic business–IT alignment and be able to relate it to the BOAT framework.
- Understand the relationship between strategic alignment and the trade-off between requirement pull and technology push in networked e-business.

10.1 Introduction

So far in this book we have discussed networked e-business from a number of perspectives: three classification dimensions and the four aspects of the BOAT framework. The emphasis has been on individual e-business scenarios, the individual business models related to these scenarios and the support required to operationalize these individual business models. A business organization, however, may be involved in more than one e-business scenario at the same time. We have already briefly discussed this in chapter 1 (see Figure 1.1). From the perspective of a business organization, these scenarios are somehow connected, as are the related business models. In other words, multiple e-business scenarios and multiple related business models can exist under the same conceptual 'umbrella' in an organization. We call this umbrella *business strategy*.

In this chapter we discuss the concept of business strategy in the context of networked e-business. We do this from two perspectives. First, we discuss the role of business strategy and its relationship to business models (section 10.2). This lays a conceptual foundation for thinking in terms of strategy. Next, we pay attention to the concept of strategic business–IT alignment and relate it to the BOAT framework (section 10.3). This provides a basis for operationalizing the concept of strategy. We end the chapter with (our last visit to) the three running cases in this book, a short summary and questions and exercises related to business strategy.

10.2 The role of business strategy

As discussed in the introduction of this chapter, this book has mainly focused on individual e-business scenarios and the business models associated with these individual e-business scenarios. A business organization can participate in multiple e-business scenarios. For large organizations the number of scenarios may be significant. The overall view on networked e-business that is shared across these scenarios is stated in a business strategy.

This discussion leads to the concept model shown in Figure 10.1. Here, each rectangle represents a concept and the lines between the concepts represent the relationships among the concepts. The numbers at the ends of a line denote the cardinality of a relationship: they indicate how many instances of one concept relate to how many instances of another concept. In the figure we see that a business organization has one business strategy that is specific for that organization (the cardinality is 1:1). A business strategy is related to all concrete business models of that company, which are specific to that company (the cardinality is 1:n, where n indicates any number greater than zero). A business organization is active in a number of markets, and a market contains a number of business organizations (cardinality $n:m$, where both n and m indicate any number greater than zero). Correspondingly, a business strategy fits in a number of markets. A concrete business model of a company fits in a number of e-business scenarios and an e-business scenario is built from a number of business models (because there are multiple parties involved that each have a business model). Finally, an e-business scenario takes place in one specific market and a market can hold a number of e-business scenarios. We discuss a practical elaboration of this concept model when we get to the case studies at the end of this chapter.

A business strategy defines an overall business view across multiple business models. This overall business view is based on the mission and vision of a business organization. Thus, we can say that a strategy defines the operational identity of an organization. Consequently, a strategy typically has a longer time horizon than specific business models. A strategy may be formulated with a time horizon of ten or twenty years, whereas the time horizon (life cycle) of a business model in the context of networked e-business may be a few years or even shorter, depending on the specific business domain. In other words, a strategy evolves, business models revolve.

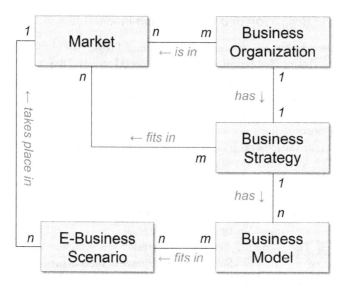

FIGURE 10.1 Business strategy and business model concepts in context.

This implies that a proper strategy specification is essential for an organization to keep convergence and synergy between its business models. This is important not only for the external positioning of a company but certainly also for the internal organization in terms of organization structures, information system architectures and information technologies. Elements of an organization used in the structures discussed in the O, A and T aspects of the BOAT framework should preferably be reusable across multiple e-business scenarios – all under the umbrella of a single strategy. In other words, organization structures, business functions and services, system architectures and deployed technology must be reusable across e-business scenarios for an organization. If reusability across e-business scenarios cannot be achieved, an organization has to build the organization structure and the information systems from scratch for each new scenario in which it participates, which obviously is detrimental to agility and efficiency.

10.3 BOAT and strategic business–IT alignment

The BOAT framework provides a structure to relate business to technology in the analysis and design of e-business scenarios (as we have seen in chapter 9). Strategic business–IT alignment models are used in general business engineering to model and analyze the interplay between the strategic design of business structures and the use of information technology. Therefore, the BOAT framework and strategic alignment models have in some respects similar goals and hence can be related to each other. We explore this relation in this section. Following, we first explain a well-known strategic business–IT alignment model: the model of Henderson and Venkatraman. Next, we discuss its relationship to the BOAT framework.

10.3.1 The Henderson and Venkatraman model

Probably the best known strategic alignment model that relates business aspects to IT aspects is that of Henderson and Venkatraman [Hend93]. They base their alignment model on two basic assumptions. First, the performance of an organization is determined by the *strategic fit* between the position of that organization in a market and its internal administrative structure. Basically, this means that the external function of an organization must be aligned with its internal operation. Second, the strategic fit is *dynamic*; that is, it changes over time as a consequence of market developments. This means that the alignment must be paid attention to on a continuous basis – this is not a one-shot analysis.

The strategic alignment model of Henderson and Venkatraman is shown in Figure 10.2 in a simplified form. The model is defined in terms of two dimensions. The first dimension distinguishes between the external (strategic) and internal (operational) levels. The second dimension distinguishes between the business and IT aspects. Taking the 'cross-product' of the two dimensions, one gets four domains of strategic choice in an organization:

- the *business strategy* describes the general strategy that an organization has in developing its business;
- the *IT strategy* describes the general strategy that an organization has in developing the way it uses IT;
- the *organizational infrastructure and processes* describe how an organization is organized in terms of 'people' structures and processes; and
- the *IT infrastructure and processes* describe how an organization is organized in terms of IT structures and processes.

The alignment model focuses on the integration in two dimensions. The *strategic fit* considers the interplay between the strategy and operational aspects of an organization (the vertical dimension in Figure 10.2, applicable to both vertical columns). The *functional integration* considers the interplay between the organizational and information technology aspects of that organization (the horizontal dimension in the figure, applicable to both horizontal rows). This results in four relationships among the cells of the model (indicated by the four arrows in the figure).[1]

Henderson and Venkatraman take the position that the alignment relationships should not be analyzed in terms of pairs of domains, as this simplifies things too much. Instead, they propose to analyze strategic alignment by looking at three domains at a time. In doing so, they describe four *perspectives* on strategic alignment (illustrated in Figure 10.3). Each perspective starts from the strategic level and proceeds to the operational level.

The *strategy execution alignment* perspective states that business strategy is first aligned with organizational infrastructure and processes and next mapped to IT infrastructure and processes – business is fully leading in this perspective. The *technology transformation alignment* perspective aligns business strategy first with IT strategy and IT strategy next with IT infrastructure and processes – here, the business–IT alignment is concentrated at the strategic level. The *competitive potential alignment*

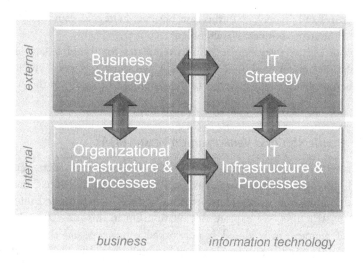

FIGURE 10.2 Simplified strategic alignment model.

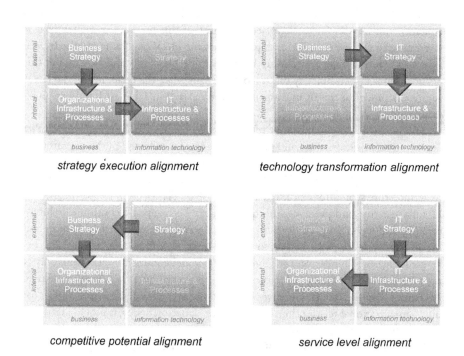

FIGURE 10.3 Four perspectives in Henderson and Venkatraman's strategic alignment model.

perspective starts from IT strategy – here, strategic alignment takes the competitive power of IT as a basis. Finally, the *service level alignment* perspective first aligns strategy and operations on the IT side and next aligns this with organizational

infrastructures and processes – in this case, business strategy does not play a significant role in strategic business–IT alignment.

The four perspectives can be seen as templates for thinking (and deciding)
about relationships in business–IT alignment. We show a practical application of
one of the perspectives when we get to our running case studies at the end of this
chapter.

10.3.2 Henderson and Venkatraman versus BOAT

As discussed in the introduction of this section, the strategic alignment model
of Henderson and Venkatraman (H&V) can be related to the BOAT framework:
they both address the relationship between business structures and information
technology structures. We explore this relationship in this subsection. Note that
the BOAT framework is aimed at networked e-business and the H&V alignment model is aimed at business in general (which obviously includes networked
e-business).

As we have seen, the H&V strategic alignment model contains four quadrants
(cells), which we can consider aspects of the model. The BOAT framework also
contains four aspects (as we have seen in most of this book). Consequently, it is
interesting to explore the relationships between the H&V quadrants and the BOAT
aspects. There is a clear relationship between these quadrants and aspects, but this
relationship is not completely one-to-one. We can relate the quadrants of the H&V
alignment model to the BOAT aspects as summarized in Table 10.1 and explained
further on.

The business strategy quadrant relates to the business (B) aspect of BOAT. The
organizational infrastructure and processes quadrant is reflected in the organization
(O) aspect of BOAT. The IT strategy quadrant pertains to both the architecture (A)
and technology (T) aspects of BOAT: strategic choices are made both with respect
to architecture structures employed and technology classes used. The same goes for
IT infrastructure and processes: this quadrant can be mapped to both the architecture (A) and technology (T) aspects of BOAT – internal architectural choices and
details of used technology belong to this quadrant.

Note that the Henderson and Venkatraman model considers architecture only at
the internal level (in the IT infrastructures and processes quadrant). As we have seen
in chapter 7, in the BOAT framework we also use architecture to shape support for
inter-organizational relationships in e-business scenarios; hence, it should clearly be
used at the external level, too.

In the wheel model of the BOAT framework (as shown in Figure 4.4), we
observe four trigger perspectives related to the choice of which BOAT aspect is
taken as leading in scenario analysis and design. This is shown in Figure 10.4. It
might be tempting to try and relate each trigger perspective of the BOAT framework to an alignment perspective of the Henderson and Venkatraman model, but
this is not a good idea for two reasons. First, the trigger perspectives each primarily
relate two aspects, whereas the alignment perspectives each relate three domains.

TABLE 10.1   Strategic alignment model and BOAT framework

	B	O	A	T
Business strategy	X			
Organization infrastructure and processes		X		
IT strategy			X	X
IT infrastructure and processes			X	X

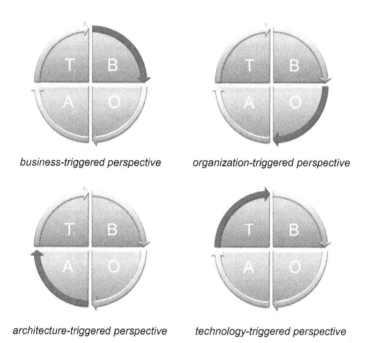

business-triggered perspective   *organization-triggered perspective*

architecture-triggered perspective   *technology-triggered perspective*

FIGURE 10.4   Four perspectives in the BOAT model.

Second, the mapping between BOAT aspects and alignment domains is not one-to-one (as shown in Table 10.1), which makes the mapping between combinations of elements even harder.

What we can observe, however, is that on the one hand there is a relationship between the business/organization triggered perspectives (of BOAT) and the business-rooted alignment perspectives (of H&V) and on the other hand a relationship between the architecture/technology triggered perspectives (of BOAT) and the IT-rooted alignment perspectives (of H&V). The first group starts from the business/organization requirements and works towards the application of IT. Hence, we can classify these as *requirements pull alignment* (see our discussion in section 1.5). The other group works from IT towards business possibilities and can likewise be classi-fied as *technology push alignment*. An overview of this grouping is given in Table 10.2.

10.3.3 Conclusion

We have seen that the alignment model of Henderson and Venkatraman and the BOAT framework can be related, but that this relationship is certainly not of a trivial, one-to-one nature. The H&V model has been developed with the strate-gic level of business design in mind. The BOAT model has been developed with a focus on tactical and operational business design (ranging from tactical business models to operational business processes). Hence, we can use a strategic alignment model, such as the H&V model, as a conceptual tool that is complementary to the BOAT framework: it can help us think about alignment of strategic issues that are only lightly covered by the BOAT framework. An important example of such issues

TABLE 10.2 Alignment and trigger perspectives grouped

is the strategic choice of information technologies (as discussed in chapter 8) to adopt – we will revisit this issue when we discuss the TTU case study at the end of this chapter. Another important example is the strategic choice to adopt a specific reference architecture, the selection of which may influence all e-business scenarios that an organization is and will be involved in.

The mapping between the H&V and BOAT models that we have discussed in this chapter helps in positioning the two approaches with respect to each other. This can, for instance, practically be applied when dealing with long-term change management issues (relate this to the discussion of change management in section 6.7).

10.4 Running cases

In this section we pay our last visit (at least in this book) to our three running case studies POSH, TTU and TraXP. We do not make complete strategic analyses of the three cases, but show an interesting element of strategy formulation or analysis for each of them. For POSH we focus on the distinction between business strategy and business models. For TTU we discuss its approach to strategic business–IT alignment. For TraXP we focus on the way it specifies its business strategy, given its service-dominant business orientation.

10.4.1 POSH

POSH has a clear vision of its strategy, in which it states that it wants to be one of the top-quality providers of office supplies in the country. In this strategy, it does not address customer segments. This has lead in the past to the formulation of one business model in one e-business scenario that covers all customer segments. Given the differences between customer segments, the consequence is friction in design choices with respect to business improvements.

Thinking explicitly about the difference between business strategy and business models, POSH is now considering making a business model per customer segment and keeping a strategy as an overarching model. Each business model will then be applied in a separate e-business scenario with its own specific design choices. The most obvious customer segments would be POSH's corporate customers and its private customers. This would lead to separate B2B and B2C business models and e-business scenarios. This is shown in Figure 10.5, which is an instantiated version of the concept model of Figure 10.1 for the POSH situation with two business models.

This is an instantiated concept model because all abstract concepts have been replaced by concrete entities. Note that the cardinalities of the relationships are all 1:1 in this diagram, because there are no sets of entities involved now.

Given the two-scenario approach, POSH can decide to modify the e-business scenarios per customer segment (and hence per business model). One modification would be the omission of the manufacturer party from the B2C scenario (see

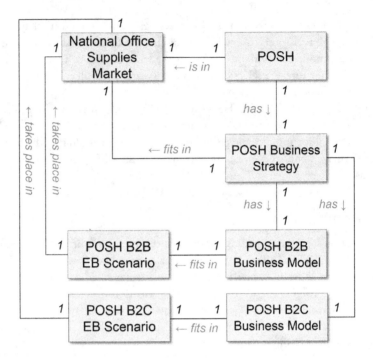

FIGURE 10.5 Instantiated concept model for POSH.

Figure 6.29), because B2C customers rarely order custom-made office furniture. This modification would reduce the scenario and simplify the B2C business processes, possibly making POSH faster and cheaper (and the business offering hence more appealing to the B2C market).

10.4.2 TTU

Strategic business–IT alignment is of utmost importance for TTU, because their business concept strongly relies on the use of advanced IT and it is in a fast-developing domain – both from business and technology perspectives. Consequently, TTU pays proper attention to strategic alignment. It has adapted the Henderson and Venkatraman model as a thinking framework.

Given its IT reliance TTU has chosen a strategic alignment perspective that is rooted in the IT column of the Henderson and Venkatraman model. As the choice of IT determines its strategic position in the interpretation and translation services market, TTU chose the *competitive potential alignment* perspective. This is illustrated in Figure 10.6.

TTU uses this figure to frame its thinking about future developments. In defining its business strategy, emphasis is placed on possibilities to define unique business propositions based on new technologies. These propositions are materialized in new concrete business models.

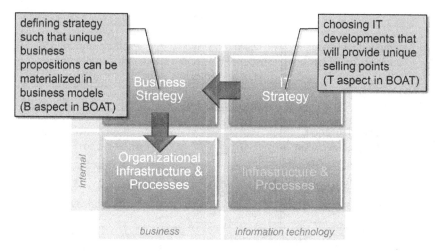

defining strategy such that unique business propositions can be materialized in business models (B aspect in BOAT)

choosing IT developments that will provide unique selling points (T aspect in BOAT)

TTU competitive potential alignment

FIGURE 10.6   Strategic alignment perspective for TTU.

10.4.3 TraXP

For TraXP we focus on the way it specifies its business strategy. As we have seen before, TraXP has organized its business from the service-dominant perspective. This implies that it has chosen to also use a service-dominant technique to specify its business strategy. The chosen technique is the *service-dominant strategy canvas* [Lüft14].

A simplified version of the TraXP strategy canvas is shown in Figure 10.7. Here we see that the canvas consists of three main regions: the specification of an (abstract) *value-in-use*, the specification of the *service ecosystem* in which TraXP operates and the specification of the main principles for *collaboration management*.

The specified value-in-use is an operationalization of TraXP's business vision shown in Figure 2.4. In the specification of the service ecosystem, we see TraXP amidst the classes of its partners and the services they provide – this is based on the ideas illustrated in Figure 2.5. In the strategy canvas a distinction is made between *core partners* that are essential to operate for TraXP and *enriching partners* that are not essential but contribute important added value to the business strategy of TraXP. The same distinction is made in the specification of collaboration management: here we see how TraXP intends to manage its collaboration with its core partners and with its enriching partners.

Based on this strategy, TraXP conceives its abstract business model specification as listed in Table 5.16 and its concrete business model radars such as the one shown in Figure 9.6.

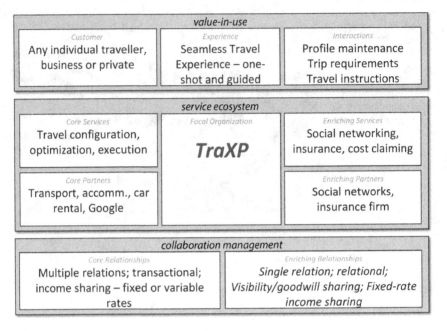

FIGURE 10.7 TraXP service-dominant business strategy.

10.5 Chapter end

For the last time in this book we end the chapter with a brief chapter summary and a set of questions and exercises to apply the theory of this chapter.

10.5.1 Chapter summary

Business strategy describes the long-term operationalization of the mission and vision of an organization (in a networked e-business context). An organization has one strategy, which is related to a set of concrete business models.

A strategy for networked e-business is related to the alignment of business (and organization) elements and IT (and architecture) elements. For this alignment, strategic business–IT alignment models can be used. The model of Henderson and Venkatraman is well-known for this purpose. This model identifies four alignment perspectives.

The four trigger perspectives of the BOAT framework and the four alignment perspectives of the Henderson and Venkatraman model can be related, but these relationships are certainly not one-to-one. They can be grouped, however, into requirements-pull and technology-push groups.

10.5.2 Questions and exercises

1   Find and get the paper on the strategic alignment model of Henderson and Venkatraman [Hend93]. Each of the four quadrants of the model has three

ingredients (as shown in Figure 1 of the paper). Discuss how each ingredient relates to the BOAT aspects.

2   Many companies now use *offshoring* in their business strategy. Find out what this exactly entails. Then discuss whether this is networked e-business as defined in this book. Analyze the relation to the B aspect elements discussed in chapter 5.

3   Find an organization that has multiple e-business models under the umbrella of a single e-business strategy. Analyze how this strategy has been specified.

4   Try and specify a service-dominant strategy canvas for TTU.

5   Try and create a service-dominant strategy canvas for a real-world business organization that operates in the service domain.

Note

1 The complete model of Henderson and Venkatraman [Hend93] also includes diagonal relationships among the four cells – we have omitted these here for reasons of clarity.

11

CONCLUDING REMARKS

Learning goals

- *Understand the tension field between separation and integration of concerns when analyzing or designing e-business scenarios.*
- *Understand the importance of change in networked e-business settings and the importance of conceptual structures in this context.*

11.1 Introduction

In this short final chapter of the book we present a few concluding remarks – they are to be interpreted as final observations after the topics discussed in the preceding ten chapters. First, we spend a few words on the tension field of separation and integration of concerns that is so typical for the complex world of networked e-business. Then, we turn our attention to dealing with change, as change is omnipresent in the field of networked e-business.

11.2 Separation and integration

Given the complexity of the networked e-business domain, a good separation of concerns is required to understand it. In this book we have presented a three-dimensional space for the classification of e-business scenarios. We have presented the BOAT framework as a basis for distinguishing aspects of networked e-business in analysis or design. These are the basic tools of this book – they are therefore repeated in Figure 11.1.

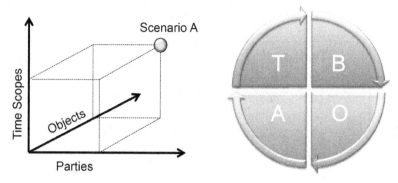

FIGURE 11.1 Main classification and analysis tools.

The BOAT framework is a conceptual tool aimed at separation of concerns – as such, it is an aid to arrive at clarity. But as the various aspects of networked e-business have an important interplay, the relationships between the aspects must be given enough attention. This is explicitly treated in this book by the sections on the four mappings between the BOAT aspects (sections 6.8, 7.8, 8.7 and 8.8). It is also reflected in the BEDD technique, which we have introduced in section 9.4. The integration of aspects is important in networked e-business to arrive at consistency in analysis or design. Consequently, a good e-business analyst (or designer, for that matter) must always consciously balance between separation and integration of aspects. An iterative analysis or design approach that alternates between separation and integration can be used to deal with scenarios of high complexity.

11.3 Dealing with change

As indicated in the beginning of this book, networked e-business is a very fast-moving domain: *the only constant in networked e-business is change*. This implies that many details have a volatile character: what is modern today may be old-fashioned tomorrow – either in terminology or in technology, perhaps even in essence. Most important in this domain is, therefore, to understand the 'grand structures' and relationships that are not that susceptible to change. Figure 11.2 presents a 'grand overview' of the main ingredients of the BOAT framework, organized into the four BOAT aspects (in the wheel configuration as shown in Figure 11.1) and augmented with the method and strategy elements (as discussed in the previous two chapters). This overview illustrates the 'grand structures' of networked e-business according to this book.

A well-structured overall view is what this book tries to convey – the focus is on important concepts, not on many details. Further details can be easily positioned within this overall view. As such, the theory presented in this book can be seen as a stable framework, the precise contents of which will evolve over time. Details in the

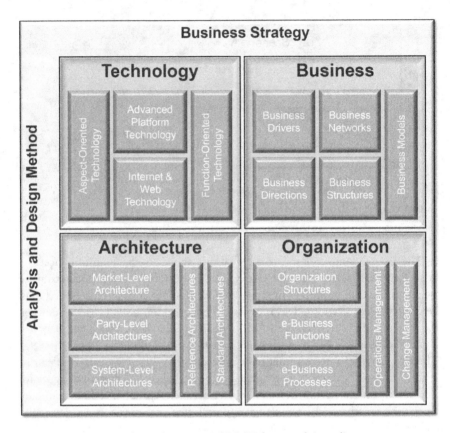

FIGURE 11.2 Augmented grand overview of BOAT framework ingredients.

networked e-business field are moving targets because they change very rapidly – they can be filled into the grand structures as they evolve. As an analogy, one can view things as a well-organized wardrobe: the overall structure (in terms of classes of clothing and the relationships between them) remains relatively stable, but the individual clothing items within the wardrobe follow trends and fashions.

Of course, to be able to analyze and design current, concrete e-business scenarios in detail, a thorough understanding of 'volatile details' is necessary, too, because they form the practical ingredients for a scenario at a certain moment in time. In terms of our analogy: to get actually dressed, one needs concrete pieces of clothing. To make concrete networked e-business designs stable over time, however, it is important to base them on non-volatile conceptual structures, which can be filled in differently as time proceeds.

REFERENCES

[Aals02] W. v.d. Aalst, K. v. Hee; *Workflow Management: Models, Methods, and Systems*; MIT Press, 2002.

[Aals11] W. v.d. Aalst; *Process Mining: Discovery, Conformance and Enhancement of Business Processes*; Springer, 2011.

[Abel00] R. Abelson; *Pets.com, Sock Puppet's Home, Will Close*; New York Times, November 8, 2000.

[Acqu08] A. Acquisti, S. Gritzalis, C. Lambrinoudakis, S. De Capitani di Vimercati; *Digital Privacy: Theory, Technologies and Practices*; Auerbach Publications, 2008.

[Ahma11] M. Ahmad; *Smartphone: Mobile Revolution at the Crossroads of Communications, Computing and Consumer Electronics*; CreateSpace Independent Publishing Platform, 2011.

[Alon99] G. Alonso, U. Fiedler, C. Hagen, A. Lazcano, H. Schuldt, N. Weiler; *WISE: Business to Business E-Commerce*; Proceedings 9th International Workshop on Research Issues in Data Engineering; IEEE, 1999; pp. 132–139.

[Alon04] G. Alonso, F. Casati, H. Kuno, V. Machiraju; *Web Services: Concepts, Architectures and Applications*; Springer, 2004.

[Ang06a] S. Angelov; *Foundations of B2B Electronic Contracting*; Ph.D. Thesis; Eindhoven University of Technology, 2006.

[Ang06b] S. Angelov, P. Grefen; *A Case Study on Electronic Contracting in On-Line Advertising – Status and Prospects*; Network-Centric Collaboration and Supporting Frameworks – Proceedings 7th IFIP Working Conference on Virtual Enterprises; Helsinki, Finland; Springer, 2006; pp. 419–428.

[Ange03] S. Angelov, P. Grefen; *The 4W Framework for B2B e-Contracting*; Networking and Virtual Organizations, Vol. 2, No. 1; Inderscience Publishers, 2003; pp. 78–97.

[Ange08] S. Angelov, P. Grefen; *An E-contracting Reference Architecture*; Journal of Systems and Software, Vol. 81, No. 11; Elsevier, 2008; pp. 1816–1844.

[Armb09] M. Armbrust c.s.; *Above the Clouds: A Berkeley View of Cloud Computing*; White Paper; Berkeley University, 2009.

[Armb10] M. Armbrust c.s.; *A View of Cloud Computing*; Communications of the ACM, Vol. 53, No. 4; ACM, 2010; pp. 50–58.

[Barr13] D. Barry; *Web Services, Service-Oriented Architectures, and Cloud Computing (2nd Edition): The Savvy Manager's Guide*; Morgan Kaufmann, 2013.

[Bass12] L. Bass, P. Clements, R. Kazman; *Software Architecture in Practice (3rd Edition)*; Addison-Wesley Professional, 2012.

[Binz13] T. Binz, U. Breitenbücher, F. Haupt, O. Kopp, F. Leymann, A. Nowak, S. Wagner; *OpenTOSCA – A Runtime for TOSCA-Based Cloud Applications*; Proceedings of the 11th International Conference on Service-Oriented Computing; Springer, 2013; pp. 692–695.

[Boh07] W. Boh, C. Soh, S. Yeo; *Standards Development and Diffusion: A Case Study of RosettaNet*; Communications of the ACM, Vol. 50, No. 12; ACM, 2007.

[Bolt01] F. Bolton; *Pure CORBA*; Sams Publishing, 2001.

[Chaf11] D. Chaffey; *E-Business and E-Commerce Management: Strategy, Implementation and Practice (5th Edition)*; Prentice Hall, 2011.

[Chan13] H. Chang; *Everyday NFC: Near Field Communication Explained*; Coach Seattle Incorporated, 2013.

[Ches06] H. Chesbrough; *Open Business Models: How to Thrive in the New Innovation Landscape*; Harvard Business Press, 2006.

[Chiu01] D. Chiu, K. Karlapalem, Q. Li; *Views for Inter-organization Workflow in an E-commerce Environment*; Proceedings 9th Working Conference on Database Semantics; IFIP, 2001; pp. 137–151.

[CIA14] *CIA World Factbook*; https://www.cia.gov/library/publications/the-world-factbook/; inspected 2014.

[Come05] D. Comer; *Internetworking with TCP/IP, Vol 1*; Prentice Hall, 2005.

[daCo13] F. daCosta; *Rethinking the Internet of Things: A Scalable Approach to Connecting Everything*; Apress, 2013.

[Dani11] I. Daniel; *E-Commerce Get It Right!*; NeuroDigital, 2011.

[Dell06] M. Dell, C. Fredman; *Direct from Dell: Strategies that Revolutionized an Industry*; Collins Business, 2006.

[Denn12] A. Dennis; *Systems Analysis and Design (5th Edition)*; Wiley, 2012.

[Dobr09] A. Dobriceanu, L. Biscu, A. Badica, C. Badica; *The Design and Implementation of an Agent-Based Auction Service*; International Journal of Agent-Oriented Software Engineering, Vol. 3, No. 2/3; Inderscience, 2009; pp. 116–134.

[Dwiv10] H. Dwivedi, C. Clark, D. Thiel; *Mobile Application Security*; McGraw-Hill Osborne Media, 2010.

[Econ10] The Economist; *Data, Data Everywhere*; Feb. 25, 2010 edition; http://www.economist.com/node/15557443; inspected 2014.

[Elli02] S. Elliott (ed.); *Electronic Commerce – B2C Strategies and Models*; Wiley, 2002.

[Evan99] P. Evans, T. Wurster; *Blown to Bits: How the New Economics of Information Transforms Strategy*; Harvard Business School Press, 1999.

[Fas07a] M. Fasli; *Agent Technology for E-Commerce*; Wiley, 2007.

[Fas07b] M. Fasli, O. Shehory (eds.); *Agent-Mediated Electronic Commerce: Automated Negotiation and Strategy Design for Electronic Markets*; Springer, 2007.

[Fenn05] J. Fenn, A. Linden; *Gartner's Hype Cycle Special Report for 2005*; Gartner, 2005.

[Fowl00] M. Fowler, K. Scott; *UML Distilled*; Addison-Wesley, 2000.

[Freu12] J. Freund, B. Rücker; *Real-Life BPMN: Using BPMN 2.0 to Analyze, Improve, and Automate Processes in Your Company*; CreateSpace Independent Publishing Platform, 2012.

[Golb13] J. Golbeck; *Analyzing the Social Web*; Morgan Kaufmann, 2013.

[Gre03a] P. Grefen; *Onzichtbare Architecturen – tussen Chaos en Structuur in e-Business*; Inaugural Lecture; Eindhoven University of Technology, 2003 (in Dutch).

[Gre03b] P. Grefen, H. Ludwig, S. Angelov; *A Three-Level Framework for Process and Data Management of Complex E-Services*; International Journal of Cooperative Information Systems, Vol. 12, No. 4; World Scientific, 2003; pp. 487–531.

[Gre13a] P. Grefen, E. Lüftenegger, E. v.d. Linden, C. Weisleder; *BASE/X: Business Agility through Cross-Organizational Service Engineering – The Business and Service Design Approach Developed in the CoProFind Project*; Beta Working Papers; Vol. 414; Eindhoven University of Technology, 2013.

[Gre13b] P. Grefen; *Networked Business Process Management*; International Journal of IT/Business Alignment and Governance; Vol. 4, No. 2; IGI Global, 2013; pp. 54–82.

[Gref00] P. Grefen, K. Aberer, Y. Hoffner, H. Ludwig; *CrossFlow: Cross-Organizational Workflow Management in Dynamic Virtual Enterprises*; Computer Systems Science & Engineering, Vol. 15, No. 5; CRL Publishing, 2000; pp. 277–290.

[Gref02] P. Grefen, S. Angelov; *On tau-, mu-, pi- and epsilon-Contracting*; Proceedings CAiSE Workshop on Web Services, e-Business, and the Semantic Web; Springer, 2002; pp. 68–77.

[Gref09] P. Grefen, N. Mehandjiev, G. Kouvas, G. Weichhart, R. Eshuis; *Dynamic Business Network Process Management in Instant Virtual Enterprises*; Computers in Industry, Vol. 60, No. 2; Elsevier, 2009; pp. 86–103.

[Gref10] P. Grefen; *Mastering e-Business*; Routledge, 2010.

[Gref14] P. Grefen; *Business Information System Architecture*; Lecture Syllabus; Eindhoven University of Technology, 2014.

[Harr13] S. Harrer, J. Lenhard, G. Wirtz; *Open Source versus Proprietary Software in Service-Orientation: The Case of BPEL Engines*; Proceedings of the 11th International Conference on Service-Oriented Computing; Springer, 2013; pp. 99–113.

[Hend93] J. Henderson, N. Venkatraman; *Strategic Alignment: Leveraging Information Technology for Transforming Organisations*; IBM Systems Journal, Vol. 32, No. 1; IBM, 1993; pp. 472–484.

[Hiatt12] J. Hiatt, T. Creasey; *Change Management: The People Side of Change*; Prosci Learning Center Publications, 2012.

[Hof01a] Y. Hoffner, S. Field, P. Grefen, H. Ludwig; *Contract-Driven Creation and Operation of Virtual Enterprises*; Computer Networks, Vol. 37, No. 2; Elsevier, 2001; pp. 111–136.

[Hof01b] Y. Hoffner, H. Ludwig, P. Grefen, K. Aberer; *CrossFlow: Integrating Workflow Management and Electronic Commerce*; SIGecom Exchanges, Vol. 2, No. 1; ACM, 2001; pp. 1–10.

[Hoff00] Y. Hoffner, H. Ludwig, C. Gülcü, P. Grefen; *Architecture for Cross-Organisational Business Processes*; Proceedings 2nd International Workshop on Advanced Issues of E-Commerce and Web-Based Information Systems; IEEE, 2000; pp. 2–11.

[Hold08] G. Holden, S. Belew, J. Elad, J. Rich; *E-Business*; Wiley Pathways, 2008.

[Howe08] J. Howe; *Crowdsourcing: Why the Power of the Crowd Is Driving the Future of Business*; Crown Business, 2008.

[Inmo01] W. Inmon, R. Terdeman, J. Norris-Montanari, D. Meers; *Data Warehousing for E-Business*; Wiley, 2001.

[ISC14] *ISC Domain Survey*; Internet Systems Consortium (ISC); https://www.isc.org/services/survey/; inspected 2014.

[ITL97] *Public Key Infrastructure Technology*; ITL Bulletin July 1997; National Institute of Standards and Technology, 1997.

[Jela08] T. Jelassi, A. Enders; *Strategies for e-Business: Concepts and Cases (2nd Edition)*; Prentice Hall, 2008.

[Jest08] J. Jeston, J. Nelis; *Business Process Management (2nd Edition): Practical Guidelines to Successful Implementations*; Butterworth-Heinemann, 2008.

[Jone07] E. Jones, C. Chung; *RFID in Logistics: A Practical Introduction*; CRC Press, 2007.

[Katz07] J. Katz, Y. Lindell; *Introduction to Modern Cryptography: Principles and Protocols*; Chapman & Hall/CRC, 2007.

[Keen00] P. Keen, C. Ballance, S. Chan, S. Schrump; *Electronic Commerce Relationships – Trust by Design*; Prentice Hall, 2000.

[Kell13] D. Kellmereit, D. Obodovski; *The Silent Intelligence: The Internet of Things*; DND Ventures LLC, 2013.

[Kirk87] P. Kirkman; *Electronic Funds Transfer Systems: The Revolution in Cashless Banking and Payment Methods*; Blackwell, 1987.

[Kost05] R. de Koster, J. Zuidema; *Commercial Returns in a Mail Order Company: The Wehkamp Case*; in: S. Flapper, J. van Nunen, L. Wassenhove; *Managing Closed-Loop Supply Chains*; Springer, 2005; pp. 97–106.

[Kou10] W. Kou; *Payment Technologies for E-Commerce*; Springer, 2010.

[Lazc01] A. Lazcano, H. Schuldt, G. Alonso, H. Schek; *WISE: Process Based E-Commerce*; Data Engineering Bulletin, Vol. 24, No. 1; IEEE, 2001; pp. 46–51.

[Leym99] F. Leymann, D. Roller; *Production Workflow: Concepts and Techniques*; Prentice Hall, 1999.

[Lind01] M. Lindstrom; *Clicks, Bricks & Brands*; Kogan Page, 2001.

[Liu07] C. Liu, Q. Li, Y. Zhang, M. Indulska, X. Zhao; *Introduction to the First Workshop on Collaborative Business Processes (CBP 2007)*; Proceedings Business Process Management Workshops; Springer, 2008; pp 181–184.

[Lüft13] E. Lüftenegger, M. Comuzzi, P. Grefen, C. Weisleder; *The Service Dominant Business Model: A Service Focused Conceptualization*; Beta Working Papers; Vol. 402; Eindhoven University of Technology, 2013.

[Lüft14] E. Lüftenegger; *Service-Dominant Business Design*; Ph.D. Thesis; Eindhoven University of Technology, 2014.

[Marc05] J. Marcus; *Amazonia: Five Years at the Epicenter of the Dot.Com Juggernaut*; New Press, 2005.

[McKa04] J. McKay, P. Marshall; *Strategic Management of e-Business*; Wiley, 2004.

[Meha10] N. Mehandjiev, P. Grefen; *Dynamic Business Process Formation for Instant Virtual Enterprises*; Springer, 2010.

[Mell11] P. Mell, T. Grance; *The NIST Definition of Cloud Computing*; National Institute of Standards and Technology, 2011.

[Mint92] H. Mintzberg; *Structure in Fives: Designing Effective Organizations*; Prentice Hall, 1992.

[Mitc03] D. Mitchell, C. Coles, B. Golisano, R. Knutson; *The Ultimate Competitive Advantage: Secrets of Continually Developing a More Profitable Business Model*; Berrett-Koehler Publishers, 2003.

[Mutc11] J. Mutch, B. Anderson; *Preventing Good People From Doing Bad Things: Implementing Least Privilege*; Apress, 2011; pp. 113–126.

[Nels02] A. Nelson, W. Nelson; *Building Electronic Commerce with Web Database Constructions*; Addison-Wesley, 2002.

[Ng12] I. Ng, G. Parry, L. Smith, R. Maull, G. Briscoe; *Transitioning from a Goods-Dominant to a Service-Dominant Logic – Visualising the Value Proposition of Rolls-Royce*; Journal of Service Management, Vol. 23, No. 3; Emerald, 2012; pp. 416–439.

[Nico13] D. Nicol; *Mobile Strategy: How Your Company Can Win by Embracing Mobile Technologies*; IBM Press, 2013.

[Norm04] T. Norman, A. Preece, S. Chalmers, N. Jennings, M. Luck, V. Dang, T. Nguyen, V. Deora, J. Shao, W. Gray, N. Fiddian; *Agent-Based Formation of Virtual Organisations*; Knowledge-Based Systems, Vol. 17, No. 2/4; Elsevier, 2004; pp. 103–111.

[OAS04] *UDDI Executive Overview: Enabling Service-Oriented Architecture*; OASIS, 2004; www.oasis-open.org; inspected 2014.

[OAS06] OASIS ebXML Joint Committee; *The Framework for eBusiness*; OASIS, 2006.

[OAS13] *Topology and Orchestration Specification for Cloud Applications Version 1.0*; OASIS, 2013; http://docs.oasis-open.org/tosca/TOSCA/v1.0/os/TOSCA-v1.0-os.html; inspected 2014.

[OGF07] OGF GRAAP Working Group; *Web Services Agreement Specification (WS-Agreement)*; Open Grid Forum, 2007.

[OMah01] D. O'Mahony, M. Peirce, H. Tewari; *Electronic Payment Systems for E-Commerce*; Artech House, 2001.

[Oste10] A. Osterwalder, Y. Pigneur; *Business Model Generation*; John Wiley and Sons, 2010.

[Paav02] J. Paavilainen; *Mobile Business Strategies: Understanding the Technologies and Opportunities*; Wireless Press, 2002.

[Papa07] M. Papazoglou; *Web Services: Principles and Technology*; Pearson, 2007.

[PaOU05] B. Parhami; *Computer Architecture: From Microprocessors to Supercomputers*; Oxford University Press, 2005.

[PáUT05] R. Párhonyi; *Micro Payment Gateways*; Ph.D. Thesis; University of Twente, 2005.

[Paul01] E. Paulson; *Inside Cisco: The Real Story of Sustained M&A Growth*; Wiley, 2001.

[Perk99] A. Perkins, M. Perkins; *The Internet Bubble*; Harper Business, 1999.

[Phil03] P. Phillips; *E-Business Strategy: Text and Cases*; MGraw-Hill, 2003.

[Piep01] R. Pieper, V. Kouwenhoven, S. Hamminga; *Behond the Hype – e-Business Strategy in Leading European Companies*; Van Haren Publishing, 2001.

[Port85] M. Porter; *Competitive Advantage: Creating and Sustaining Superior Performance*; Free Press, 1985.

[Prov13] F. Provost, T. Fawcett; *Data Science for Business: What You Need to Know about Data Mining and Data-Analytic Thinking*; O'Reilly Media, 2013.

[Rao95] A. Rao, M. Georgeff; *BDI-agents: From Theory to Practice*; Proceedings of the 1st International Conference on Multiagent Systems; AAAI, 1995; pp. 312–319.

[Rauc95] R. Raucci; *Mosaic for Windows: A Hands-on Configuration and Set-up Guide to Popular Web Browsers*; Springer, 1995.

[Rich08] L. Richardson, S. Ruby; *RESTful Web Services*; O'Reilly Media, 2008.

[Rose08] M. Rosen, B. Lublinsky, K. Smith, M. Balcer; *Applied SOA: Service-Oriented Architecture and Design Strategies*; Wiley, 2008.

[Rose09] RosettaNet Program Office; *Overview, Clusters, Segments, and PIPS, Version 02.07.00*; RosettaNet, 2009.

[Scha14] T. Schadler, J. Bernoff, J. Ask; *The Mobile Mind Shift: Engineer Your Business to Win in the Mobile Moment*; Groundswell Press, 2014.

[Schi14] H. Schildt; *Java: The Complete Reference (9th Edition)*; McGraw-Hill Osborne Media, 2014.

[Soko95] P. Sokol; *From EDI to Electronic Commerce: A Business Perspective*; McGraw-Hill, 1995.

[Spea14] M. Spears; *The Ultimate Guide to Marketing a Business in the Second Life World*; Self-Published, 2014.

[Spur00] C. Spurgeon; *Ethernet: The Definitive Guide*; O'Reilly Media, 2000.

[Stev94] W. Stevens; *TCP/IP Illustrated, Volume 1: The Protocols*; Addison-Wesley Professional, 1994.

[Strö00] M. Ströbel; *Dynamic Outsourcing of Services*; Research Report RZ 3236; IBM Research, 2000.

[Tale07] N. Taleb; *The Black Swan: The Impact of the Highly Improbable*; Random House, 2007.

[Tayl09] R. Taylor, N. Medvidovic, E.M. Dashofy; *Software Architecture: Foundations, Theory, and Practice*; Wiley, 2009.

[Terd07] D. Terdiman; *The Entrepreneur's Guide to Second Life: Making Money in the Metaverse*; Sybex, 2007.

[Thom02] E. Thomsen; *OLAP Solutions: Building Multidimensional Information Systems*; Wiley, 2002.

[Turb02] E. Turban, D. King, J. Lee, M. Warkentin, H.M. Chung; *Electronic Commerce 2002: A Managerial Perspective*; Prentice Hall, 2002.

[Turb10] E. Turban, L. Volonino; *Information Technology for Management*; Wiley, 2010.

[Vacc04] J. Vacca; *Public Key Infrastructure: Building Trusted Applications and Web Services*; Auerbach Publications, 2004.

[VanH03] D. VanHoose; *E-Commerce Economics*; Thomson – South-Western, 2003.

[VanS03] C. Van Slyke, F. Bélanger; *E-Business Technologies*; Wiley, 2003.

[Varg08] S. Vargo, R. Lusch; *Service-Dominant Logic: Continuing the Evolution*; Journal of the Academy of Marketing Science, Vol. 36; Springer, 2008; pp. 1–10.

[Vets08] I. Vetsikas, N. Jennings; *Towards Agents Participating in Realistic Multi-Unit Sealed-Bid Auctions*; Proceedings 7th International Joint Conference on Autonomous Agents and Multiagent Systems; IFAAMAS, 2008; pp. 1621–1624.

[Wade12] W. Wade; *Scenario Planning: A Field Guide to the Future*; Wiley, 2012.

[Wang08] T. Wang, B. Kratz, J. Vonk, P. Grefen; *A Survey on the History of Transaction Management: From Flat to Grid Transactions*; Distributed and Parallel Databases, Vol. 23, No. 3; Springer, 2008; pp. 235–270.

[Wein52] J. Weiner; *Operating Experience with UNIVAC Systems*; Transactions of the I.R.E. Professional Group on Electronic Computers, Vol. PGEC-1, No. 1; IEEE, 1952; pp. 33–46.

[Weis01] J. Weise; *Public Key Infrastructure Overview*; Sun BluePrints OnLine, Sun Microsystems, 2001.

[WfM94] *Glossary: A Workflow Management Coalition Specification*; Workflow Management Coalition, 1994.

[Why01] W.S. Whyte; *Enabling eBusiness: Integrating Technologies, Architectures and Applications*; Wiley, 2001.

[Wik14a] *Event-driven Process Chain*; Wikipedia; http://en.wikipedia.org/wiki/Event-driven_process_chain; inspected 2014.

[Wik14b] *Telepresence*; Wikipedia; http://en.wikipedia.org/wiki/Telepresence; inspected 2014.

[Wik14c] *History of the Internet*; Wikipedia; http://en.wikipedia.org/wiki/History_of_the_internet; inspected 2014.

[Wik14d] *X/Open XA*; Wikipedia; http://en.wikipedia.org/wiki/X/Open_XA; inspected 2014.

[Wik14e] *Web 2.0*; Wikipedia; http://en.wikipedia.org/wiki/Web_2.0; inspected 2014.

[Wik14f] *SABRE*; Wikipedia, 2009; http://en.wikipedia.org/wiki/Sabre_(computer_system); inspected 2014.

[Wik14g] *Society for Worldwide Interbank Financial Telecommunication*; Wikipedia; http://en.wikipedia.org/wiki/Society_for_Worldwide_Interbank_Financial_Telecommunication; inspected 2014.

[Wik14h] *Waterfall Model*; Wikipedia; http://en.wikipedia.org/wiki/Waterfall_model; inspected 2014.

[Wik14i] *Web Ontology Language*; Wikipedia; http://en.wikipedia.org/wiki/Web_Ontology_Language; inspected 2014.

[Wik14j] *Pets.com*; Wikipedia; http://en.wikipedia.org/wiki/Pets.com; inspected 2014.

[Wik14k] *Interplanetary internet*; Wikipedia; http://en.wikipedia.org/wiki/Interplanetary_internet; inspected 2014.

[Wik14l] *Venn Diagram*; Wikipedia; http://en.wikipedia.org/wiki/Venn_diagram; inspected 2014.

[Wik14m] *Swim Lane*; Wikipedia; http://en.wikipedia.org/wiki/Swim_lane; inspected 2014.

[Wik14n] *Social Network Analysis*; Wikipedia; http://en.wikipedia.org/wiki/Social_network_analysis; inspected 2014.

[Wik14o] *UNIVAC*; Wikipedia; http://en.wikipedia.org/wiki/UNIVAC; inspected 2015.

[Xu04] Lai Xu; *Monitorable Multi-party Contracts for E-Business*; Ph.D. Thesis; Tilburg University, 2004.

[Yee12] J. Yee, S. Oh; *Technology Integration to Business: Focusing on RFID, Interoperability, and Sustainability for Manufacturing, Logistics, and Supply Chain Management*; Springer, 2012.

[Zach02] J. Zachman; *The Zachman Framework for Enterprise Architecture*; Zachman International, 2002.

[Zhao09] X. Zhao, C. Liu, T. Lin; *Enhancing Business Process Automation by Integrating RFID Data and Events*; Proceedings On the Move to Meaningful Internet Systems: OTM 2009; Springer, 2009; pp. 255–272.

INDEX

Printed in the United States
by Baker & Taylor Publisher Services